MANAGEMENT ACCOUNTING

A Practical Approach

Gail Sheppard

Gill & Macmillan

Gill & Macmillan Ltd
Hume Avenue
Park West
Dublin 12
with associated companies throughout the world
www.gillmacmillan.ie

978 07171 4996 4

Index compiled by Helen Litton
Print origination in Ireland by Carole Lynch
Printed by GraphyCems, Spain

The paper used in this book is made from the wood
pulp of managed forests. For every tree felled, at
least one tree is planted, thereby renewing natural
resources.

A CIP catalogue record for this book is available
from the British Library.

CONTENTS

ACKNOWLEDGMENTS

Thanks to all those who helped in the preparation of this book at its various stages. Special thanks to my family, friends and colleagues for their encouragement and support.

1 Introduction

Learning outcomes of Chapter 1

At the end of this chapter, you will be able to:

- understand the principles of management accounting and its position in the organisation
- explain the differences between management and financial accounting
- discuss the history and development of management accounting
- discuss the changing role of management accounting
- explain the need to allocate costs
- classify costs into direct and indirect costs; period and product costs; variable, fixed, semi-variable and stepped costs; decision-making costs and non-manufacturing costs

Introduction

In this chapter the term 'management accounting' will be explained and the role of the management accountant will be defined. The differences between management and financial accounting will be discussed.

You will learn about the history of management accounting and how this has developed to fit the needs of strategic decision-making in businesses.

Management accounting terminology, which will be used throughout the book, will be defined.

The principles of management accounting

CIMA Official Terminology defines management accounting as:

> ... the application of the principles of accounting and financial management to create, protect, preserve and increase value for the stakeholders of for-profit and not-for-profit enterprises in the public and private sector.
> Management Accounting is an integral part of management. It requires the identification, generation, presentation, interpretation and use of relevant information to:

- Inform strategic decisions and formulate business strategy
- Plan long, medium and short-run operations
- Determine capital structure and fund that structure
- Design reward strategies for executives and shareholders
- Inform operational decisions
- Control operations and ensure the efficient use of resources
- Measure and report financial and non-financial performance to management and other stakeholders
- Safeguard tangible and intangible assets
- Implement corporate governance procedures, risk management and internal controls.

The definition of management accounting is a long one, but its position in the organisation can be summarised into the following areas:

(a) Planning

Management accounting is concerned with achieving the objectives of the organisation. The objectives should stem from the mission statement and strategies of the organisation, which are then translated into budgets. Budgets set a benchmark from which the organisation can measure whether it is achieving its objectives. **Chapter 6: Budgetary Planning and Control** will cover planning in an organisation.

(b) Decision-making

Management accounting provides detailed and timely information which enables managers to make decisions. The management accountant needs to discern which information is relevant to the decision. **Chapter 10: Relevant Costing and Decision-Making** will cover the decision-making process from a quantitative perspective. Marginal costing information is used to make short-term decisions and this is covered in **Chapter 8: Marginal and Absorption Costing** and **Chapter 9: Cost Volume Profit Analysis. Chapter 11: Capital Investment Decisions** sets out appraisal techniques which can be used to make decisions which affect the medium- to long-term future of the organisation.

(c) Reporting

Management accounting is concerned with reporting information for internal use in the organisation. This allows managers to set objectives, control activities, measure performance and make decisions. In profit-making organisations, management accounting is used to report on the main objective of the organisation, i.e., to make profit. In not-for-profit organisations and the public sector, management accounting is used to measure performance and to see if the objectives are being met.

Chapter 7: Standard Costing and Variance Analysis provides a means of measuring actual outcomes against budget and analysing results. This allows managers to take corrective action to ensure the organisation will achieve its stated objectives.

(d) Performance measurement

Management accounting is used to measure performance. In profit-making organisations this is easy as the aim is to make a profit. Quantitative analysis using standard costing will allow measurement of actual costs, revenues and profit against budgets.

In more recent times there has been a move to measure performance not only in terms of quantitative performance but also in terms of qualitative performance. Customer satisfaction, research and development, and employee skills are important for the continued growth of organisations. Qualitative measures have been incorporated into performance reports using the balanced scorecard.

Performance measurement in not-for-profit organisations and the public sector measures whether objectives have been achieved and whether there is value for money. Economy, efficiency and effectiveness are important performance measurement criteria.

All these issues are discussed in **Chapter 12: Performance Measurement and Issues in Accounting**.

(e) Control of operations and efficient use of resources

Management accounting is used to control operations and ensure efficient use of resources. **Chapter 2: Product Costing – Materials and Labour, Chapter 3: Product Costing – Overheads** and **Chapter 5: Process Costing** provide a means of costing products, services and inventories.

Chapter 4: Activity-Based Costing provides a more modern approach to product costing which results in more accurate product costing.

Differences between management accounting and financial accounting

Most organisations provide management accounting and financial accounting information. Both sets of accounting systems rely on the same basic financial data. Management accounting is concerned with the provision of detailed accounting information on all aspects of the organisation, e.g., sales by product, sales by regions, sales by employee and sales by customer. Management accounting information contains both quantitative and qualitative information. Financial accounting information is summarised and reports on the organisation as a whole, e.g., sales are reported in total. It mainly contains quantitative information.

Management accounting information is used to make decisions which affect the short-, medium- and long-term future of the organisation. It is used to measure performance and to control different aspects of the organisation. Management accounting uses past information or historic information as well as estimates of future costs and revenues to make decisions. Financial accounting reports on the financial consequences of past activities, usually over the last financial year. The information contained in financial accounts is historic information and is standard in its format.

The systems used to gather information and report information in a management accounting system are more informal than those in a financial accounting system, which are regulated by the International Accounting Standards Board (IASB) and which are highly standardised. This is to ensure that all financial regulations have been complied with and compliance can be easily verified.

Management accounting information is reported on regularly and in as much detail as required. Timeliness is of the essence as decisions may need to be made quickly. Managers might decide to make decisions based on estimates rather than wait for more precise figures. Financial accounting information is usually reported only once a year as part of the year-end accounts but it must be precise as information must be verifiable.

Management accounting information is sensitive and organisations would not want it to get into the hands of competitors, so it is kept within the organisation and is not publicly available. Organisations may be obliged to publish financial information as it is necessary for outside parties such as the Revenue Commissioners, banks and the Companies Registration Office.

Summary of the differences between management accounting and financial accounting

	MANAGEMENT ACCOUNTING	FINANCIAL ACCOUNTING
Level of detail:	Provides detailed information – quantitative and qualitative	Provides high-level information – quantitative
Use of historic and future information:	Uses historic and future estimates	Uses only historic information
Estimates v precise data:	Uses estimates to assist decision-making	Uses precise data to prepare financial reports
Accounting systems:	Informal non-regulated accounting systems	Formal standardised accounting systems regulated by International Financial Reporting Standards (IFRSs)
Timing:	Regular reporting, usually every month or more frequently if required	Annual reporting
Sensitivity of information:	Very detailed and highly sensitive information	Less detailed information which is published in the public domain

The history and development of management accounting

Management accounting came about before financial accounting, according to Grahame Steven (2002). It became more organised during the Industrial Revolution. Johnson and Kaplan (1987) write that in the early 19th century, accountants were concerned with the cost of labour. In pre-factory times, workers were paid 'piece rates' for work carried out at home. This changed when workers were centralised in factories. Work contracts were substituted for piece rates and overhead items such as hauling and repair work began to be supplied internally, not subcontracted.

Johnson and Kaplan (1987) write that the first American business organisations to develop management accounting systems were the mechanised integrated cotton textile factories that appeared after 1812. They used cost accounts to ascertain the direct labour and overhead costs of converting raw material into finished yarn and fabric.

Andrew Carnegie of the Carnegie Steel Company between 1872 and 1902 stated that his operating strategy was to push his own direct costs below those of his competitors. This was to enable him to charge prices that would always ensure enough demand to keep his plants running at full capacity. This required frequent information showing his direct costs relative to those of his competitors.

The development of railroads in the 19th century led to internal accounting systems designed to provide information and control. The railroad companies devised cost accounting systems to evaluate and control the internal processes by which resources were converted into the transport service. A basic measurement of performance developed was the 'ton-mile'. Another measurement of performance developed was the 'operating ratio'. This is a ratio of operating expenses to revenues that railroad companies studied, indicating how variations in the business of diverse sub-units would affect the railroad companies' total performance.

In the last quarter of the 19th century, the American economy witnessed an incredible outpouring of standardised, mass-produced goods. Marshall Fields in Chicago collected departmental accounting information on both gross margins and inventory turnover.

Macintosh (1994) uses the following definition to describe management accounting:

> ... the process of identification, measurement, accumulation, analysis, preparation, interpretation and communication of information that assists executives in fulfilling organisational objectives ... a formal mechanism for gathering and communicating data for the ends of aiding and co-ordinating collective decisions in light of the overall goals or objectives of an organization.

Steven (2002) states that there was little need for external reporting and financial accounting until the mid-19th century as there was little or no legal requirement about what should be provided and when it should be issued.

In summary, the Industrial Revolution brought about a need for a more formal accounting approach to assist managers to plan and make decisions. This developed into the management accounting practices that exist today.

Changing role of management accounting

Johnson and Kaplan stated as far back as 1987 in 'Relevance Lost' that management accounting systems were no longer serving the information needs of managers. When managers are no longer receiving accurate information on the efficiency and effectiveness of internal operations, the business becomes vulnerable to outside competition.

Johnson and Kaplan state that the obsolescence of management accounting information came about due to:

(1) Total quality control

Traditionally manufacturing accepted a level of defects and rejected units and strived to limit this level by focusing on inspection. The availability of new technology in manufacturing and innovative practices developed by Japanese manufacturers in the 1970s led to a practice of 'total quality manufacturing'. Johnson and Kaplan state that with total quality, the only acceptable quality level was zero defects. In the 1980s, US manufacturers found that adopting a zero defect policy enabled them to gain competitive advantage.

(2) Just-in-time inventory systems

Traditionally manufacturing adopted economic order quantity (EOQ) as a means of inventory control. Japanese manufacturing developed a system of inventory control called just-in-time (JIT). This reduced factory set-up times, developed relationships with suppliers, reduced inventory holding levels and improved factory layouts. JIT resulted in great improvements in productivity.

(3) Computer-integrated manufacturing systems

Developments in production technology such as robots and computer-aided manufacturing have resulted in improved quality and reliability.

(4) High-technology products: short product life cycles

Many products have a very short product life cycle and companies compete in these industries by being product innovators. Their goals are continually to introduce high-performance products, products delivered in a timely fashion, customised or niche products.

(5) Deregulation: competition in transportation and service industries

Deregulation of transport and service industries in the 1980s resulted in increased competition in these sectors. Organisations that traditionally were never concerned about product profitability or customer service had to respond to competition. They state that deregulation will lead to an increased demand for excellent cost measurement and management systems.

In **Chapter 12: Performance Measurement and Issues in Accounting**, we will discuss how developments in management accounting have strived to cope with these changes.

Why do we need to allocate costs?

Management accounting attributes costs to cost objects, i.e., the item being costed, be it a product or service. This is necessary for inventory valuation, insurance valuation, setting prices which are based on cost, planning and control, performance evaluation and decision-making.

Costing systems allocate costs to cost objects. Upchurch in *Cost Accounting Principles and Practice* (2002) states that allocating costs to products falls into two categories: (1) specific order costing and (2) continuous operation costing. This topic is discussed in detail in **Chapter 2: Product Costing – Materials and Labour.**

Cost classification

The aim of classifying costs is to impose an ordered structure on an organisation's costs. Cost classification is about grouping together costs that have the same attributes. This should be relevant to managers' information needs. For example, in **Chapter 10: Relevant Costing and Decision-Making**, costs are classified into relevant and irrelevant costs, and in **Chapter 9: Cost Volume Profit Analysis**, costs are classified into variable costs, fixed costs and semi-variable costs.

Grouping costs according to attributes is a subjective process and may change from organisation to organisation. The following list is by no means exhaustive but attempts to classify costs according to their use in this book.

(1) Cost classification: direct and indirect costs

A direct cost is directly and exclusively related to the cost object, for example the raw material costs incurred in making a chair. Direct costs are further classified as direct materials, direct labour and direct expenses. The sum of all direct costs is called 'prime cost'.

An indirect cost, also known as an overhead, cannot be directly or exclusively related to the cost object, e.g., the salary of the supervisor in the factory where the chair is made. In production, indirect costs are referred to as production or manufacturing overheads. Indirect costs are further classified as indirect materials, indirect labour and indirect expenses. This topic is discussed further in **Chapter 2: Product Costing – Materials and Labour** and **Chapter 3: Product Costing – Overheads**.

(2) Cost classification: product cost and period cost

A product cost is the cost of making a product or service. It will contain both direct and indirect costs. For example, the product cost of the chair will include direct costs, e.g., raw materials, and some indirect costs, e.g., part of the supervisor's salary. Unsold finished goods inventory will be valued at the product cost and listed on the balance sheet. When the finished goods are sold, they are released as an expense in the income statement and matched against sales revenue.

A period cost is any cost other than a product cost which is incurred during the accounting period. An example would be selling and distribution overheads and administration overheads. They are treated as an expense in the income statement in the period in which they are incurred. This topic is covered in **Chapter 8: Marginal and Absorption Costing**.

(3) Cost classification: variable, fixed, semi-variable and stepped costs

This topic is covered in **Chapter 9: Cost Volume Profit Analysis**.

Variable cost

A variable cost varies with the level of activity. For example, if we produce a chair, the more chairs we produce, the more raw materials we will have to purchase. If we do not produce any chairs, we will not incur any raw material costs. Raw materials are classified as a variable cost. If raw materials are €50 per chair, then:

NUMBER OF CHAIRS		€
Zero	0 x €50 =	0
10	10 x €50 =	500
20	20 x €50 =	1 000
30	30 x €50 =	1 500

This can be represented on a graph where the variable cost line is an upward sloping line as follows:

Figure 1.1: *Variable cost graph*

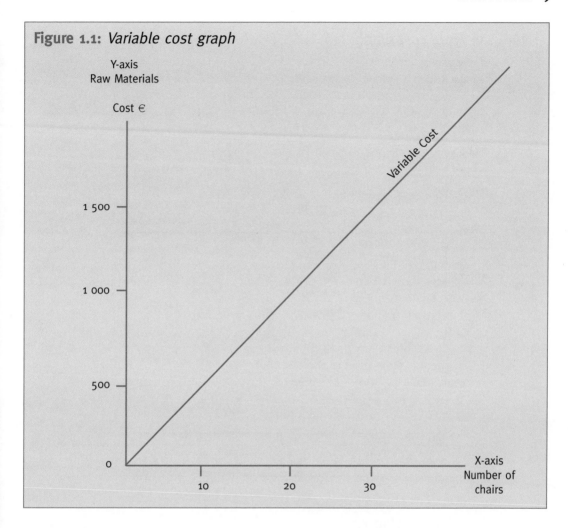

Fixed cost

A fixed cost remains the same or fixed regardless of the level of activity. For example, if the annual rent on the factory where the chairs are produced is €5 000, it will remain the same regardless of whether 10 chairs are produced or 10 000.

The fixed cost line is represented as a horizontal line on the graph:

Figure 1.2: *Fixed cost graph*

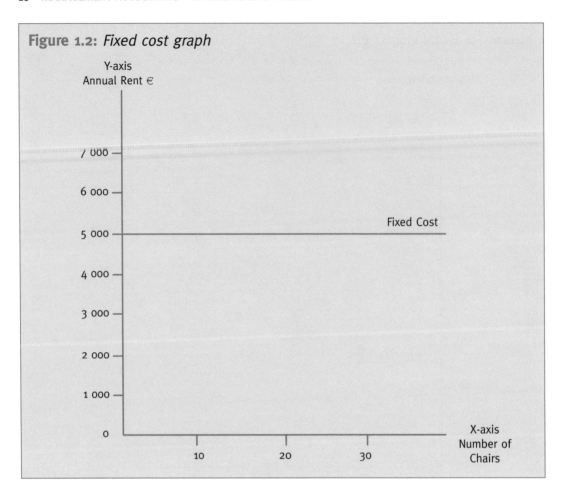

Semi-variable cost

A semi-variable cost contains both a fixed and a variable element. An example would be telephone costs. The telephone line rental is the fixed cost, and the cost of the calls made is the variable cost. The more calls that are made, the more variable cost there will be. If the line rental is €200 and the call cost is €0.50 per call, the semi-variable cost will be:

NUMBER OF CALLS	VARIABLE COST + FIXED COST	SEMI-VARIABLE COST €
Zero	(0 x €0.50) + €200 =	200
100	(100 x €0.50) + €200 =	250
200	(200 x €0.50) + €200 =	300
300	(300 x €0.50) + €200 =	350

The semi-variable line on a graph will be an upward sloping line. Even when the level of activity is zero, in this case when no calls are made, the semi-variable cost will be €200. The semi-variable line will start at €200 on the Y-axis and extend upwards as the number of calls made increases:

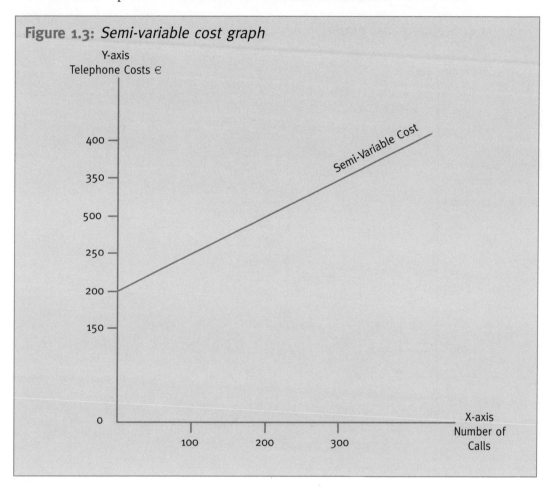

Figure 1.3: *Semi-variable cost graph*

Stepped cost

We have assumed that fixed costs remain fixed at all levels of activity. But in fact fixed costs may increase when a certain level of activity is reached. This is referred to as a stepped cost. For example, if production activity decreases in a factory, a supervisor might continue to be employed in the hope that activity will pick up. If activity does not pick up, he or she may be made redundant. Similarly, if activity increases, an additional supervisor may have to be recruited, but this may take some time. The current supervisor may have to take on extra duties until this happens. When the new supervisor is recruited the fixed costs will suddenly increase.

For example, where a supervisor is paid €50 000 to supervise activity levels within the range of 0 to 500 units, if activity levels increase beyond 500 units, from 501 to 1 000 units, another supervisor will be hired and the total supervisor costs will be €100 000 (€50 000 x 2). If activity levels increase beyond 1 000 units from 1 001 to 1 500 units, then a third supervisor will be hired and the supervisor costs will be €150 000 (€50 000 x 3). This can be represented on a graph as follows:

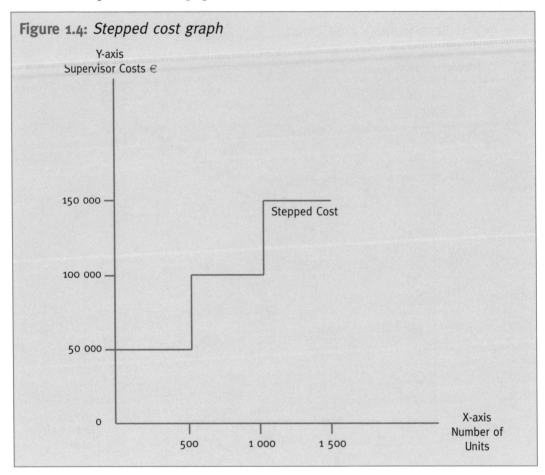

Figure 1.4: *Stepped cost graph*

(4) Cost classification: decision-making

In **Chapter 10: Relevant Costing and Decision-Making**, it is stated that decisions regarding the future of the organisation should be based on relevant information.

When deciding on whether a cost or revenue is relevant to the decision, the following question should be asked: if I go ahead with this decision, will I incur this cost or revenue? If the answer is yes, then the cost is considered to be an avoidable cost or avoidable revenue and is relevant to the decision. If the answer is no, then the cost or revenue is considered to be unavoidable – it will be incurred regardless of the decision made and is irrelevant to the decision.

Decisions which a business will make are based on future costs relevant to that decision. Past costs or 'historic costs' are not relevant as they have occurred or are committed. Past costs are ignored in decision-making. Another name for a past cost is a 'sunk cost'.

Future decisions made by the organisation should include opportunity costs. An opportunity cost is the potential benefit that is forgone when one course of action is taken above another.

(5) Cost classification: non-manufacturing costs

In **Chapter 8: Marginal and Absorption Costing**, non-manufacturing or production costs are classified as:

1 Selling and distribution costs. Examples include sales commissions, sales salaries, shipping and advertising costs.
2 Administration expenses. Examples include clerical costs such as placing orders, secretarial, accounting and public relations costs.

Chapter summary

In this chapter the principles of management accounting and its position in the organisation were explained. The differences between management and financial accounting were discussed.

The student was introduced to the history and development of management accounting and how the role of management accounting has changed in recent times.

The need to allocate costs to cost objects was discussed and the student was introduced to different cost classifications which can assist the management accountant in the management of the organisation.

Test questions

Question 1

An office administrator in a theatre company is applying for an Arts Council grant for an upcoming performance. The performance will take place over two weeks and there will be 16 performances. The terms of the grant only cover direct costs associated with the performance. You are asked to assist the administrator in highlighting the direct costs and indirect costs from the following list of costs:

- Annual rent on office €5 000
- Hire of theatre for two weeks €1 000
- Hire of props assistant for the two weeks of the performance and one week of rehearsal €2 000
- Hire of costumes for performance €750

- Cost per programme printed €5
- Royalty payments €500 regardless of the number of performances
- Office administrator's salary for the two weeks €800

Question 2

Alan Arklow makes and sells clay pots. He is budgeted to produce 1 500 pots in February but he believes that he may receive a last-minute order which would increase this to 2 000 pots. The following costs are estimated:

- Clay for each pot costs €10
- Rent on the workshop is €500 per month
- Telephone line rental is €75 per month and each call made costs €0.10; Alan makes on average one call for each clay pot made
- Alan has one full-time apprentice working with him who earns a salary of €700 per month

Required

a   Classify each of the above costs as fixed, variable or semi-variable
b   Using your classification in (a) above, plot your results onto a fixed cost graph, variable cost graph and semi-variable cost graph

Question 3

The following are a list of costs which a hairdressing salon incurs. You are required to state whether they are variable, fixed or semi-variable costs:

- Salary of owner of the salon €50 000 per annum
- Hair colouring costs €35 per head
- Conditioning treatments cost €10 per head
- Rent on salon €1 500 per month
- Telephone costs of salon landline
- Salary of head stylist €1 000 per month plus bonus €10 per conditioning treatment sold

For answers and additional test questions, see www.gillmacmillan.ie. Search for Management Accounting and click on the link in the right-hand column.

2 Product Costing – Materials and Labour

Learning outcomes of Chapter 2

At the end of this chapter, you will be able to:

* explain the different costing methodologies
* discuss the components of product costing
* calculate the issues of inventory using FIFO, LIFO and weighted average pricing methods
* discuss and calculate the traditional approach to managing inventory – economic order quantity
* understand the modern approaches to managing inventory – just-in-time and materials requirement planning
* calculate labour costs in product costing

Introduction

Costs such as materials, labour and overheads need to be allocated to products in production in the business. This is necessary for inventory valuation and insurance purposes. Upchurch in *Cost Accounting Principles and Practice* (2002) states that allocating costs to products falls into two categories: (1) specific order costing and (2) continuous operation costing.

(1) Specific order costing

In specific order costing, usually a unique or one-off product is being produced for a customer so it is easier to track costs to products as they move through the manufacturing cycle. Examples of specific order costing are:

Job costing

This costing system applies to a single task, product or service charged to one customer. It is identifiable with and made to the specific requirements of a customer and priced accordingly. It is normally of a short duration and is completed within one accounting period. Cost accumulation is straightforward as costs such as labour and materials are collected and allocated to the job as it progresses. Examples where job costing would be appropriate would be building work, e.g., an extension on a house, or printing of brochures by a printing company.

Batch costing

This is a variation of job costing. It occurs when units are batched into production runs where products share common attributes. For example, in the production of table lamps, the early part of the production process may be common but as the lamps enter the final production stages they may be batched into units which have a cream lampshade, a blue lampshade, etc. Costs are allocated to each batch or production run.

Contract costing

Contract costing is similar to job costing except that the work being carried out is of a much larger nature and of a longer duration. Contracts would normally span a number of accounting periods, progress payments would be made at different stages of the contract and this would require legal documents setting out details of the contract to be drawn up. Examples where contracts would be appropriate would be in large construction projects such as building a hospital or bridge. In this situation architects' certificates would be required as proof that work has been carried out before any payments are made.

(2) Continuous operation costing

In continuous operation costing similar products are produced on a mass scale. It is more difficult to allocate costs to cost objects as the individual objects or products may not be identifiable until the end of the manufacturing cycle. Examples of continuous operation costing are:

Process costing

Process costing involves the mass production of a single product. It is used in food processing and oil refining. It is uneconomical to trace the individual costs incurred in making a single product, so an average cost per unit is calculated instead and each individual product's cost is based on this average. Process costing is dealt with in Chapter 5.

Service costing

Products being made in manufacturing differ from a service provided by a service company. Take, for example, a loaf of bread made by a manufacturer:

the bread is a tangible product and all costs involved in its manufacture – direct materials, direct labour, direct expenses and overheads – form the basis of the product cost. The customer purchases the finished product (a tangible product).

Contrast this with a service provider, e.g., a hairdresser. A customer enters the hairdresser and asks for a service, e.g., a haircut. The product (haircut) is not a tangible product; it is a service rendered to the customer who partakes while the service is being provided. The customer pays for a service, e.g., cut and blow dry, blow dry, colour (an intangible product).

A hospital, for example, provides a service to the public, i.e., treating and curing patients. How would costs be allocated to these services and how would the performance of these services be measured? Perhaps the hospital would allocate costs per number of out-patient clinics or the number of operations carried out. This would allow it to measure performance over different periods and against different hospitals.

A law firm, for example, also provides a service to its clients. A case undertaken for a client would represent a 'job'. All costs associated with the case are gathered – the time lawyers spent on the case (direct labour cost), legal forms (direct material cost) and a portion of secretary salaries, rent, heat and light (overheads). This forms the cost of the job or case charged to the client.

Activity-based costing (ABC) can be used to allocate costs to services and the balanced scorecard can be used to measure performance. ABC will be dealt with in Chapter 4 and the balanced scorecard is discussed in Chapter 12.

The components of product costing

A cost will need to be established for products for inventory valuation purposes and also to establish a selling price. The product cost will contain the following components:

(1) Direct material costs

This is the cost of the raw materials used in making the product. Material costs are classified as a direct cost.

(2) Direct labour costs

This is the labour cost of staff used in making the product. Labour costs are classified as a direct cost.

(3) Direct expenses

A direct expense is any cost other than materials and labour which is directly related to the product being produced. An example would be the hire of special equipment for a specific job.

(4) Production overhead costs

Production or manufacturing overheads are classified as indirect costs. They may include the labour cost of the supervisor on the factory floor. He or she may supervise the production of many different products and his or her labour cost cannot be traced directly back to the product being produced. Production overheads can include indirect materials, indirect labour and indirect expenses.

(5) Non-manufacturing costs

Non-manufacturing or non-production costs are classified as indirect costs. They may include marketing, selling and administration costs which are necessary for the running of the business but are not directly related to production of products. Examples of marketing costs include the salaries and travel expenses of sales staff, and advertising costs. Examples of administration costs include general management salaries and costs of running the personnel and finance departments.

All of the costs incurred in producing a product are added together to arrive at the product cost:

Direct materials

+

Direct labour

+

Direct expenses

=

Prime cost

+

Production overhead costs

=

Production cost

+

Non-manufacturing costs

=

Total cost/full cost

The sum of all direct costs is called the prime cost.

In this chapter we will use methods to allocate materials and labour into products being costed. In Chapter 3 we use methods to allocate overheads into products being costed.

The traditional approach to accounting for inventory in product costing

In a manufacturing process raw materials are in constant use. There is a link between the purchasing department, the stores warehouse and the production department.

When inventory levels fall to their reorder level in the warehouse a **purchase requisition** for the reorder quantity is sent to the purchasing department. A suitable supplier is selected and a **purchase order** for the reorder quantity is sent to the supplier and a copy to the warehouse.

When the materials are delivered, the warehouse receiving person checks the **delivery note** and the inventory against the purchase order to ensure the delivery is correct. **A goods received note** is signed by the warehouse receiving person and sent to the accounts department and a copy to the purchasing department. The **supplier's invoice** is checked against the goods received note to ensure the quantity and type of inventory received is correct. The supplier is then paid.

The inventory is coded in the warehouse and the inventory level on the stores accounts system is updated. When inventory is required in production, a **stores requisition order** is issued by the production department to the stores warehouse. The inventory is moved to production. The inventory code is scanned by a hand-held computer device and the inventory levels in the stores accounts system are updated.

Inventory levels are maintained to ensure there is no 'stock-out' in production whereby production is ready to receive inventory but the warehouse is awaiting a delivery of inventory from the supplier. Maintaining a minimum inventory level is very costly because inventory must be stored and staff must be employed to maintain the inventory, and it may need to be refrigerated or heated.

Stock-takes are carried out to ensure physical inventory levels match the inventory levels on the stores accounts system. Stock-takes can be carried out periodically. For example, once a year when the auditors are checking inventory levels, all the inventory is counted at one time, possibly in one day or over a weekend. Alternatively, stock-takes can be carried out continually, whereby different sections of inventory are counted on a regular basis – for example, daily or weekly – thus preventing a total shutdown of the warehouse.

Pricing the issues of inventories

A value needs to be placed on inventory when it is moved to production for the manufacture of products. Placing a value is also necessary for closing inventory valuation and insurance purposes. Inventory will also be moved from the warehouse to production in rotation, i.e., the oldest inventory will be moved first, then the next oldest and so on.

Inventory levels change constantly and inventory is replenished regularly. Inventory prices from suppliers will fluctuate as economic conditions change. At what price should we value inventory? The price at which we purchased the oldest inventory or the most recent price we paid for inventory?

There are three methods of valuing inventories:

1   First in, first out or FIFO
2   Last in, first out or LIFO
3   Weighted average

IAS 2 Inventories (*International GAAP 2009*) allows either a FIFO or a weighted average method to be used for financial reporting. The LIFO method is not an acceptable method under IAS 2. For management accounting purposes any of the three methods can be used for inventory valuation.

(1) First in, first out (FIFO)

IAS 2 states that 'the FIFO method probably gives the closest approximation to actual cost flows, since it is assumed that when inventories are sold or used in a production process, the oldest are sold or used first. Consequently the balance of inventory on hand at any point represents the most recent purchases or production.'

(2) Last in, first out (LIFO)

IAS 2 states that 'the most recent purchases or production are used first. It is an attempt to match current costs with current revenues so that the profit and loss account excludes the effects of holding gains. LIFO is no longer permitted for published accounts but it is allowable under US GAAP.'

(3) Weighted average

IAS 2 states that weighted average 'involves the computation of an average unit cost by dividing the total cost of units by the number of units. The average unit cost then has to be revised with every receipt of inventory or, alternatively, at the end of predetermined periods.'

Example 2.1

The following production and inventory information has been provided for Lily Ltd:

2 April	Issued to production	4 000 kg
7 April	Purchased	5 000 kg @ €20 per kg
10 April	Purchased	5 000 kg @ €18 per kg
15 April	Issued to production	4 000 kg
20 April	Issued to production	4 000 kg
24 April	Purchased	2 000 kg @ €21 per kg

The opening inventory on 1 April is 10 000 kg valued at €19 per kg.

Required

Prepare statements showing the amount charged to production and the value of inventory held after each inventory transaction using:

a   The FIFO method
b   The LIFO method
c   The weighted average method

Solution to Example 2.1

a The FIFO method

Date	RECEIPTS			ISSUES			BALANCE		
	Kg	Price €	Value €	Kg	Price €	Value €	Kg	Price €	Value €
1 Apr							10 000	19.00	190 000
2 Apr				4 000	19.00	76 000	6 000	19.00	114 000
7 Apr	5 000	20.00	100 000				6 000	19.00	114 000
							5 000	20.00	100 000
							11 000		214 000
10 Apr	5 000	18.00	90 000				6 000	19.00	114 000
							5 000	20.00	100 000
							5 000	18.00	90 000
							16 000		304 000
15 Apr				4 000	19.00	76 000	2 000	19.00	38 000
							5 000	20.00	100 000
							5 000	18.00	90 000
							12 000		228 000
20 Apr				2 000	19.00	38 000	3 000	20.00	60 000
				2 000	20.00	40 000	5 000	18.00	90 000
				4 000		78 000	8 000		150 000
24 Apr	2 000	21.00	42 000				3 000	20.00	60 000
							5 000	18.00	90 000
							2 000	21.00	42 000
							10 000		192 000

Using FIFO the closing inventory value is €192 000 and closing inventory is 10 000 units. The value of inventory issued is:

	€
2 April	76 000
15 April	76 000
10 April	78 000
Total value of inventory issued	230 000

Drury (2008) states that during periods of inflation, using FIFO, the earliest inventories that have the lowest purchase price will be issued first. This assumption leads to a lower cost of sales calculation and therefore a higher profit than would be obtained by using either of the other methods.

b The LIFO method

Date	RECEIPTS Kg	RECEIPTS Price €	RECEIPTS Value €	ISSUES Kg	ISSUES Price €	ISSUES Value €	BALANCE Kg	BALANCE Price €	BALANCE Value €
1 Apr							10 000	19.00	190 000
2 Apr				4 000	19.00	76 000	6 000	19.00	114 000
7 Apr	5 000	20.00	100 000				6 000	19.00	114 000
							5 000	20.00	100 000
							11 000		214 000
10 Apr	5 000	18.00	90 000				6 000	19.00	114 000
							5 000	20.00	100 000
							5 000	18.00	90 000
							16 000		304 000
15 Apr				4 000	18.00	72 000	6 000	19.00	114 000
							5 000	20.00	100 000
							1 000	18.00	18 000
							12 000		232 000
20 Apr				1 000	18.00	18 000	6 000	19.00	114 000
				3 000	20.00	60 000	2 000	20.00	40 000
				4 000		78 000	8 000		154 000
24 Apr	2 000	21.00	42 000				6 000	19.00	114 000
							2 000	20.00	40 000
							2 000	21.00	42 000
							10 000		196 000

Using LIFO the closing inventory value is €196 000 and closing inventory is 10 000 units. The value of inventory issued is:

	€
2 April	76 000
15 April	72 000
10 April	78 000
Total value of inventory issued	226 000

Drury (2008) states that during periods of inflation, using LIFO, the latest and higher prices are assigned to the cost of sales and therefore lower profits will be reported compared with using either FIFO or weighted average.

c The weighted average method

Date	RECEIPTS Kg	Price €	Value €	ISSUES Kg	Price €	Value €	BALANCE Kg	Price €	Value €
1 Apr							10 000	19.00	190 000
2 Apr				4 000	19.00	76 000	6 000	19.00	114 000
7 Apr	5 000	20.00	100 000				6 000	19.00	114 000
							5 000	20.00	100 000
							11 000	19.454	214 000
10 Apr	5 000	18.00	90 000				11 000	19.454	214 000
							5 000	18.00	90 000
							16 000	19.00	304 000
15 Apr				4 000	19.00	76 000	12 000	19.00	228 000
20 Apr				4 000	19.00	76 000	8 000	19.00	152 000
24 Apr	2 000	21.00	42 000				8 000	19.00	152 000
							2 000	21.00	42 000
							10 000	19.40	194 000

The weighted average price will need to be recalculated every time inventory is purchased. In Example 2.1 part (c) above, new inventory was purchased on 7 April. The weighted average is calculated:

$$\frac{\text{Closing inventory value}}{\text{Closing inventory units}} \quad \frac{€214\ 000}{11\ 000\ \text{units}} = €19.454 \text{ per unit}$$

More inventory is purchased on 10 April and the weighted average is recalculated:

$$\frac{\text{Closing inventory value}}{\text{Closing inventory units}} \quad \frac{€304\ 000}{16\ 000\ \text{units}} = €19 \text{ per unit}$$

When inventory is next issued on 15 April it is issued at the most recent weighted average price, i.e., €19 per unit. Finally, on 24 April after more inventory is purchased, the weighted average is again recalculated:

$$\frac{\text{Closing inventory value}}{\text{Closing inventory units}} \quad \frac{€194\ 000}{10\ 000\ \text{units}} = €19.40 \text{ per unit}$$

Using weighted average, the closing inventory value is €194 000 and closing inventory is 10 000 units. The value of inventory issued is:

	€
2 April	76 000
15 April	76 000
10 April	76 000
Total value of inventory issued	228 000

Using weighted average, Drury (2008) states that during periods of inflation the cost of sales and the closing inventory will fall somewhere between the values recorded for the FIFO and LIFO methods.

Points to note about Example 2.1

- The number of units issued and the closing units will always be the same with the three methods.
- The profits of a company will be affected by the method of inventory valuation used during periods of inflation and deflation.
- FIFO and weighted average are acceptable under IAS 2 and LIFO is not.

Managing inventory levels using economic order quantity

The traditional approach to managing inventory levels has been to use the economic order quantity (EOQ) approach. There is a trade-off when managing inventory levels in a business between carrying too much inventory and incurring high inventory holding costs and carrying too little inventory and incurring high inventory ordering costs.

Inventory holding costs are costs associated with storing inventory, e.g., the cost of rent on the warehouse, the cost of heating or refrigerating inventory and the cost of the staff managing the warehouse.

Inventory ordering costs are costs associated with ordering inventory, e.g., the administration costs of placing orders with suppliers and the accounting costs of paying orders.

If a company decides to reduce the amount of inventory it stores, it will reduce its inventory holding costs. It will have to order inventory more frequently to prevent 'stock-outs' where production ceases when inventory runs out. Inventory ordering costs will increase.

Economic order quantity

The economic order quantity (EOQ) model is an attempt to set an order size which minimises the holding costs and ordering costs. It can be found by means of a formula:

$$\text{EOQ} = \sqrt{\frac{2 \times \text{total demand} \times \text{cost per order}}{\text{Holding cost per unit}}}$$

The total demand is the total demand for the period in question, be it annual demand, monthly demand, weekly demand or daily demand. It is calculated using the maximum usage per day.

An assumption built into the EOQ model is that the holding cost per unit will remain constant. Holding costs may increase as stock levels increase. It also assumes that the ordering cost is constant as is the cost per order. All of these costs can fluctuate.

Lead time

The lead time is the time that lapses between placing an order and receiving the inventory. If the rate of usage of inventory is constant in production, the lead time can be determined with reasonable certainty.

Reorder level

The reorder level is the point or level at which an order should be placed with the supplier to replenish inventory. It can be determined using the following formula:

Reorder level = maximum usage x maximum lead time

Maximum stock level

Storey in *Introduction to Cost and Management Accounting* (2002) states that the maximum stock level is calculated by reducing the reorder level to the least amount on the assumption that the supplier delivers the inventories in the quickest time. The EOQ is added to this. Holding excess inventories ties up working capital and is costly. Therefore the formula uses the minimum usage and minimum lead time. The formula is:

Maximum stock level = reorder level –
(minimum usage x minimum lead time) + EOQ

Minimum stock level (where there is no safety stock)

The reason for setting the minimum stock level is to prevent a stock-out where inventory is required in production but is not available in the warehouse. The formula uses the average usage and average lead time. If the minimum usage and minimum lead time were to be used the company might risk a stock-out. The formula is:

Minimum stock level = reorder level – (average usage x average lead time)

Safety stock

Where delivery of inventories is irregular or suppliers unreliable, a business may decide to keep a buffer stock or safety stock. Seal, Garrison and Noreen in *Management Accounting* (2008) state that the size of safety stock is determined by deducting average usage from the maximum usage that can reasonably be expected during the lead time.

Minimum stock level (where there is safety stock)

Storey in *Introduction to Cost and Management Accounting* (2002) states that where a safety stock level is to be maintained, the minimum stock level will be set higher. The formula is:

Minimum stock level = reorder level + safety stock
– (average usage x average lead time)

Example 2.2*

The following information is available for a company which holds inventories:

Cost per kg	€20
Holding costs per annum	8% of cost
Cost per order	€600
Average usage per day	400 kg
Maximum usage per day	800 kg
Minimum usage per day	200 kg
Maximum lead time	8 days
Minimum lead time	2 days

The company operates a five-day-week manufacturing cycle and operates for 50 weeks per year. Management are anxious about inventory holding costs and have asked you to calculate the following:

Required

a Economic order quantity
b Reorder level
c Minimum stock level assuming no safety stock
d Maximum stock level

* Based on question 3 in IATI Costing & Budgeting, Summer 2007.

Solution to Example 2.2

a Economic order quantity

$$EOQ = \sqrt{\frac{2 \times \text{total demand} \times \text{cost per order}}{\text{Holding cost per unit}}}$$

$$EOQ = \sqrt{\frac{2 \times (800 \text{ kg} \times 5 \text{ days} \times 50 \text{ weeks}) \times €600}{8\% \times €20}}$$

$$= \sqrt{\frac{2 \times 200\,000 \text{ kg} \times €600}{€1.6}}$$

$$= \sqrt{\frac{240\,000\,000}{€1.60}}$$

$$= 12\,247 \text{ kg (to the nearest kg)}$$

b Reorder level

$$\begin{aligned}
\text{Reorder level} \ &= \ \text{maximum usage x maximum lead time} \\
&= \ \text{800 kg x 8 days} \\
&= \ \text{6 400 kg}
\end{aligned}$$

c Minimum stock level assuming no safety stock

$$\begin{aligned}
\text{Minimum stock level} \ &= \ \text{reorder level} - (\text{average usage x average lead time}) \\
&= \ \text{6 400 kg} - \left(\text{400 kg} \times \frac{\text{8 days} + \text{2 days}}{2}\right) \\
&= \ \text{4 400 kg}
\end{aligned}$$

d Maximum stock level

$$\begin{aligned}
\text{Minimum stock level} \ &= \ \text{reorder level} - (\text{minimum usage x minimum lead time}) + \text{EOQ} \\
&= \ \text{6 400 kg} - (\text{200 kg x 2 days}) + \text{15 492 kg} \\
&= \ \text{21 492 kg}
\end{aligned}$$

Managing inventory using just-in-time

Just-in-time (JIT) is a Japanese philosophy which states that inventory should not be held, as it is a cost burden, but should arrive from the supplier just as it is needed in production.

JIT endeavours to reduce holding costs and inward inspection costs, and to have zero defects in production. It operates a 'pull through' system where inventory is ordered only when it is required in production, and production occurs only in response to customer demand. This is in contrast to a 'push' system where inventory acts as a buffer between production, purchases and sales.

If suppliers do not deliver on time, production will halt and deadlines will not be met. The company will need to consider the location of the supplier, as frequent small deliveries are required. JIT relies on building relationships with a few reliable suppliers who deliver defect-free inventory.

JIT is suitable for production processes in which there are short set-up times, where customer demand is constant and there are no downtimes due to poor quality inventory.

Managing inventory using materials requirement planning

CIMA Official Terminology defines materials requirement planning (MRP) as 'a system that converts a production schedule into a listing of the materials and components required to meet that schedule, so that adequate stock levels are maintained and items are available when needed'.

Materials requirement planning, now known as MRP I, originated in the 1960s. It is a computerised system which co-ordinates the planning of inventory used in production and the timing of inventory purchases. The components and sub-components of the finished product may take different lengths of time to produce and MRP takes account of this. The operation of an MRP system involves the following:

(1) A master production schedule

This schedule is produced from known customer orders and sets out how many units of each product are required from production and by when.

(2) A bill of materials

A bill of materials is produced for every product produced by the company. It lists the components, sub-components and raw materials which make up the product. The master production schedule uses the bill of materials to establish the timing for purchasing and production of these components, sub-components and raw materials.

(3) An inventory file

Inventory files will contain information on the availability of components, sub-components and raw materials.

MRP aims to produce a planned schedule of components, sub-components and raw materials required for production.

Material resource planning, or MRP II, is an extension of MRP I. *CIMA Official Terminology* defines MRP II as 'an expansion of materials requirement planning (MRP) to give a broader approach than MRP to the planning and scheduling of resources, embracing areas such as finance, logistics, engineering and marketing'.

MRP II systems aim to integrate purchases, planning, inventory control and accounting systems through a common computer system.

Accounting for labour costs in product costing

The labour costs incurred in manufacturing must be traced to the products being produced to determine the total product cost. Employees will record their working time on a time sheet or a clock card system. The time sheet will enable them to distinguish between productive hours, overtime hours and idle time hours, for example where a machine breaks down and production is suspended. The time sheet should also detail the job or products being produced. Once it has been signed off by a supervisor it will be used (i) to generate the employees' pay slips and (ii) to form the basis of direct and indirect labour costs.

Basic pay

Basic pay is calculated by multiplying hours worked by rate per hour. In the past this was how businesses paid staff. There is now a tendency to provide a contract to staff and to pay them a salary. This provides job protection for staff and avoids the exploitation by employers of staff members. Staff remuneration now tends to be a fixed cost rather than a variable cost.

Idle time

Idle time occurs where staff are available and ready to work but cannot do so as a result of a machine breaking down, inventory being unavailable or a bottleneck in production. The cost of idle time is calculated by multiplying the idle time hours by the labour rate per hour. If the idle time is unexpected, e.g., owing to a machine breakdown, then it should be treated as an indirect labour cost charged to the idle time overhead account for the production department. If the idle time is expected, e.g., the time staff spend travelling to a job, then the cost of the idle time should be treated as a direct labour cost.

Overtime

Overtime occurs where work is performed outside normal working hours. An overtime premium is added to the normal hourly rate. The overtime premium is usually at 'time and a half', where the overtime premium is half that of the normal hourly rate, or at 'double time', where the overtime premium equals that of the normal hourly rate.

The normal time element of overtime is treated as direct labour and the overtime premium, if it is a result of lack of labour hours or machine hours, is treated as an overhead or indirect labour. The reason for this is that comparing the labour cost of work performed in overtime with similar work performed in normal time would give an artificially inflated view of labour cost. If the work is carried out in overtime as a request of the customer, the overtime premium would be charged as a direct cost to that customer's job.

Example 2.3*

An employee works a 40-hour week and earns €20 per labour hour. During week 5, because of a machine breakdown, 10 hours of overtime were worked by the employee at 'time and a half'. The machine was out of commission for eight hours and this has been recorded as idle time.

Required

a   During week 5 calculate how much of the employee's wages would be classified as direct labour

b   During week 5 calculate how much of the employee's wages would be classified as indirect labour

* Based on question 3 in CPA Professional 2 Management Accounting, April 2008.

Solution to Example 2.3

a   During week 5 calculate how much of the employee's wages would be classified as direct labour. The direct labour cost would consist of the hours worked in normal time:

		€
Productive hours 32 hours x €20	=	640
Normal time element of overtime: 10 hours x €20	=	200
Total direct labour cost		840

b   During week 5 calculate how much of the employee's wages would be classified as indirect labour. The indirect labour cost would consist of the overtime premium element of overtime and the idle time hours:

		€
Overtime premium: 10 hours x (€20 x 0.5)	=	100
Idle time hours: 8 hours x €20	=	160
Total indirect labour cost		260

Remuneration and labour incentive schemes

There are two approaches to remuneration: (1) a time-based system, and (2) an output-based system. Employers may decide to implement a labour incentive scheme to increase productivity, improve staff morale and attract more experienced staff to the business.

(1) Time-based system

Using a time-based scheme the employee is paid an hourly rate based on the number of hours worked. To increase productivity, management may introduce a premium bonus scheme as a way of rewarding more productive employees. Employees are awarded a bonus based on the time saved in completing a task:

Standard time to complete a task – actual time taken to complete the task
= time saved x premium bonus

Standard time is the time it should take to complete a task. Standards are discussed in Chapter 7. The details of the actual time taken to complete a task should be available on the employee's time sheet or clock card.

A time-based system is appropriate where activities vary and output is difficult to measure such as in an office. It is also appropriate where quality of output is important.

(2) Output-based system

Using an output-based scheme the employees are paid a rate per unit based on the number of units they produce:

Units produced x piecework rate

As an incentive the employees may be guaranteed a minimum percentage of their basic pay. This percentage will be negotiated between staff, unions and management.

An output-based system is appropriate where a series of repetitive tasks is carried out, such as on a production line. It is important to ensure quality controls are in place as quality can suffer if output increases.

Problems with labour incentive schemes

Labour incentive schemes encourage an increase in output, but as output increases quality can suffer, rejects can occur and re-works may need to take place. Businesses need to ensure they have quality control procedures in place, such as regular inspections, to counteract this.

Output in non-manufacturing departments, e.g., finance, may be difficult to quantify and labour incentive schemes may be subjective. This can result in employee dissatisfaction and loss of morale.

Labour incentive schemes may cause stress amongst employees where competition arises.

Example 2.4

Management are considering introducing an incentive scheme for staff working in production. Employees work a 40-hour week and are paid €12 per hour. Their output is as follows:

Staff member A:	325 units
Staff member B:	350 units
Staff member C:	475 units

Required

a   Calculate the basic pay for each employee

b Calculate the wages paid to each employee if a piecework scheme is introduced. The piecework rate is €0.75 per unit and they are guaranteed 70% of their basic pay. State the amount each staff member will receive in wages

c Calculate the wages paid to each employee if a premium bonus scheme is introduced. The standard time taken to complete each unit is seven minutes and a bonus of 80% is paid on time saved

Solution to Example 2.4

a Calculate the basic pay for each employee:

Basic pay = hours worked x labour rate per hour
40 hours x €12 per hour = €480

Currently each employee receives €480 per week in basic pay regardless of their productivity.

b Calculate the wages paid to each employee if a piecework scheme is introduced and state the amount each staff member will receive in wages

Calculate the piecework amount by multiplying the units produced by the piecework rate per unit:

Staff member A: 325 units x €0.75 = €243.75
Staff member B: 350 units x €0.75 = €262.50
Staff member C: 475 units x €0.75 = €356.25

Staff are guaranteed a minimum of 70% of their basic pay which is:

70% x €480 = €336

Under the piecework scheme staff members A and B will be paid the guaranteed minimum pay of €336. Staff member C will be paid the piecework amount of €356.25.

c Calculate the wages paid to each employee if a premium bonus scheme is introduced

The standard time set to complete a unit is seven minutes. Calculate the standard time it should have taken to complete the actual units and compare it with the actual time taken to determine whether there was a saving:

	UNITS		STAND MINS		TOTAL STAND MINS		60 MINS		STAND HOURS	ACTUAL HOURS	SAVING IN HOURS
A	325	X	7	=	2 275	/	60	=	37.92	40	–
B	350	X	7	=	2 450	/	60	=	40.83	40	0.83
C	475	X	7	=	3 325	/	60	=	55.42	40	15.42

Staff member A will not receive a premium bonus as it should have taken him 37.92 hours to complete 325 units but it took him 40 hours. He will receive the basic pay of €480.

Staff members B and C will receive premium bonuses as they completed their units in less time than the standard hours allowed. The premium bonus is calculated as follows:

Time saved x labour rate per hour x 80%

The bonus is paid in addition to their basic pay.

Staff member B:
Premium bonus:	0.83 hours x €12 x 80%	=	€ 7.97
Basic pay:			€480.00
Total wages paid:			€487.97

Staff member C:
Premium bonus:	15.42 hours x €12 x 80%	=	€148.03
Basic pay:			€480.00
Total wages paid:			€628.03

Labour efficiency

The labour efficiency ratio indicates whether staff completed the work in less time or more time than anticipated. The ratio is calculated as follows:

$$\frac{\text{Standard hours taken to produce actual units}}{\text{Actual hours taken}} \times 100$$

If the ratio is greater than 100 then staff were more efficient than anticipated; if less than 100 they were less efficient than anticipated.

Labour turnover

Employees leave and new employees are recruited. It costs to recruit new employees and there are administration costs and disruption to the business when employees leave. Labour turnover is a measure of the number of employees leaving and being recruited in a period, expressed as a percentage of the total number of employees:

$$\frac{\text{Number of employees replaced during the period}}{\text{Total number of staff employed during the period}} \times \frac{100}{1}$$

The labour turnover percentage provides an insight into employee satisfaction and it can be compared with similar businesses in the same industry.

Chapter summary

This chapter began by introducing different costing methodologies that can be adopted by businesses. Two important elements of product costing were discussed – materials and labour.

The costing of materials was explained using the FIFO, LIFO and weighted average methods. The traditional approach to managing inventories was discussed under economic order quantity and more modern approaches to managing inventories were discussed under just-in-time and materials requirement planning.

The costing of labour and issues such as idle time, overtime, labour turnover and incentive schemes were discussed. Categorising labour costs into direct labour and indirect labour was also examined.

Test questions

Question 1

The following inventory and production information has been provided for Earley Ltd:

1 June	Opening inventory	1 000 kg	At €10 per kg
10 June	Bought	500 kg	At €12 per kg
12 June	Issued	800 kg	
15 June	Bought	700 kg	At €15 per kg
20 June	Issued	600 kg	
24 June	Bought	1 000 kg	At €14 per kg
26 June	Issued	900 kg	

Required

Prepare a statement showing the value of issues and the value of inventory using each of the following methods:

a   First in, first out (FIFO)
b   Last in, first out (LIFO)
c   Weighted average

Question 2

A company has the following receipts and issues of inventory during the month of October:

1 Oct	Opening balance	100 litres	Valued at €5 per litre
11 Oct	Receipts	150 litres	At €5.50 per litre
12 Oct	Issued	100 litres	
17 Oct	Receipts	100 litres	At €6 per litre
22 Oct	Issued	75 litres	

Required

Prepare a statement showing the value of issues and the value of inventory using each of the following methods:

a First in, first out (FIFO)
b Last in, first out (LIFO)
c Weighted average

Question 3

The following information relates to two products produced by a company:

	IBOD	MPY
Cost per kg	€2.50	€1
Maximum usage per day	100 kg	2 500 kg
Minimum usage per day	25 kg	1 250 kg
Maximum lead time	15 days	6 days
Minimum lead time	5 days	3 days
Storage costs per annum	8% of cost	
Cost per order	€100	
Production period	125 days	

Required

You are required to calculate the following for each product:

a Economic order quantity
b Reorder level
c Minimum stock level
d Maximum stock level

Notes to students

1   Calculate each of the formulas for the two products.
2   The average usage and the average lead time will both need to be calculated as they are not given in the question.
3   The total demand in the EOQ formula should be based on maximum usage.
4   There is no mention of safety stock so the minimum stock level formula will be:

Minimum stock level = reorder level – (average usage x average lead time)

For answers and additional test questions, see www.gillmacmillan.ie. Search for Management Accounting and click on the link in the right-hand column.

3 Product Costing – Overheads

Learning outcomes of Chapter 3

At the end of this chapter, you will be able to:

- discuss the traditional approach to overhead absorption into product costs
- calculate overhead absorption rates using five methods of overhead absorption
- calculate the price of a job for a customer and work out the profit using mark-up and margin
- discuss when to use a plant-wide overhead absorption rate and when to use individual overhead absorption rates
- discuss the use of budgeted information to calculate overhead absorption rates and calculate under- and over-absorption of overheads
- calculate non-production overhead absorption rates
- use the repeated distribution method and specified order of closing method to reallocate service centre costs
- discuss the criticisms of the traditional approach to overhead absorption

Introduction

In Chapter 2 product costing and the costing approaches to materials and labour were discussed. In Chapter 3 we will discuss the traditional approach to overhead absorption. This is a method of allocating production and production-related overheads or indirect costs to products. If product values didn't include some overhead costs then they would be undervalued. Overhead absorption is a means of allocating a small amount of overheads, such as rent of the factory premises, to the products in production.

Allocating overheads into products using the traditional approach

In this chapter we will discuss how production overheads such as rent on the factory or the supervisor's salary can be apportioned to products in production. Overheads are also described as indirect costs and products are described as cost objects.

As products are being produced they will move through different production departments or cost centres. For example, consider a factory producing furniture such as a table. The table starts off as a raw material, i.e., wood. It moves from the Warehouse into the Cutting Department where it is cut into the various components of the table. It is now considered to be work in progress. The components then move to the Assembly Department where they are assembled into a table. The table then moves to the Finishing Department where it is varnished and finished and becomes a finished good. The finished table is then sold to the customer.

When deciding how much to charge for the table, all the costs involved in making it will need to be gathered. Raw materials will need to be ordered for production. The costs of materials will be available from invoices. Material costs are a direct cost. Staff working in production will sign in and out and their hours will be recorded using a labour costing system. The labour costs involved in producing the tables can be calculated by multiplying labour hours by the labour rate per hour. Labour costs are a direct cost. Materials and labour costing were discussed in Chapter 2.

Production overheads such as rent on the factory and the supervisor's salary, which are not directly related to the tables in production, are an indirect cost. If we only cost the tables with the materials and labour costs we will have undercosted the table as we are ignoring production overhead costs. After all, we would not be able to produce the tables if we didn't pay the rent on the factory or we didn't have supervisors on the factory floor. But the rent refers to the whole of the factory and several products may be in production such as chairs, beds and tables. An equitable method of allocating the production overhead costs to products needs to be established. The traditional method used is called the overhead absorption method.

Overhead absorption method

When absorbing production overhead costs into products a number of steps need to be carried out:

1 Allocate and apportion production overheads to production and service cost centres.
2 Reapportion service centre costs to production centres.
3 Calculate overhead absorption rates for each production centre.
4 Use overhead absorption rates to cost products.

Each of these steps is discussed below.

(1) Allocate and apportion production overheads to production and service cost centres

Initially we will consider an example of allocating and apportioning production overheads to production cost centres, i.e., production departments, only. Service cost centres, i.e., service departments, will be dealt with in step 2.

Using the example of manufacturing tables mentioned above, each table moves through the factory as follows:

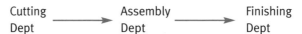

Some production overheads can be allocated directly to a production cost centre. Consider the running costs of a machine in the Cutting Department. The machine is only in the Cutting Department, so any costs associated with the running of it can be allocated directly to the Cutting Department.

Other production overhead costs such as factory rent need to be split or apportioned over production cost centres. Rent on the whole of the factory, i.e., Cutting Department, Assembly Department and Finishing Department, is an overhead cost and is paid regularly, e.g., monthly, quarterly or annually. A fair method of apportioning rent to each department would be by floor area. The bigger the floor area or space a department occupies in the factory, the higher the allocation of rent to that department.

Consider the factory supervisor's salary. He or she supervises staff on the factory floor, and his or her salary is considered to be an overhead cost. What would be a fair method of allocating the supervisor's salary to each production department? Possibly in proportion to the number of staff working in each department, or the labour hours used? After all, the more staff there are in a department, the more time the supervisor will spend in the department, so more of his or her salary should be allocated to that department.

There are no hard and fast rules for apportioning production overhead costs to cost centres. Common sense usually prevails. Some common methods of apportioning production overheads are as follows:

PRODUCTION OVERHEAD	METHOD OF APPORTIONMENT
Rent	Floor area
Production supervisor's salary	Number of staff or labour hours
Depreciation of machinery	Machine value
Canteen costs	Number of staff or labour hours
Insurance costs	Machine value

Example 3.1

A company has three production cost centres: Cutting, Assembly and Finishing. Production overheads at 31 December along with the basis of apportionment to each cost centre are as follows:

PRODUCTION OVERHEAD	AMOUNT €	METHOD OF APPORTIONMENT
Rent	42 000	Floor area
Depreciation of machinery	19 000	Value of machinery
Supervisor's salary	5 000	Number of employees
Insurance costs of machinery	9 500	Value of machinery
Canteen costs	20 000	Number of employees

The following information is also given:

	CUTTING	ASSEMBLY	FINISHING	TOTAL
Floor area sq. m.	10 500	8 000	2 500	21 000
Number of employees	25	15	10	50
Value of machinery €	50 000	20 000	25 000	95 000

Required

Prepare an overhead apportionment schedule for the month of December.

Solution to Example 3.1

Overhead apportionment schedule

OVERHEAD	BASIS OF APPORTIONMENT	TOTAL €	CUTTING €	ASSEMBLY €	FINISHING €
Rent (w1)	Floor area	42 000	21 000	16 000	5 000
Depreciation of machinery (w2)	Value of machinery	19 000	10 000	4 000	5 000
Supervisor's salary (w3)	Number of employees	5 000	2 500	1 500	1 000
Insurance costs of machinery (w4)	Value of machinery	9 500	5 000	2 000	2 500
Canteen costs (w5)	Number of employees	20 000	10 000	6 000	4 000
Total		95 500	48 500	29 500	17 500

Workings

(w1) Allocate rent using floor area. First calculate the rent per square metre of floor area:

$$\frac{\text{Rent}}{\text{Total floor area}}$$

$$\frac{€42\ 000}{21\ 000\ \text{sq. m.}} = €2\ \text{per square metre of floor area}$$

Next, allocate the rent over all of the departments by multiplying €2 by the number of square metres in each department:

	TOTAL	CUTTING	ASSEMBLY	FINISHING
Floor area sq. m.	21 000	10 500	8 000	2 500
x	x	x	x	x
Rent per sq. m.	€2	€2	€2	€2
=	=	=	=	=
Rent apportioned to each department	€42 000	€21 000	€16 000	€5 000

(w2) Allocate depreciation of machinery using the value of machinery. First calculate the depreciation per €1 of machine value:

$$\frac{\text{Depreciation of machinery}}{\text{Total value of machinery}}$$

$$\frac{€19\ 000}{€95\ 000} = €0.20\ \text{per €1 of machinery value}$$

Next, allocate the depreciation over all of the departments by multiplying €0.20 by the machine value in each department:

	TOTAL	CUTTING	ASSEMBLY	FINISHING
Machine value	€95 000	€50 000	€20 000	€25 000
x	x	x	x	x
Depreciation per €1 of machine value	€0.20	€0.20	€0.20	€0.20
=	=	=	=	=
Depreciation apportioned to each department	€19 000	€10 000	€4 000	€5 000

(w3) Allocate supervisor's salary using number of employees. First calculate the supervisor's salary per employee:

$$\frac{\text{Supervisor's salary}}{\text{Total number of employees}}$$

$$\frac{€5\ 000}{50} \quad = \quad €100 \text{ per employee}$$

Next, allocate the supervisor's salary over all of the departments by multiplying €100 by the number of employees in each department:

	TOTAL	CUTTING	ASSEMBLY	FINISHING
Number of employees	50	25	15	10
X	X	X	X	X
Supervisor's salary per employee	€100	€100	€100	€100
=	=	=	=	=
Supervisor's salary apportioned to each department	€5 000	€2 500	€1 500	€1 000

(w4) Allocate the insurance of machinery using the value of machinery. First calculate the insurance cost per €1 of machine value:

$$\frac{\text{Insurance costs of machinery}}{\text{Total value of machinery}}$$

$$\frac{€\ 9\ 500}{€95\ 000} \quad = €0.10 \text{ per } €1 \text{ of machine value}$$

Next, allocate the depreciation over all of the departments by multiplying €0.10 by the machine value in each department:

	TOTAL	CUTTING	ASSEMBLY	FINISHING
Machine value	€95 000	€50 000	€20 000	€25 000
X	X	X	X	X
Insurance cost of machinery per €1 of machine value	€0.10	€0.10	€0.10	€0.10
=	=	=	=	=
Insurance cost of machinery apportioned to each department	€9 500	€5 000	€2 000	€2 500

(w5) Allocate the Canteen costs using the number of employees. First calculate the Canteen costs per employee:

$$\frac{\text{Canteen costs}}{\text{Total number of employees}}$$

$$\frac{€20\ 000}{50} \quad = \quad €400\ \text{per employee}$$

Next, allocate the Canteen costs over all of the departments by multiplying €400 by the number of employees in each department:

	TOTAL	CUTTING	ASSEMBLY	FINISHING
Number of employees	50	25	15	10
x	x	x	x	x
Canteen cost per employee	€400	€400	€400	€400
=	=	=	=	=
Canteen cost apportioned to each department	€20 000	€10 000	€6 000	€4 000

(2) Reapportion service centre costs to production centres

We have considered the apportionment of production overheads into production cost centres such as the Cutting, Assembly and Finishing departments. But there are also service cost centres. Examples of service cost centres would be the Canteen (it feeds staff), the Warehouse (it stores materials) and the Cleaning Department (it cleans the factory). These service cost centres also consume overheads and they should be allocated overheads in the same way as production cost centres.

While products being produced in the factory do not move through service cost centres as they are being produced, the products would not be able to be produced unless service cost centres such as the Canteen or Warehouse existed. If product costs do not contain a portion of service costs, the product cost will not reflect the whole cost incurred in producing it and products will be undercosted.

Using the traditional method of overhead absorption, service department costs are reallocated to production departments. As products pass through production, a portion of service department costs is allocated to them.

The method chosen to allocate service department costs to production departments should reflect the benefit the production department receives from the service department. For example, a service department such as the Canteen could use the number of employees to reallocate its costs to production. Example 3.2 will use the direct reapportionment approach to reapportion service department costs to production cost centres only. Further on we will consider the specified order of closing and the repeated distribution methods.

Example 3.2

Eiremotive produces components for the aircraft industry. Components pass through three production cost centres: Metal Cutting, Fitting and Painting. There are also two service cost centres: Warehouse and Canteen.

Budgeted overhead costs for the year are as follows:

	€
Rent	6 400
Telephone charges	1 600
Depreciation	9 000
Factory supervisor's salary	12 000
Training costs (note 1)	3 550
Total overheads	32 550

Note 1: Training costs are allocated to cost centres as follows:

	€
Metal Cutting	1 400
Fitting	850
Painting	600
Warehouse	400
Canteen	300
Total training costs	3 550

The following information is also available regarding the production and service cost centres:

	METAL CUTTING	FITTING	PAINTING	WARE-HOUSE	CANTEEN	TOTAL
Floor area (sq. m.)	1 500	900	300	300	200	3 200
Value of machines €	12 000	5 000	4 000	2 000	1 000	24 000
Direct labour hours	1 600	900	500			3 000
Machine hours	2 000	750	200			2 950

The Warehouse costs should be reapportioned equally among the production cost centres. The Canteen costs should be reapportioned using direct labour hours.

Required

a Prepare an overhead apportionment schedule showing the budgeted overhead cost for each cost centre

b Reapportion service cost centre costs into production cost centres

Solution to Example 3.2

a Prepare an overhead apportionment schedule showing the budgeted overhead cost for each cost centre

OVERHEAD	BASIS OF APPORTIONMENT	TOTAL €	METAL CUTTING €	FITTING €	PAINTING €	WARE-HOUSE €	CANTEEN €
Rent (w1)	Floor area	6 400	3 000	1 800	600	600	400
Telephone charges (w2)	Floor area	1 600	750	450	150	150	100
Depreciation (w3)	Value of machines	9 000	4 500	1 875	1 500	750	375
Factory supervisor's salary (w4)	Direct labour hours	12 000	6 400	3 600	2 000	–	–
Training costs (w5)	Already allocated	3 550	1 400	850	600	400	300
Total		32 550	16 050	8 575	4 850	1 900	1 175
(b) Reapportion service department costs:							
Warehouse (w6)	Apportion equally	–	633	633	634	(1 900)	–
Canteen (w7)	Direct labour hours	–	627	353	195	–	(1 175)
Total		32 550	17 310	9 561	5 679	0	0

Workings

(w1) Rent

The most obvious method of allocating rent is to use floor area. The more floor area a cost centre occupies, the more rent it should be allocated. First calculate the rent per square metre of floor area:

$$\frac{\text{Rent}}{\text{Total floor area}}$$

$$\frac{€6\ 400}{3\ 200\ \text{sq. m.}} = €2 \text{ per square metre of floor area}$$

Next, allocate the rent over all of the departments by multiplying €2 by the number of square metres in each department:

	TOTAL	METAL CUTTING	FITTING	PAINTING	WARE-HOUSE	CANTEEN
Floor area sq. m.	3 200	1 500	900	300	300	200
x	x	x	x	x	x	x
Rent per sq. m.	€2	€2	€2	€2	€2	€2
=	=	=	=	=	=	=
Rent apportioned to each department	€6 400	€3 000	€1 800	€600	€600	€400

(w2) Telephone charges

The most obvious method of allocating telephone charges to cost centres would be to use an estimate of telephone calls in each cost centre. We are not given this information here so we could use floor area or direct labour hours. If we use direct labour hours we are assuming that the more labour in a department, the higher the telephone costs are. If we use floor area we are assuming that the more floor area a department occupies, the greater the likelihood that more telephone calls will be made in it.

There are also likely to be telephones in the Warehouse and Canteen but there are no direct labour hours in these cost centres. If we use direct labour hours we will not allocate any telephone costs to these service cost centres. The more suitable allocation method is floor area. First calculate the telephone charges per square metre of floor area:

Telephone charges
Total floor area

$$\frac{€1\ 600}{3\ 200\ sq.\ m.} \quad = \quad €0.50 \text{ per square metre of floor area}$$

Next, allocate the telephone charges over all of the departments by multiplying €0.50 by the number of square metres in each department:

	TOTAL	METAL CUTTING	FITTING	PAINTING	WARE-HOUSE	CANTEEN
Floor area sq. m.	3 200	1 500	900	300	300	200
x	x	x	x	x	x	x
Telephone charges per sq. m.	€0.50	€0.50	€0.50	€0.50	€0.50	€0.50
=	=	=	=	=	=	=
Telephone charges apportioned to each department	€1 600	€750	€450	€150	€150	€100

(w3) Depreciation

According to *CIMA Official Terminology*, depreciation is the allocation of the depreciable amount of an asset over its life. The only asset mentioned in the example is machines. The more valuable a machine the more it will be depreciated, so we will use the value of machines as an allocation method.

First calculate the depreciation cost per €1 of machine value:

$$\frac{\text{Depreciation}}{\text{Total value of machinery}}$$

$$\frac{€\ 9\ 000}{€24\ 000} \quad = \quad €0.375 \text{ per €1 of machine value}$$

Next, allocate the depreciation over all of the departments by multiplying €0.375 by the machine value in each department:

	TOTAL	METAL CUTTING	FITTING	PAINTING	WARE-HOUSE	CANTEEN
Value of machines	€24 000	€12 000	€5 000	€4 000	€2 000	€1 000
x	X	X	X	X	X	X
Depreciation per €1 of machine value	€0.375	€0.375	€0.375	€0.375	€0.375	€0.375
=	=	=	=	=	=	=
Depreciation apportioned to each department	€9 000	€4 500	€1 875	€1 500	€750	€375

(w4) Factory supervisor's salary

As the title suggests, the factory supervisor is supervising staff on the factory floor. This salary cost should be allocated based on direct labour hours. The more direct labour hours (or staff) there are in a department, the more time will be spent by the factory supervisor in supervising them. Use direct labour hours to allocate the factory supervisor's salary.

First calculate the supervisor's salary per direct labour hour:

$$\frac{\text{Supervisor's salary}}{\text{Total direct labour hours}}$$

$$\frac{€12\ 000}{3\ 000} \quad = \quad €4 \text{ per direct labour hour}$$

Next, allocate the supervisor's salary over all of the departments by multiplying €4 by the number of direct labour hours in each department:

	TOTAL	METAL CUTTING	FITTING	PAINTING	WARE-HOUSE	CANTEEN
Direct labour hours	3 000	1 600	900	500		
x	x	x	x	x		
Supervisor's salary per direct labour hour	€4	€4	€4	€4		
=	=	=	=	=		
Supervisor's salary apportioned to each department	€12 000	€6 400	€3 600	€2 000		

(w5) Training costs

Training costs have already been allocated and are slotted into each cost centre as outlined in the question.

b Reapportion service cost centre costs into production cost centres

In the question we are told to reapportion the Warehouse costs equally among the production cost centres, while the Canteen costs should be reapportioned using direct labour hours:

(w6) Warehouse

The total of overheads in the Warehouse is €1 900 and we are to apportion the cost equally to the three production cost centres:

$$\frac{€1\ 900}{3\ \text{production cost centres}} = €633 \text{ per cost centre}$$

€633 should be allocated to each of the production cost centres – Metal Cutting and Fitting, and the balance of €634 is allocated to Painting. €1 900 should be deducted from the Warehouse.

(w7) Canteen

The total overheads in the Canteen are €1 175 and these are to be apportioned to the production cost centres using direct labour hours. First calculate the Canteen costs per direct labour hours:

$$\frac{\text{Canteen}}{\text{Total direct labour hours}}$$

$$\frac{€1\ 175}{3\ 000} = €0.3917 \text{ (rounded) per direct labour hour}$$

Next, allocate the Canteen costs over all of the departments by multiplying €0.3917 by the number of direct labour hours in each department:

	TOTAL	METAL CUTTING	FITTING	PAINTING	WARE-HOUSE	CANTEEN
Direct labour hours	3 000	1 600	900	500		
x	x	x	x	x		
Canteen costs per direct labour hour	€0.3917	€0.3917	€0.3917	€0.3917		
=	=	=	=	=		
Canteen costs (rounded)	€1 175	€627	€353	€195		

Allocate the Canteen costs to each of the production cost centres as calculated above. Note that the figures are rounded; the rounding difference is insignificant. €1 175 should be deducted from the Canteen Department.

All overheads are now allocated to the production cost centres.

(3) Calculate overhead absorption rates for each production centre

Now that we have allocated and apportioned all overheads to production cost centres (including service cost centre reapportionment), we need to establish a method of allocating overheads to products as they pass through production cost centres. The traditional approach uses five different methods of allocating overheads to products:

1 Machine hours
2 Labour hours
3 Units of output
4 Direct labour cost %
5 Direct material cost %

The most frequently used methods are time-based ones – machine hours and labour hours. The logic is that the more time a product spends in a department measured in labour hours or machine hours, the more overhead cost it should be allocated.

An overhead absorption rate (OAR) is calculated by dividing the cost centre overheads by machine hours or labour hours or one of the other three methods of absorption that may be used. Different overhead absorption rates may be used for each production cost centre. The most appropriate method for that production cost centre should be used. For example, if the cost centre is more labour-intensive, i.e., has more labour hours than machine hours, an OAR based on labour hours should be used. If the cost centre is more machine-intensive, i.e., has more machine hours than labour hours, an OAR based on machine hours should be used.

Example 3.3

Calculate appropriate overhead absorption rates for each of the production departments – Metal Cutting, Fitting and Painting – using the information and solution to Example 3.2.

Solution to Example 3.3

The total overheads allocated to the production cost centres in the solution to Example 3.2 were:

	METAL CUTTING	FITTING	PAINTING	TOTAL
Total overheads €	17 310	9 561	5 679	32 550

The machine hours and labour hours in Example 3.2 were:

	METAL CUTTING	FITTING	PAINTING	TOTAL
Direct labour hours	1 600	900	500	3 000
Machine hours	2 000	750	200	2 950

The overhead absorption rates are calculated as follows:

Metal Cutting

The Metal Cutting Department appears to be more machine-intensive as more machine hours are incurred in production than labour hours. As the aircraft components pass through the Metal Cutting Department, overheads should be allocated using machine hours:

$$\frac{\text{Overheads in Metal Cutting Department}}{\text{Machine hours in the Metal Cutting Department}} = \text{OAR}$$

$$\frac{\text{€17 310}}{\text{2 000}} = \text{€8.655 per machine hour}$$

This means that for every one machine hour an aircraft component requires in the Metal Cutting Department, €8.655 is added on to the component cost to cover overheads.

Fitting

The Fitting Department appears to be more labour-intensive as more labour hours are incurred in production than machine hours. As the aircraft components pass through the Fitting Department, overheads should be allocated using labour hours:

$$\frac{\text{Overheads in Fitting Department}}{\text{Labour hours in the Fitting Department}} = \text{OAR}$$

$$\frac{€9\ 561}{900} = €10.623 \text{ (rounded) per labour hour}$$

This means that for every one labour hour a component requires in the Fitting Department, €10.623 is added on to the component cost to cover overheads.

Painting

The Painting Department appears to be more labour-intensive as more labour hours are incurred in production than machine hours. As the aircraft components pass through the Painting Department, overheads should be allocated using labour hours:

$$\frac{\text{Overheads in Painting Department}}{\text{Labour hours in the Painting Department}} = \text{OAR}$$

$$\frac{€5\ 679}{500} = €11.358 \text{ (rounded) per labour hours}$$

This means that for every one labour hour a component requires in the Painting Department, €11.358 is added on to the component cost to cover overheads.

(4) Use overhead absorption rates to cost products

The next step is to allocate overheads to products. If, for example, overheads are being absorbed on a machine hour basis and the OAR is €5 per machine hour, where a product requires four machine hours to be produced in that department, then €20 (OAR €5 x 4 machine hours) will be absorbed into each unit produced.

Example 3.4

Using the information and solutions to Examples 3.2 and 3.3 above:

a   Calculate the amount of overhead absorbed into each aircraft component. Additional information is as follows:

Each aircraft component requires the following:

	METAL CUTTING	FITTING	PAINTING
Direct labour hours	5	9	4
Machine hours	10	3	2

b   Calculate the total production cost of an aircraft component using your answer to (a) above if direct materials cost €100 and direct labour costs €350

Solution to Example 3.4

a   Calculate the amount of overhead absorbed into each aircraft component.
    As the aircraft component passes though each production department, overhead will be absorbed into it as follows:

Metal Cutting

Overheads are absorbed into each component using machine hours in the Metal Cutting Department. The OAR is €8.655 per machine hour. The overhead cost per component is calculated as follows:

OAR per machine hour x number of machine hours

€8.655 x 10 machine hours = €86.55 per component

Fitting

Overheads are absorbed into each component using labour hours in the Fitting Department. The OAR is €10.623 per labour hour. The overhead cost per component is calculated as follows:

OAR per labour hour x number of labour hours

€10.623 x 9 labour hours = €95.61 (rounded to two decimal places) per component

Painting

Overheads are absorbed into each component using labour hours in the Painting Department. The OAR is €11.358 per labour hour. The overhead cost per component is calculated as follows:

OAR per labour hour x number of labour hours

€11.358 x 4 labour hours = €45.43 (rounded to two decimal places) per component b Calculate the total production cost of an aircraft component using your answer to (a) above if direct materials cost €100 and direct labour costs €350

Total cost of an aircraft component:

	€	€
Direct materials		100.00
Direct labour		350.00
Prime cost		450.00
Overheads:		
Metal Cutting	86.55	
Fitting	95.61	
Painting	45.43	227.59
Total production cost		677.59

Profit mark-up and margin

The total production cost can be used to value unsold finished stock and also to set a price for the component. Using a cost plus pricing approach, the selling price for the component is set by adding on profit to the total cost:

Total cost
Add: Profit
Equals: Selling price

Profit can be calculated using a mark-up or margin. The percentage used depends on the demand for the product, competition in the market, the pricing objectives of the company and the costs incurred in producing the product.

Profit mark-up

Profit is expressed as a percentage of cost and is calculated by adding on a percentage mark-up to cost. For example, where the total cost of a product is €100 and the profit mark-up is 25%, the profit is calculated as follows:

Total cost x 25% = profit
€100 x 25% = €25

The selling price is calculated as follows:

Total cost   €100
Add: Profit   € 25
Equals: Selling price   €125

Profit margin

Profit is expressed as a percentage of sales. Using the example above, if the total cost of a product is €100 and the profit margin is 20%, the selling price and profit are calculated as follows:

If the profit margin is 20% of sales this means that sales are 100%. The total cost is calculated by deducting the profit margin percentage from 100%:

$$100\% - 20\% = 80\%$$

The total cost is 80% of sales. If €100 equals 80% then calculate 100%:

$$\frac{€100}{80} \quad \times \quad 100 \quad = €125$$

In summary:

Total cost	€100
Add: Profit	€ 25
Equals: Selling price	€125

Example 3.5

In Example 3.4 the total cost of an aircraft component was calculated as:

	€	€
Direct materials		100.00
Direct labour		350.00
Prime cost		450.00
Overheads:		
Metal Cutting	86.55	
Fitting	95.61	
Painting	45.43	227.59
Total production cost		677.59

Required

Calculate the selling price and profit of an aircraft component using:

a   A mark-up of 10%
b   A margin of 25%

Solution to Example 3.5

a   Calculate the selling price and profit of an aircraft component using a mark-up of 10%
The profit mark-up is 10% of total production cost:

10% x €677.59 = €67.76 (rounded to two decimal places).

The selling price is calculated as follows:

Total production cost	€677.59
Add: Profit	€ 67.76
Equals: Selling price	€745.35

b   Calculate the selling price and profit of an aircraft component using a margin of 25%
If the profit margin is 25% of sales this means that sales are 100%. The total cost is calculated by deducting the profit margin percentage from 100%:

100% − 25% = 75%

The total cost is 75% of sales. If €677.59 equals 75% then calculate 100%:

$$\frac{€677.59}{75} \quad \text{x} \quad 100 \quad = \quad €903.45 \text{ (rounded)}$$

If the selling price is €903.45 and the total production cost is €677.59, then the profit is the difference, i.e., €225.86 (€903.45 – €677.59).
In summary:

Total production cost	€677.59
Add: Profit	€225.86
Equals: Selling price	€903.45

Other methods of absorbing overheads

So far we have only used machine hours and labour hours to absorb overheads into products. The choice of method used should reflect what 'drives' the cost or causes it to occur. In Example 3.4 we saw that the Metal Cutting Department incurred more machine hours in producing the component than labour hours, so a machine hour overhead absorption method was appropriate. The Fitting and Painting Departments incurred more labour hours in producing the component than machine hours, so a labour hour overhead absorption method was appropriate.

If the method used to absorb overheads does not 'drive' the cost, then it will result in inaccurate allocation of overheads and ultimately distorted product costs.

Traditionally direct labour hours and direct labour costs were used as overhead absorption methods in manufacturing. This was because the most

significant cost in manufacturing was labour cost. There are no rules that
state which method should be used. Management should decide which
method is the most appropriate for the company and which method will help
achieve the objectives of the company.

In Example 3.4 machine hours and labour hours were used to absorb
overheads. There are three other methods which can be used:

1   Units of output
2   Direct labour cost %
3   Direct material cost %

Example 3.6

A window manufacturing company prepared the following budgeted
information for the year ended 31 December 2010:

	€
Direct materials	400 000
Direct labour	125 000
Direct expenses	22 500
Production overhead	100 000

The budget is based on the manufacture of 5 000 windows for the year.

A request for a quote has been received from a customer for the supply of
20 windows and the management accountant has prepared the following
quote based on the actual costs for the windows:

	€
Direct materials	1 300
Direct labour	600
Direct expenses	100

Required

a   Calculate the following budgeted production overhead absorption rates
and explain when they would be appropriate to use:
(i)   units of output
(ii) direct labour cost %
(iii) direct material cost %
b   Calculate the total production cost of the quote using the three different
overhead absorption rates calculated in (a) above

Solution to Example 3.6

a Calculate the following budgeted production overhead absorption rates and explain when they would be appropriate to use:

(i) Units of output

Using units of output the budgeted production OAR is calculated as follows:

$$\frac{\text{Budgeted production overhead}}{\text{Budgeted units of output}}$$

Using the budgeted information for the company the OAR is calculated as follows:

$$\frac{€100\ 000}{5\ 000\ \text{windows}} = €20 \text{ per window}$$

For every window produced €20 is added to the total cost to cover production overheads.

The units of output method would be suitable where every unit produced in a department is identical.

(ii) Direct labour cost %

Using direct labour cost % the budgeted production OAR is calculated as follows:

$$\frac{\text{Budgeted production overhead}}{\text{Budgeted direct labour cost}} \times \frac{100}{1}$$

Using the budgeted information for the company the OAR is calculated as follows:

$$\frac{€100\ 000}{€125\ 000} \times \frac{100}{1} = 80\% \text{ of direct labour cost}$$

For every €1 of direct labour cost incurred in producing a window €0.80 (80% x €1) is added to the total cost to cover production overheads.

If the direct labour % method is used, more overhead will be allocated to a product if higher-paid employees are producing it and less if lower-paid employees are producing it. If higher-paid staff are employed in production do they necessarily incur higher overheads? Are overheads being 'driven' by labour costs? An analysis of overheads would reveal this. Higher-paid staff possibly could generate higher overheads, e.g., they may have bigger offices or company cars.

(iii) Direct material cost %

Using direct material cost % the budgeted production OAR is calculated as follows:

$$\frac{\text{Budgeted production overhead}}{\text{Budgeted direct material cost}} \times \frac{100}{1}$$

Using the budgeted information for the company the OAR is calculated as follows:

$$\frac{€100\ 000}{€400\ 000} \times \frac{100}{1} = 25\% \text{ of direct material cost}$$

For every €1 of direct material cost incurred in producing a window €0.25 (25% x €1) is added to the total cost to cover production overheads.

The direct material % would only be suitable where overhead costs are 'driven' by material costs. For example, this method would be used where materials handling costs are a significant part of overheads.

b Calculate the total production cost of the quote using the three different overhead absorption rates calculated in (a) above

	(i) UNITS OF OUTPUT €	(ii) DIRECT LABOUR COST % €	(iii) DIRECT MATERIAL COST % €
Direct materials	1 300	1 300	1 300
Direct labour	600	600	600
Direct expenses	100	100	100
Prime cost	2 000	2 000	2 000
Production overheads	(w1) 400	(w2) 480	(w3) 325
Total production cost	2 400	2 480	2 325

Workings

(w1) Using the units of output method calculated in (a) part (i) the OAR was €20 per window. The quote is for the supply of 20 windows; the amount of production overhead absorbed into the order would be:

OAR x number of windows
€20 x 20 windows = €400

(w2) Using the direct labour cost % method calculated in (a) part (ii) the OAR was 80% of direct labour cost. The amount of production overhead absorbed into the quote would be:

OAR x direct labour cost of the quote
80% x €600 = €480

(w3) Using the direct materials cost % method calculated in (a) part (iii) the OAR was 25% of direct materials cost. The amount of production overhead absorbed into the quote would be:

OAR x direct material cost of the quote
25% x €1 300 = €325

Plant-wide or individual overhead absorption rates?

A company can use individual overhead absorption rates for each cost centre or one plant-wide overhead absorption rate. Plant-wide overhead absorption rates are also referred to as blanket overhead absorption rates. They refer to a single overhead absorption rate for the whole of the company.

Plant-wide rates are not recommended where some departments are more 'overhead-intensive' than others. If products spend more time in these departments, they should be allocated more overheads. In this situation individual overhead absorption rates should be used. Plant-wide rates should only be used where products consume overheads in the same proportion in each department.

Example 3.7

A company produces two different products – X and Y – which pass through the Assembly and Packaging Departments. Overheads are absorbed on a machine hour basis. Budgeted information is as follows:

	BUDGETED OVERHEAD €	BUDGETED MACHINE HOURS
Assembly	50 000	1 000
Packaging	20 000	500
Total	70 000	1 500

The standard machine hours required to produce X and Y are as follows:

	X	Y
Assembly	7	4
Packaging	1	4
Total	8	8

Required

a   Calculate individual overhead absorption rates for the Assembly and Packaging Departments, using machine hours
b   Calculate the amount of overheads allocated to X and Y using the answer to (a) above
c   Calculate a plant-wide overhead absorption rate using machine hours
d   Calculate the amount of overheads allocated to X and Y using the answer to (c) above
e   Discuss your findings

Solution to Example 3.7

a   Calculate individual overhead absorption rates for the Assembly and Packaging Departments, using machine hours

$$OAR = \frac{\text{Budgeted overhead in each cost centre}}{\text{Budgeted machine hours in each cost centre}}$$

Assembly Department:

$$\frac{€50\ 000}{1\ 000\ \text{machine hours}} = €50 \text{ per machine hour in Assembly Department}$$

Packaging Department:

$$\frac{€20\ 000}{500\ \text{machine hours}} = €40 \text{ per machine hour in Packaging Department}$$

b   Calculate the amount of overheads allocated to X and Y using the answer to (a) above

Overhead allocated to X (using individual rates):

		€
Assembly	7 hours x €50	350
Packaging	1 hours x €40	40
Overhead cost per unit		390

Overhead allocated to Y (using individual rates):

		€
Assembly	4 hours x €50	200
Packaging	4 hours x €40	160
Overhead cost per unit		360

c Calculate a plant-wide overhead absorption rate using machine hours

$$\text{OAR} = \frac{\text{Budgeted total overheads}}{\text{Budgeted total machine hours}}$$

$$= \frac{\text{\euro}70\ 000}{1\ 500\ \text{machine hours}} = \text{\euro}46.67 \quad \text{(rounded to two decimal places) per machine hour}$$

d Calculate the amount of overheads allocated to X and Y using the answer to (c) above

Overhead allocated to X (using plant-wide rate):

		€
Overhead cost per unit	8 hours x €46.67	373.36

Overhead allocated to Y (using plant-wide rate):

		€
Overhead cost per unit	8 hours x €46.67	373.36

e Discuss your findings
When individual rates are applied, X is allocated more overhead cost per unit (€390) because it requires more machine hours in the Assembly Department where overheads are higher.
   A plant-wide rate masks this, as the rate of €46.67 per machine hour is applied to the total machine hours required to make each product. The difference in the consumption of overheads in each department is averaged out in the rate of €46.67, and X is under-costed and Y over-costed.

Budgeted or actual overhead absorption rates?

In Example 3.6 we used budgeted or predetermined information to calculate overhead absorption rates. Why not use actual information? The reason is that actual information on overheads will not be known with certainty until all invoices relating to overheads have been accounted for. For example, rent may be paid monthly, quarterly or annually, heating and lighting may be paid every two months, and supervisors' salaries will usually be paid monthly.
   If actual overhead costs are used to calculate overhead absorption rates, should they be calculated monthly, every two months, quarterly or annually? If we calculate them monthly we may not capture all overheads as they are not yet accounted for in the financial accounts. As a result, any job quotes prepared based on actual overhead absorption rates may be too low. But it is unrealistic to delay job quotes until the annual accounts when we are sure all overheads have been accounted for.

This problem can be overcome by using budgeted overhead information to calculate overhead absorption rates. A budget is a predetermined plan in which all elements of costs, revenues and activities are planned and provide a yardstick against which to measure actual costs, revenues and activities. Budgeting will be discussed in more detail in Chapter 6.

In Example 3.6 the direct costs in the quote are actual costs. When preparing a quote for a job it should be easy to gather the actual costs of materials, labour and expenses required to do the job. The overhead cost is absorbed into the quote using an overhead absorption rate. The overhead absorption rate is based on budgeted information because the business will not know what the actual overheads are until the year-end accounts. If overheads are not included in the quote, the business will under-cost the job.

Overhead costs in the job quote is calculated by multiplying the budgeted OAR by the actual labour hours, if labour hours are used to absorb overheads. Remember that the budgeted OAR is based on the budgeted production overheads and the budgeted labour hours. The likelihood is that the actual overheads and labour hours for the year will be different from the budgeted overheads and labour hours calculated at the beginning of the year. So job quotes made during the year may include too much overhead or too little. This is known as under-absorption or over-absorption of overheads.

If overheads are under-absorbed, the amount of overhead actually incurred in the year was greater than the amount of overhead absorbed into jobs for the year. The accounting treatment is to treat the amount of under-absorbed overhead as a period cost and subtract it from profit in the income statement.

If overheads are over-absorbed, the amount of overhead incurred in the year was less than the amount of overhead absorbed into jobs for the year. The accounting treatment is to add it as miscellaneous revenue to profit in the income statement.

Assuming there was no error in the overhead absorption rate or some change in the business which would render the under- or over-absorbed amount a normal event, we can charge or credit these under-/over-absorbed amounts to the profit and loss account each period, rather than making adjustments to the overhead wherever it was charged to products – a process called pro-rating the overhead.

Overheads can be variable or fixed. Where overheads are fixed, the overhead absorption method is especially important as the cost being absorbed is fixed relative to the volume of output. If labour hours are used, the fixed overheads will not grow as the number of labour hours incurred increases. If the budgeted OAR is €5 per labour hour, it is assumed that actual overheads incurred will be €5 for every labour hour worked. If the budgeted labour hours are set too low in the first place, the OAR will be overstated, which may result in overstated inventory values and selling prices.

In this chapter we use five different methods to absorb overheads. IAS 2 (Ch 20:s2.2.1 pg 1293) states that 'the allocation of fixed production overheads is to be based on the normal capacity of the facilities'. Normal capacity is defined as 'the production expected to be achieved on average over a number of periods or seasons under normal circumstances'. In **Chapter**

8: Marginal and Absorption Costing, we use only 'normal capacity' to absorb overheads.

The under-absorption and over-absorption of fixed production overheads can be further subdivided into a fixed overhead volume variance and a fixed overhead expenditure variance. This is discussed in further detail in Chapter 7. This problem does not affect variable production overheads as, by definition, variable overheads will vary with the level of activity.

Example 3.8

A company has produced the following budgeted information for two production departments for the forthcoming year:

	POLISHING	FINISHING
Budgeted overheads	€80 000	€10 000
Budgeted labour hours	10 000	1 000
Budgeted machine hours	5 000	2 000

It is company policy to absorb overheads on a labour hour basis in the Polishing Department and on a machine hour basis in the Finishing Department. Overhead absorption rates are calculated at the beginning of the year for use in job quotes and for inventory valuation purposes. At the year end the following information was reported:

	POLISHING	FINISHING
Actual overheads	€100 000	€8 000
Actual labour hours	12 000	1 500
Actual machine hours	6 000	2 500

Required

Calculate the amount of under- or over-absorbed overhead for each department.

Solution to Example 3.8

Overheads are absorbed on a labour hour basis in the Polishing Department. The OAR is:

$$\frac{\text{Budgeted overheads in Polishing Department}}{\text{Budgeted labour hours in Polishing Department}}$$

$$\frac{€80\ 000}{10\ 000\ \text{labour hours}} = €8 \text{ per labour hour}$$

Overheads are absorbed on a machine hour basis in the Finishing Department. The OAR is:

$$\frac{\text{Budgeted overheads in Finishing Department}}{\text{Budgeted machine hours in Finishing Department}}$$

$$\frac{€10\ 000}{2\ 000\ \text{labour hours}} = €5 \text{ per machine hour}$$

Calculate the amount of under- or over-absorbed overhead in each department:

	POLISHING €			FINISHING €
Overhead absorbed: OAR x actual labour hours €8 x 12 000	96 000	Overhead absorbed: OAR x actual machine hours €5 x 2 500		12 500
Actual overhead	(100 000)			(8 000)
Under-/over-absorbed overhead	(4 000) Under			4 500 Over

The Polishing Department has under-absorbed overhead for the year. €4 000 should be treated as a period cost and written off against profit in the income statement.

The Finishing Department has over-absorbed overhead for the year. €4 500 should be credited as miscellaneous income and added to profit in the income statement.

Non-production overheads

So far in this chapter when referring to overheads we mean production overheads. Other, non-production, overheads exist. IAS 2 (Ch 20:s2.2.1 pg 1294) states that other non-production costs should be included in inventories only to the extent that they bring them into their present location and condition. IAS 2 (Ch 20:s2.2.1 pg 1294) states a number of examples of costs which are disallowed. These include storage costs, unless those costs are necessary in the production process prior to a further production stage; administration costs that do not contribute to bringing inventories to their present location and condition; and selling costs.

For internal decision-making, non-production overheads should be absorbed into product costs. They could be absorbed on the basis of their production costs, both direct and indirect:

$$\frac{\text{Budgeted non-production overheads}}{\text{Budgeted production costs}} \times \frac{100}{1}$$

Each product would be allocated with non-production overheads at a percentage of its total production cost. This method suggests that non-production overheads are principally production-related, which may not be the case. Activity-based costing (ABC) provides a more satisfactory method of assigning non-production overheads to products. ABC is covered in Chapter 4.

Other methods of reapportioning service centre costs

In Example 3.2 we used the direct reapportionment method to reapportion service costs to production cost centres. Two other methods exist: (1) repeated distribution method and (2) specified order of closing method.

(1) Repeated distribution method

This method is used where there are reciprocal services between service departments. Each time Service Department 1's costs are cleared out, a small amount is allocated to Service Department 2 as well as to the production departments. And each time Service Department 2's costs are cleared out, a small amount is allocated back into Service Department 1 as well as to the production departments. With this method the reapportionment of the two service departments is repeated a number of times until the amount to be reapportioned is so small that it can be divided among the production departments. This is illustrated in the following example:

Example 3.9

A company has two production departments, A and B, and two service departments, X and Y. Overheads have already been allocated to the four departments and are listed below. The percentages of X's service department costs, which are to be reapportioned to A, B and Y, are listed below, as are the percentages of Y's service department costs, which are to be reapportioned to A, B and X.

DEPARTMENT	OVERHEADS €	REAPPORTION X'S COSTS	REAPPORTION Y'S COSTS
A	120 000	60%	50%
B	75 000	20%	40%
X	50 000	–	10%
Y	65 000	20%	–
Total	310 000	100%	100%

Required

Prepare an overhead apportionment schedule and reapportion service department costs into production departments.

Solution to Example 3.9 (using repeated distribution method)

OVERHEAD	BASIS OF APPORTIONMENT	TOTAL €	DEPARTMENT A €	DEPARTMENT B €	DEPARTMENT X €	DEPARTMENT Y €
Overheads	Already allocated	310 000	120 000.00	75 000.00	50 000.00	65 000.00
Reapportion service department costs:						
First reapportionment:						
X	% given		30 000.00	10 000.00	(50 000.00)	10 000.00
Y	% given		37 500.00	30 000.00	7 500.00	(75 000.00)
Second reapportionment:						
X	% given		4 500.00	1 500.00	(7 500.00)	1 500.00
Y	% given		750.00	600.00	150.00	(1 500.00)
Third reapportionment:						
X	% given		90.00	30.00	(150.00)	30.00
Y	% given	(note 1)	15.00	12.00	3.00	(30.00)
Department X split evenly			1.50	1.50	(3.00)	0
Total		310 000	192 856.50	117 143.50	0	0

Note 1: After the third reapportionment there is only A3 left in Department X. As this is a very insignificant amount it can be split evenly between the two production departments.

(2) Specified order of closing method

Using this method the service department which does the most work for other service departments is closed off first, then the next and so on. Returns are not made to service departments whose costs have already been closed off.

Solution to Example 3.9 (using specified order of closing method)

In Example 3.9 20% of Service Department X's work is done for Service Department Y, but only 10% of Service Department Y's work is done for Service Department X. Using this method Service Department X should be closed off first.

OVERHEAD	BASIS OF APPORTIONMENT	TOTAL €	DEPARTMENT A €	DEPARTMENT B €	DEPARTMENT X €	DEPARTMENT Y €
Overheads	Already allocated	310 000	120 000.00	75 000.00	50 000.00	65 000.00
Reapportion service department costs:						
First reapportionment:						
X	% given		30 000.00	10 000.00	(50 000.00)	10 000.00
Y	(note 1)		41 666.67	33 333.33	0	(75 000.00)
Total		310 000	191 666.67	118 333.33	0	0

Note 1: Service Department Y is reallocated next but returns are not made to Service Department X as it has been closed off. The proportions of Service Department Y have changed: 50% out of 90% or 5/9 are allocated to Department A and 40% out of 90% or 4/9 are allocated to Department B.

It may be argued that, because Service Department Y's costs are greater than Service Department X's costs, Y should be closed off first and then X. This would also be acceptable.

Summary of solutions to Example 3.9

TOTAL OVERHEADS USING	DEPARTMENT A €	DEPARTMENT B €
(1) Repeated distribution method	192 856.50	117 143.50
(2) Specified order of closing method	191 666.67	118 333.33
Difference	1 189.83	(1 189.83)

The differences are very small between the two methods. There is justification for using the specified order of closing method as it is simpler and quicker to calculate than the repeated distribution method where calculations are being done manually. But many businesses use computer software and spreadsheets to do these calculations, so the more accurate repeated distribution method can be performed at the touch of a button.

Criticisms of the traditional approach

1   When originally developed the traditional approach assumed that labour costs and materials costs were the most significant costs in a business. Today overheads are the most significant cost in a business. Manufacturing is more automated and driven by technology, overhead costs associated with this are now significant and labour costs are now less important in the manufacturing process.

2   The traditional approach uses volume-based drivers to absorb overheads. This assumes that all overheads are related to volume, such as machine hours, units and labour hours. This is not the case with all overheads. Consider machine set-ups, a non-volume-based overhead. It is not driven by labour hours, machine hours or units. It would not be correct to allocate machine set-up costs using a volume-based driver.

3   Non-production and service costs, e.g., customer service costs, after-sales service costs and advertising costs, were insignificant or non-existent when the traditional approach was developed. Service costs may not include materials costs or machine hours, so these methods would not be appropriate. The traditional method fails to allocate non-production and service costs well to products.

4   Manufacturing is becoming more flexible and responsive to market demand. A variety of products are produced and manufacturing is driven by customers' wishes. The traditional approach is rigid and inflexible; it cannot cope with complex product mixes.

Chapter summary

This chapter began by discussing the traditional approach to overhead absorption into product costs. The calculation of overhead absorption rates using five methods was illustrated.

Job costing was demonstrated using a profit mark-up and margin. Plant-wide and individual overhead absorption rates were illustrated and recommendations were put forward for their use.

The reasons for using budgeted and not actual overhead absorption rates were examined. The chapter illustrated how to calculate under-absorption and over-absorption of overheads. Non-production overheads were discussed and the calculation of absorption rates was demonstrated.

Methods of reallocating service centre costs were illustrated – repeated distribution method and specified order of closing method.

The chapter concluded by discussing the criticisms of the traditional approach to overhead absorption.

Test questions

Question 1

A company has three production departments – A, B and C. Budgeted overheads for the forthcoming year are as follows:

OVERHEAD	€
Rent	31 000
Supervisor's salary	45 000
Heat and light	15 500
Cleaners' wages	15 000
Machine depreciation	18 000
Machinery maintenance	5 250
Total	129 750

Other information is available as follows:

	TOTAL	A	B	C
Floor area sq. m.	6 200	3 100	1 240	1 860
Number of employees	36	18	8	10
Machine value €	180 000	90 000	18 000	72 000
Hours spent on machine repairs	300	198	60	42

In addition to the above information it is ascertained that the cleaners spend equal amounts of time cleaning each department. The management accountant is unsure of how to apportion overheads to each production department.

Required

Prepare an overhead apportionment schedule apportioning the overheads between the three production departments. Use the most appropriate basis of apportionment for each type of overhead.

Notes to students

1 You must decide the most appropriate method of apportioning overheads. Look at the language used in the question and see if there is information available which will allow you to apportion overheads among departments.
2 There are only production departments in this question so there is no need to reapportion service department costs.
3 You are not required to calculate any OARs.

Question 2

A company has two production departments – Preparing and Finishing – and two service departments – Maintenance and Canteen. The following budgeted information is available:

OVERHEAD	BASIS OF APPORTIONMENT	€
Rent	Floor area	75 000
Telephone costs	Direct labour hours	7 500
Light and heat	Floor area	18 750
Supervisor's salary	Direct labour hours	45 000
Machine running costs	(note 1)	2 000
Machine depreciation	Value of machinery	12 000
Total		160 250

Note 1: Machine running costs are to be apportioned equally between the two production departments.

The following information is also available:

	TOTAL	PREPARING	FINISHING	MAINTENANCE	CANTEEN
Floor area sq. m.	7 500	2 000	4 000	1 000	500
Direct labour hours	6 000	3 000	3 000	–	–
Value of machinery	16 000	6 000	10 000	–	–
Machine hours	6 000	2 000	4 000	–	–

Maintenance costs should be reapportioned to the production departments using the value of machinery. Canteen costs should be reapportioned using direct labour hours.

Required

a Prepare an overhead apportionment schedule showing the budgeted overhead cost for each cost centre
b Reapportion the costs of the service cost centre into the production cost centres
c Calculate appropriate overhead absorption rates for the Preparing and Finishing Departments

Notes to students

1 In part (c) decide which of the five methods of absorbing overheads is appropriate for each department.
2 Remember you do not need to use the same method in the Preparing Department as you do in the Finishing Department.

Question 3

A company has three production departments – A, B and C – and two service departments – X and Y. It allocates budgeted overheads across departments in the following percentages:

DEPARTMENTS	PERCENTAGES
A	50%
B	20%
C	15%
X	7.5%
Y	7.5%

The budgeted overheads for the forthcoming year are €100 000. Other budgeted information is as follows:

	TOTAL	A	B	C	X	Y
Machine hours	7 500	2 000	3 000	2 000	500	–
Units of output	3 000	–	–	3 000	–	–
Labour hours	5 000	1 000	3 250	500	–	250

Required

a Prepare an overhead apportionment schedule, apportioning overheads using the percentages given
b Reapportion X's costs using labour hours and Y's costs using machine hours
c Calculate overhead absorption rates as follows:
  (i) a machine hour rate in Department A
  (ii) a labour hour rate in Department B
  (iii) a units of output rate in Department C

Notes to students

1 There is no need to do a detailed apportionment of overheads in this question – just divide the overheads across each department using the percentages given.
2 The repeated distribution method of reapportioning service department costs is required in this question.

For answers and additional test questions, see www.gillmacmillan.ie. Search for Management Accounting and click on the link in the right-hand column.

4 Activity-Based Costing

Learning outcomes of Chapter 4

At the end of this chapter, you will be able to:

- discuss the principles of activity-based costing (ABC)
- implement an ABC approach to product costing
- compare and discuss the traditional approach and the ABC approach to product costing
- discuss the use of ABC in service industries
- discuss the use of ABC in the public sector
- understand the benefits and drawbacks of the ABC approach

Introduction

In Chapter 3 the traditional approach to allocating overheads to product costs was discussed. Cooper and Kaplan in 'Measure Costs Right: Make the Right Decisions' (1988: 96) outlined the activity-based costing approach. They noted that when the traditional method was devised, labour costs and materials costs were the most significant costs in a business. Manufacturing is now more automated and driven by technology, overhead costs associated with this are now significant and labour costs are less important in the manufacturing process.

The traditional approach uses volume-based drivers to absorb overheads, e.g., machine hours, labour hours and units. It assumes that all overheads are driven by volume. This is not the case with overheads such as set-up costs. Set-up costs refer to the costs of setting up machines for production, where machines need to be recalibrated for the next production run. Set-up costs will be the same regardless of the number of units produced: they are not volume-driven. A volume-based driver would therefore distort the overall product costs. The ABC approach would use a non-volume-based driver such as the number of machine set-ups to allocate set-up costs to products.

In recent times there has been an increase in service costs such as customer service costs. These costs are not volume-driven; they do not increase as labour hours or machine hours increase. Using a traditional approach such as labour or machine hours to absorb service costs into products would result in distorted product costs.

When the traditional approach was developed, businesses had a narrow range of products. In recent times product ranges have become more diverse and businesses are developing new and more complex products and services. Managing a diverse product range requires the consumption of more overheads in terms of more supervision and more complex manufacturing processes. The ABC approach is more suited to costing more complex production processes.

The ABC approach aims to allocate overheads to products based on activities. This involves more calculations and time to gather the information but it results in more accurate product costing. Prices charged for products reflect the effort put into making the product.

Implementation of ABC

The traditional approach uses four steps to allocate costs to cost objects, as described in Chapter 3:

1 Allocate and apportion production overheads to production and service cost centres.
2 Reapportion service centre costs to production centres.
3 Calculate overhead absorption rates for each production centre.
4 Use overhead absorption rates to cost products.

The ABC approach uses five steps to allocate costs to cost objects:

(1) Identify activities

An activity is a task, e.g., activities in production would be: inspection, order processing, purchasing and materials handling.

Seal, in *Management Accounting* (2008), states:

> … an activity is any event that causes the consumption of overhead resources. The costs of carrying out these activities are assigned to the products that cause the activities.

The first task in introducing an ABC system is to ask managers and supervisors to identify their activities. This may result in a long list of activities but the more activities that can be identified, the more accurately products will be costed.

However, this will lead to a complex ABC system which will be costly and time-consuming to maintain. It may be decided to combine similar activities to reduce the complexity of the system.

(2) Allocate overhead costs to activity cost pools

The next step is to identify all costs associated with an activity. For example, if an activity is a machine set-up, all the costs associated with setting up machines should be identified. When these costs are combined they are called an activity cost pool. Some of these costs will be readily identifiable with activities. If they are not, assistance may be required from managers or supervisors who may be able to identify how costs should be allocated over activities.

(3) Select cost drivers

CIMA Official Terminology defines a cost driver as 'a factor influencing the level of cost ... [it] denote[s] the factor which links activity resource consumption to product outputs, for example the number of purchase orders would be a cost driver for procurement cost'. Questions that should be asked in selecting cost drivers are: How readily available is the information about them? How easily quantifiable is it? Considerations in the selection of cost drivers would be the ready availability of information and the ease with which it can be quantified.

The number of cost drivers, for example the number of set-ups, should be ascertained. For the purposes of this chapter the number of cost drivers is referred to as cost driver transactions. This information may be readily available or a system may need to be put in place to capture it. Again, managers or supervisors may be able to advise on methods of gathering this information.

Drury in *Cost & Management Accounting: An Introduction* (2006) identifies two types of cost drivers:

1 Transaction drivers such as the number of set-ups or the number of purchase orders. They count the number of times an activity is performed. The problem with transaction drivers is that they assume that the same quantity of resources is required every time an activity is performed.
2 Duration drivers, which represent the length of time required to perform an activity. An example would be the number of maintenance hours which drives the maintenance costs.

(4) Calculate cost driver rates

The cost driver rates are obtained by dividing the activity cost pools by the cost driver transactions.

(5) Assign cost driver rates to cost objects

If, for example, machine set-ups have been identified as an activity and a cost driver rate has been calculated per machine set-up, the next step is to assign the machine set-up costs to the cost object or product. This assumes that the number of cost driver transactions or machine set-ups has already been measured for each product. The ease of measuring cost driver transactions for cost objects must be a consideration in part (3) when selecting cost drivers.

To illustrate these five steps the following example will be used:

Example 4.1

A company sells three different products, Alpha, Beta and Gamma, and has provided you with the following information:

	ALPHA	BETA	GAMMA	TOTAL
Direct materials (per unit)	€5 750	€7 300	€9 160	
Direct labour (per unit)	€2 360	€2 920	€3 460	
Units produced	4 000	8 000	10 000	22 000
Number of production runs for the period	2 000	3 000	1 000	6 000
Number of purchase orders placed for the period	5 000	8 000	10 000	23 000
Machine hours for the period	500 000	800 000	1 000 000	2 300 000

Information on the breakdown of overheads is as follows:

PRODUCTION OVERHEADS	€
Set-ups	1 488 000
Materials handling	1 380 000
Inspection	1 980 000
Machining	2 760 000
Total	7 608 000

The company has been using a machine hour method to absorb overheads at a rate of €3.308 per machine hour. The management accountant has recently attended a seminar on activity-based costing and is considering implementing an ABC system in the company.

Required

a   Using the traditional overhead absorption approach, prepare a statement showing the total overhead cost for the production of products Alpha, Beta and Gamma, the overhead cost per unit and the total cost per unit

b   Using ABC, prepare a statement showing the total overhead cost for the production of products Alpha, Beta and Gamma, the overhead cost per unit and the total cost per unit

c Comment on the reasons for any differences in the costs in your answers to (a) and (b)

Solution to Example 4.1

a The OAR has already been worked out in the question so the next step is to allocate overheads to Alpha, Beta and Gamma:

	ALPHA	BETA	GAMMA	TOTAL €
OAR €	3.308	3.308	3.308	
x	x	x	x	
Machine hours	500 000	800 000	1 000 000	
=	=	=	=	
Total overhead costs €	1 654 000	2 646 400	3 308 000	7 608 400*
/	/	/	/	
No. of units	4 000	8 000	10 000	
=	=	=	=	
Overhead cost per unit €	413.50	330.80	330.80	
Direct materials €	5 750.00	7 300.00	9 160.00	
Direct labour €	2 360.00	2 920.00	3 460.00	
Total cost per unit €	8 523.50	10 550.80	12 950.80	

* Rounding difference.

b Using the five steps in the ABC approach mentioned above, the activities and activity cost pools need to be identified. These have been provided already in the question. They are:

PRODUCTION OVERHEADS/ACTIVITIES	ACTIVITY COST POOLS €
Set-ups	1 488 000
Materials handling	1 380 000
Inspection	1 980 000
Machining	2 760 000
Total	7 608 000

The next step is to select cost drivers. It is necessary to identify what is causing costs to occur. Appropriate cost drivers for activities are:

PRODUCTION OVERHEADS/ACTIVITIES	COST DRIVERS	REASON FOR COST DRIVER SELECTION
Set-ups	Number of production runs	Set-up costs are driven by the number of production runs – the more production runs, the more set-up costs are incurred
Materials handling	Number of orders	Materials handling costs are driven by the number of orders made – the more orders made, the more materials handling costs such as warehouse labour costs are incurred
Inspection	Units produced	Inspection costs are driven by the number of units produced – the more units produced, the more inspection costs such as quality control checks are incurred
Machining	Machine hours	Machining costs are driven by the number of machine hours used – the more machine hours used, the more machining costs such as machine running costs are incurred

The next step is to calculate cost driver rates by dividing the activity cost pools by the cost driver transactions:

ACTIVITIES	ACTIVITY COST POOLS €	COST DRIVERS	COST DRIVER TRANSACTIONS	COST DRIVER RATES €
Set-ups	1 488 000	No. of production runs	6 000	(w1) 248
Materials handling	1 380 000	No. of purchase orders	23 000	(w2) 60
Inspection	1 980 000	Units produced	22 000	(w3) 90
Machining	2 760 000	Machine hours	2 300 000	(w4) 1.20

Workings

(w1) Set-ups

$$\frac{\text{Activity cost pool}}{\text{Cost driver transactions}} = \frac{€1\,488\,000}{6\,000}$$
$$= €248 \text{ per production run}$$

(w2) Materials handling

$$\frac{\text{Activity cost pool}}{\text{Cost driver transactions}} = \frac{€1\,380\,000}{23\,000}$$
$$= €60 \text{ per purchase order}$$

(w3) Inspection

Activity cost pool		€1 980 000
Cost driver transactions	=	22 000
	=	€90 per unit produced

(w4) Machining

Activity cost pool		€2 760 000
Cost driver transactions	=	2 300 000
	=	€1.20 per machine hour

The last step is to assign cost driver rates to cost objects:

OVERHEADS	ALPHA €	BETA €	GAMMA €	TOTAL €
Set-ups (w5)	496 000	744 000	248 000	1 488 000
Materials handling (w6)	300 000	480 000	600 000	1 380 000
Inspection (w7)	360 000	720 000	900 000	1 980 000
Machining (w8)	600 000	960 000	1 200 000	2 760 000
Total overhead costs	**1 756 000**	**2 904 000**	**2 948 000**	**7 608 000**
/	/	/	/	
No. of units	4 000	8 000	10 000	
=	=	=	=	
	€	€	€	
Overhead cost per unit	**439**	**363**	**294.80**	
Direct materials	5 750	7 300	9 160.00	
Direct labour	2 360	2 920	3 460.00	
Total cost per unit	**8 549**	**10 583**	**12 914.80**	

Workings

(w5) Set-ups

	ALPHA	BETA	GAMMA
Cost driver rate (w1)	€248	€248	€248
x	x	x	x
No. of production runs	2 000	3 000	1 000
=	=	=	=
Set-up cost	€496 000	€744 000	€248 000

(w6) Materials handling

	ALPHA	BETA	GAMMA
Cost driver rate (w2)	€60	€60	€60
x	x	x	x
No. of orders	5 000	8 000	10 000
=	=	=	=
Materials handling cost	€300 000	€480 000	€600 000

(w7) Inspection

	ALPHA	BETA	GAMMA
Cost driver rate (w3)	€90	€90	€90
x	x	x	x
No. of units	4 000	8 000	10 000
=	=	=	=
Inspection cost	€360 000	€720 000	€900 000

(w8) Machining

	ALPHA	BETA	GAMMA
Cost driver rate (w4)	€1.20	€1.20	€1.20
x	x	x	x
No. of machine hours	500 000	800 000	1 000 000
=	=	=	=
Machining cost	€600 000	€960 000	€1 200 000

c   Comment on the reasons for any differences in the costs in your answer to (a) and (b)

Summary of total costs per unit:

TOTAL COST PER UNIT	ALPHA €	BETA €	GAMMA €
(b) ABC approach	8 549.00	10 583.00	12 914.80
(a) Traditional approach	8 523.50	10 550.80	12 950.80
Difference	25.50	32.20	(36.00)

Comments

The traditional approach uses a volume-based driver, i.e., machine hours, to absorb overheads into products. The result is that Gamma, which is a high-volume product, i.e., it has 1 000 000 machine hours, is over-costed, and Alpha and Beta, which are lower-volume products, are under-costed. ABC drills into the detail of the resource consumption by each product and captures it using multiple OAR and carefully selected drivers.

The ABC approach allocates costs to products using cost drivers that cause the cost to occur. Gamma uses the lowest number of production runs per unit (1 000 production runs/10 000 units = 0.10 production runs per unit), while Alpha uses 0.50 production runs per unit (2 000 production runs/4 000 units) and Beta uses 0.375 production runs per unit (3 000 production runs/8 000 units). Therefore Gamma is allocated the least amount of set-up costs per unit of the three products. The ABC approach recognises that Alpha and Beta require more production runs per unit and are therefore allocated more of the set-up costs per unit.

Activity-based management

ABC provides more accurate product costing information. It has evolved from a product costing approach into a management approach, called activity-based management (ABM). Kaplan and Cooper (1998: 137) refer to ABM as actions that can be taken, on a better informed basis, with activity cost information.

The aim is to achieve the same results but with lower costs, thus increasing profitability. Companies which use ABM should be able to make better-quality decisions. Jones and Dugdale (2002: 159) state that the acronym used to describe activity-based management has evolved into ABC/M (activity-based costing/management).

ABC in service companies

Kaplan and Cooper (1998: 228) state that, while ABC had its origin in manufacturing companies, many service organisations are obtaining great benefits from it. Clarke and Mullins (2001: 5) note that service companies face the same changing environment and cost management practices that manufacturing companies do.

For service industries such as banks, airlines and telecommunications companies, a significant proportion of their costs are fixed in the short term. This is compared with manufacturing industries, for which a significant proportion of costs are variable costs such as materials and labour. Managers can have difficulty in linking fixed costs to services. Kaplan and Cooper (1998: 229) state that managers in service companies knew neither the costs of their services nor the cost of servicing their different types of customers.

Once managers observe that there is a link between committing resources in advance of providing services or activities, ABC will enable them to make better decisions on the services they offer.

Kaplan and Cooper (1998: 230) note that, until recently, service industries were state-owned monopolies and were protected from competition. As a result there was no need for detailed costing systems and customer analysis. With deregulation, service industries are exposed to competition and need to acquire more knowledge of costs and customer profitability. ABC can provide this knowledge.

Kaplan and Cooper (1998: 231) also state that managers of service companies require information to improve the quality, timeliness and efficiency of the activities they perform. Clarke and Mullins (2001: 5) note that in service companies 'the challenge is to make the less expensive service also the preferred service among customers'. More timely and accurate information provided by ABC will support this challenge.

Service companies involve a wider range of activities than manufacturing companies and staff are involved in a wide range of tasks. ABC allows service companies to focus on the most important tasks that will add value to the products and services provided.

ABC and the public sector

Jackson and Lapsley (2003: 363) write that there has been a great deal of accounting innovation in the public sector and new techniques such as activity-based costing have been introduced. Research was carried out in the form of a survey of public-sector accountants in Scotland which included questions about the accounting techniques and practices being used in their organisations. 54% of respondents working in local authorities reported that ABC had been implemented in their organisation. 55% of respondents working in healthcare indicated that ABC had been implemented and 17% of respondents working in government agencies had implemented it.

Recent research by Doyle, Duffy and McCahey (2009: 7) analyses the extent of ABC/M adoption in Irish hospitals. The researchers surveyed financial controllers in Irish public and private hospitals. The findings showed that 55% of respondents, both public and private, had implemented or had considered implementing activity-based costing.

Doyle et al. (2009: 17) state that of the responses received from public hospitals, 37.5% stated that the overriding reason for implementation of ABC/M was the possibility of achieving more accurate costing information. Better use of resources was also a central factor in introducing ABC systems in the public hospital environment with respondents either strongly agreeing (33.3%) or agreeing (22.2%) with this option.

Benefits of ABC

1   ABC results in more accurate costing. Doyle et al. (2009: 19) state that, of hospitals surveyed, respondents on average agree that the use of an ABC system enables more accurate costing and improves insight into cost causation.
2   ABC leads to better decision-making. Clarke and Mullins (2001: 10), in research carried out on ABC in the non-manufacturing sector, found that of the respondents to a survey, 60% stated that ABC had resulted in improved decision-making in their company.
3   ABC results in improved measurement of a business's performance. Overheads are more fairly allocated and products more accurately costed using ABC. Costs which need to be more tightly controlled are identified.
4   ABC is used to identify and eliminate activities that do not add value to product. Clarke and Mullins (2001: 10) state that 60% of respondents believe that ABC encourages a greater understanding of opportunities available to reduce costs.

Drawbacks of ABC

1   There can be difficulties in gathering all of the data required for an ABC system. Doyle et al. (2009: 26) state that data needed to establish the ABC system are time-consuming and expensive to gather. Of the Irish hospitals surveyed, approximately 55% found this impeded the successful implementation of ABC, while 33% of those surveyed did not find this a major problem and 11% were inconclusive in their decision.
2   It can be costly to implement and operate an ABC system. The costs involved include hiring consultants, buying software and training staff. If no in-house expertise exists, outside consultants will need to be hired to design and implement the ABC system. Doyle et al. (2009: 16) state that 42% of respondents surveyed in Irish hospitals used external consultants to design ABC/M software and 33% used in-house expertise.
3   There can be resistance to change by staff, or lack of top management support. Doyle et al. (2009: 34) state that 56% of respondents surveyed in Irish hospitals stated that ABC/M was initiated and driven by the accounting department and not by senior hospital management. This may have accounted for the low adoption of activity-based costing practices among respondents (55% of responding hospitals have implemented ABC/M or have applied ABC principles in costing some hospital activities).
4   Identifying cost drivers may be difficult. Clarke, Thorley Hill and Stevens (1999: 456) cite one of the major problems in implementing ABC as the identification and selection of cost drivers.
5   There has been a great deal of research in the area of ABC and evidence gathered on its adoption. Innes, Mitchell and Sinclair (2000) conducted a survey of companies which mirrored a similar survey carried out five years earlier. Both surveys were based on the *Times 1 000* publication. Table 2 is summarised below:

TABLE 2 ABC ADOPTION STATUS	1999 SURVEY		1994 SURVEY	
	n	%	n	%
Currently using ABC	31	17.5	74	21.0
Currently considering ABC adoption	36	20.3	104	29.6
Rejected ABC after assessment	27	15.3	47	13.3
No consideration of ABC to date	83	46.9	127	36.1
Total	177	100.0	352	100.0

Innes et al. (2000) write that Table 2 indicates that both use of and interest in ABC had shown no increase over the preceding five years; the proportion of ABC users and those currently considering its use had both fallen to 17.5% and 20.3%, from 21.0% and 29.5% respectively. In addition, a slightly higher proportion claimed to have rejected ABC after assessment in 1999, and there was also a higher percentage of companies that had not even considered its use.

Chapter summary

This chapter introduced ABC, which was developed in the 1980s to counteract the problems with the traditional method of overhead absorption. The difference between the two approaches can be explained by way of an analogy. For example, consider a restaurant bill for 10 people. If the traditional absorption costing method was used, the bill would be split evenly between the 10 people. But this ignores the fact that some may have had only two courses and others three courses. A fairer method of splitting the bill would be to total up the cost of the courses consumed individually and then everyone pays for what they have consumed. This is activity-based costing.

ABC was demonstrated in the chapter and the use of ABC in the public sector and service industries was discussed. Finally the benefits and drawbacks of ABC were discussed.

Test questions

Question 1

A company currently uses an overhead absorption rate based on direct labour hours. The following costings have been prepared for its three products:

PER UNIT	A135 €	B160 €	C243 €
Prime costs	3.75	4.89	11.450
Overhead costs	2.00	1.00	2.466
Total costs	5.75	5.89	13.916
Selling price	10.00	12.00	16.000
Profit/(loss)	4.25	6.11	2.084

The company is considering implementing an activity-based costing system. Managers of departments have collected the following data:

OVERHEADS/ACTIVITIES	ACTIVITY COST POOLS €	COST DRIVERS
Machine set-ups	2 996	Number of machine set-ups
Machinery costs	8 985	Number of machine hours
Quality checks	2 100	Number of inspections
Order processing	885	Number of orders processed
Total	14 966	

Other information available:

	A135	B160	C243	TOTAL
Number of machine set-ups	500	625	373	1 498
Number of machine hours	1 245	1 250	500	2 995
Number of inspections	20	35	15	70
Number of orders processed	2 200	1 130	210	3 540
Units produced and sold	5 000	2 500	1 000	8 500

Required

a Calculate the total unit cost, to two decimal places, and profit for the three products using activity-based costing
b Comment on your findings

Notes to students

1 Present the information in the way the question requires it, i.e., the unit cost and unit profit.
2 Comment on the results for each of the three products.

Question 2

O'Brien Ltd manufacture shoes and produce three styles – the SANDAL, the RUNNER and the BOOT. They have recently implemented an activity-based costing system. The following data have been collected:

OVERHEADS/ACTIVITIES	ACTIVITY COST POOLS €
Sales and marketing costs	67 500
Customer order costs	273 125
Inspection costs	420 000
Machining costs	860 000
Total	1 620 625

	SANDAL	RUNNER	BOOT	TOTAL
Prime cost (per unit)	€35.00	€49.00	€77.00	
Units produced	25 000	15 000	12 500	52 500
No. sales calls	1 000	1 500	500	3 000
No. customer orders	12 500	20 000	25 000	57 500
Machine hours	25 000	15 000	10 000	50 000

Required

a   Prepare a statement showing the total overhead cost of products SANDAL, RUNNER and BOOT. Show the overhead cost per unit and the total cost per unit (to two decimal places)
b   Calculate the selling price per unit (to two decimal places) for each of the three products on the basis of:
(i)   10% mark-up on cost
(ii) 20% margin on selling price

Notes to students

1   You are not required to work out the overhead costs per unit using the traditional overhead absorption method in this question.
2   It is up to you to decide on the most appropriate cost driver for each activity cost pool. Look at the language of each of the activity cost pools and see if there is a cost driver using similar language, e.g., sales and marketing costs are driven by the number of sales calls.

Question 3

Decco Ltd uses a plant-wide overhead absorption rate using labour hours to allocate overheads to products. The company is considering using an activity-based costing system to allocate overheads to products.

The following information is available for the company:

OVERHEADS/ACTIVITIES	ACTIVITY COST POOLS €
Materials ordering	85 000
Maintenance	79 000
Set-up	31 000
Total	195 000

The management accountant has ascertained that materials ordering costs are driven by the quantity of materials ordered, maintenance costs are driven by machine hours and set-up costs are driven by the number of machine set ups.

PRODUCTS	ASD	QWE	ZXC	TOTAL
Prime cost (per unit)	€12.80	€10.00	€9.60	
Total units produced	1 250	2 000	1 875	5 125
Total materials (kg)	100 000	70 000	170 000	340 000
Total machine set-ups	20	80	60	160
Total labour hours	8 000	4 000	12 000	24 000
Total machine hours	6 500	2 000	4 000	12 500

Required

a   Calculate, to two decimal places, the total cost per unit for each product using the traditional overhead absorption approach
b   Calculate, to two decimal places, the total cost per unit for each product using the activity-based costing approach
c   Comment on the reasons for any differences in the costs in your answers to (a) and (b)

Notes to students

1   A plant-wide or blanket OAR is required for part (a) – this will be calculated using the total overheads divided by the total labour hours.
2   In part (c) it is useful to show a comparison of the results of parts (a) and (b) as a starting point to your comments.

For answers and additional test questions, see www.gillmacmillan.ie. Search for Management Accounting and click on the link in the right-hand column.

5 Process Costing

Learning outcomes of Chapter 5

At the end of this chapter, you will be able to:

- explain the difference between job costing and process costing
- calculate the unit cost and value finished goods
- calculate the unit cost and value finished goods where units pass through more than one process
- define normal losses, abnormal losses and abnormal gains and show their accounting treatment
- explain the concept of equivalent units and prepare a statement of equivalent units
- calculate the unit cost and value finished goods and closing work in progress (WIP) where closing WIP has cost elements with different levels of completeness
- calculate the unit cost, value finished goods and closing WIP where there are previous process costs
- calculate the unit cost, value finished goods and closing WIP where there is work in progress at the beginning and end of the process, using the weighted average and first in, first out (FIFO) methods
- define joint and by-product costs and allocate joint costs to products using different methods

Introduction

This chapter explains how units are valued where process costing is used. The difference between job costing and process costing is explained and situations where process costing is used are demonstrated.

The accounting treatments of normal losses, abnormal losses, abnormal gains and where units pass through more than one process are explained. Where there are unfinished units at the beginning and end of the period, the reader is shown how to use the concept of equivalent units to value unfinished units.

The chapter concludes by defining joint and by-product costs and illustrates how joint costs are allocated to products using different methods.

Difference between job costing and process costing

In **Chapter 2: Product Costing – Materials and Labour**, it was explained that job costing is an example of specific order costing and process costing is an example of continuous operation costing.

Job costing applies to a single task, product or service charged to one customer. It is normally of a short duration and is completed within one accounting period. Cost accumulation is straightforward as costs such as labour and materials are collected and allocated to the job as it progresses. Examples where job costing is used would be building work, e.g., an extension on a house or the printing of brochures by a printing company.

Process costing involves the mass production of a single product. It is used in food processing and oil refining. It is uneconomical to trace the individual costs incurred in making a single product to that product, so an average cost per unit is calculated instead. Each individual product's cost is based on this average.

Tracing costs to units of output in process costing

In the examples used in this chapter, output from the process is called 'output' where it will go to the next process, or 'finished goods' where it is fully finished and available to sell. Typically the costs involved in process costing are similar to those involved in job costing – materials, labour and overheads. Instead of costing each job or unit separately as we do in job costing, we calculate an average cost per unit. It would be uneconomical to cost each unit of output in process costing separately.

To value the output from each process we draw up a 'T-account', called the Process Account. In general we debit and credit the Process Account with the following information:

DEBIT	PROCESS ACCOUNT	CREDIT
– Opening work in progress		– Output to the next process or finished goods
– Input cost: Materials Labour		– Normal loss
– Overheads		
– Abnormal gain		– Abnormal loss
		– Closing work in progress

Example 5.1

A manufacturing company produces units which go through one process. 1 000 units are added at the start of the process and 1 000 units of finished goods are produced. Materials costing €2 000, labour costing €1 000 and overheads costing €500 are added into the process. You are required to calculate the average cost per unit and the value of finished goods for the month of June and prepare the Process Account.

Solution to Example 5.1

Carry out the following steps when preparing the Process Account:

1   Open up a Process Account and put the input into the process on the debit side and the output from the process on the credit side.
2   The number of units on both sides of the Process Account should balance. If they do not balance, then check to see if there are any losses or gains. Notice that there are 1 000 units on the debit and credit side of the account.
3   Calculate the average cost per unit using the following formula:

$$\frac{\text{Input costs}}{\text{Number of units of output}}$$

$$\frac{\text{€2 000 + 1 000 + 500}}{\text{1 000 units}} \quad = \quad \text{€3.50 per unit}$$

4   Value the finished goods at the average cost per unit:

   1 000 units x €3.50 = €3 500

This is used to value the finished goods for insurance purposes and to formulate a pricing policy for the units.

5   The Process Account should balance on both sides:

DEBIT			PROCESS ACCOUNT		CREDIT
	UNITS	€		UNITS	€
Materials	1 000	2 000	Finished goods	1 000	3 500
Labour		1 000			
Overheads		500			
	1 000	3 500		1 000	3 500

Where units go through more than one process

In process costing, units may go though several processes before they become fully finished. For example, in the food processing industry where ready-made pizzas are prepared, the process would look something like this:

	PROCESS 1			PROCESS 2	PROCESS 3	FINISHED GOODS
	——————————————→			——————→	——————→	
Raw materials Process 1: flour, water and eggs	Pizza base is baked		Raw materials Process 2: tomatoes and cheese	Topping added	Pizzas are packaged	Pizzas are ready for sale

The raw materials are added into Process 1, the pizza base is baked, the topping is added in Process 2 and the pizza is packed in Process 3. The output from Process 3 goes to finished goods where it is ready for sale.

Example 5.1.a

Using the information from Example 5.1, the output from the Process Account (which is Process 1) now forms the input into Process 2. In Process 2, further labour costs of €1 000 are added and overheads of €750 are incurred. You are required to prepare the Process 2 Account.

Solution to Example 5.1.a

1   The output from Process 1 – on the credit side of the account – was 1 000 units at a value of €3 500. This forms the input into the debit side of Process 2.
2   The inputs into Process 2 – labour and overheads – go onto the debit side of Process 2.
3   The 1 000 units are processed further in Process 2 and when they finish the process they will be viewed as finished goods and this will be credited to the Process 2 Account.
4   The units column should balance on each side of the Process 2 Account. If it does not, check to see if there are any losses or gains. In this example the units column balances on both sides.
5   Calculate the average cost per unit using the following formula:

$$\frac{\text{Input costs}}{\text{Number of units of output}}$$

$$\frac{€3\ 500 + 1\ 000 + 750}{1\ 000\ \text{units}} = €5.25\ \text{per unit}$$

6   Value the finished goods at the average cost per unit:

$$1\ 000\ \text{units} \times €5.25 = €5\ 250$$

This will be used to value the finished goods for insurance purposes and will also be used to formulate a pricing policy for the units.

7   The Process 2 Account should balance on both sides:

DEBIT		PROCESS 2 ACCOUNT			CREDIT
	UNITS	€		UNITS	€
Process 1	1 000	3 500	Finished goods	1 000	5 250
Labour		1 000			
Overheads		750			
	1 000	5 250		1 000	5 250

Where there are normal losses

A normal loss may occur as part of the normal production process. Examples of a normal loss are evaporation of milk through the pasteurisation process and sawdust left over from the wood-cutting process. The cost of the normal loss is passed on to the customer in the price of the units.

Example 5.2

A manufacturing company produces units which go through one process. A total of 1 000 units are added at the start of the process. Materials costing €2 000, labour costing €1 000 and overheads costing €500 are added into the process. As part of the process the company expects to have a normal loss of 200 units. You are required to calculate the average cost per unit and the value of finished goods for the month of June and to prepare the Process Account.

Solution to Example 5.2

1   Open up a Process Account and put the input into the process on the debit side. The normal loss will go onto the credit side of the Process Account and the output from the process on the credit side. The company inputs 1 000 units and has a normal loss of 200 units. The expected output from the process is 800 units:

	Units
Input	1 000
Less: Normal loss	(200)
Expected output (finished goods)	800

2   Where there is a normal loss, the average cost per unit formula will have to be adjusted. The input costs will now be divided by the expected output, i.e., the input units minus the normal loss units. This ensures that

the cost of the normal loss is passed on to the customer in the average cost per unit. Calculate the average cost per unit as follows:

$$\frac{\text{Input costs}}{\text{Expected output}}$$

$$\frac{€2\ 000 + 1\ 000 + 500}{1\ 000\ \text{units} - 200\ \text{units}} = €4.375 \text{ per unit}$$

3 Value the finished goods at the average cost per unit:

$$800 \text{ units} \times €4.375 = €3\ 500$$

This will be used to value the finished goods for insurance purposes and will also be used to formulate a pricing policy for the units.

4 The normal loss will be valued at nil in the Process Account as the cost is being passed on to the customer in the average cost per unit.

5 The Process Account should balance on both sides:

DEBIT			PROCESS ACCOUNT		CREDIT
	UNITS	€		UNITS	€
Materials	1 000	2 000	Finished goods	800	3 500
Labour		1 000	Normal loss	200	0
Overheads		500			
	1 000	3 500		1 000	3 500

Where there is a normal loss which can be sold for scrap

Sometimes losses can be sold for scrap, for example sawdust can be sold to stables or butchers. If this happens, then the cost of the normal loss passed on to the customer should be reduced by the scrap sales. A 'Normal Loss/Scrap Sales Account' should be opened and the scrap sales should be transferred to it.

Where a normal loss occurs and there are scrap sales, the average cost per unit will be:

$$\frac{\text{Input costs} - \text{scrap sales from normal loss}}{\text{Expected output}}$$

Example 5.2.a

Using the information in Example 5.2, the opportunity has arisen to sell the normal loss units for scrap value of €2 per unit. Prepare the Process Account and the Normal Loss/Scrap Sales Account.

Solution to Example 5.2.a

1   The normal loss will be credited to the Process Account as 200 units and the scrap sales will be credited as €400 (200 units x €2).

2   The average cost per unit will now have to adjust to take account of the scrap sales. The input costs will be reduced by the amount of the total scrap sales. Calculate the average cost per unit as follows:

$$\frac{\text{Input costs} - \text{scrap sales from normal loss}}{\text{Expected output}}$$

$$\frac{€2\,000 + 1\,000 + 500 - 400}{1\,000 \text{ units} - 200 \text{ units}} = €3.875 \text{ per unit}$$

3   Value the finished goods at the average cost per unit:

$$800 \text{ units} \times €3.875 = €3\,100$$

This will be used to value the finished goods for insurance purposes and to formulate a pricing policy for the units.

4   The Process Account should balance on both sides:

DEBIT		PROCESS ACCOUNT			CREDIT
	UNITS	€		UNITS	€
Materials	1 000	2 000	Finished goods	800	3 100
Labour		1 000	Normal loss	200	400
Overheads		500			
	1 000	3 500		1 000	3 500

5   Open up a Normal Loss/Scrap Sales Account. Transfer the normal loss, i.e., 200 units at a value of €400, from the Process Account to the debit side of the Normal Loss/Scrap Sales Account. On the credit side of this account show the receipt of the scrap sales from the normal loss into the Bank Account.

DEBIT		NORMAL LOSS/SCRAP SALES ACCOUNT			CREDIT
	UNITS	€		UNITS	€
Process Account	200	400	Bank Account	200	400

Where there are abnormal losses

An abnormal loss is an unexpected loss which does not occur as part of the normal production process. It occurs where the actual loss exceeds the normal loss. The abnormal loss is valued at the average cost per unit and transferred to an Abnormal Loss Account. It should then be written off as an expense in the income statement for the period.

Example 5.2.b

Using the information in Example 5.2, the situation has arisen where the actual loss is 300 units. Losses cannot be sold for scrap. You are required to calculate the average cost per unit and prepare the Process Account and the Abnormal Loss Account.

Solution to Example 5.2.b

1   In Example 5.2 it was stated that the normal loss was 200 units. The actual loss is 300 units so the abnormal loss is:

	Units
Actual loss	300
Less: Normal loss	(200)
Abnormal loss	100

The output from the process will be:

	Units
Input	1 000
Less: Actual loss	(300)
Expected output (finished goods)	700

2   The average cost per unit will be:

$$\frac{\text{Input costs}}{\text{Expected output}}$$

$$\frac{€2\ 000 + 1\ 000 + 500}{1\ 000\ \text{units} - 200\ \text{units}} = €4.375\ \text{per unit}$$

3   Value the finished goods at the average cost per unit:

$$700\ \text{units} \times €4.375 = €3\ 062.50$$

This will be used to value the finished goods for insurance purposes and to formulate a pricing policy for the units.

4   The normal loss will be valued at zero in the Process Account, and as there are no scrap sales there is no need to prepare a Normal Loss/Scrap Sales Account.

5   The abnormal loss will be valued at the average cost per unit in the Process Account. It is an unexpected loss and will not be passed on to the customer in the average cost per unit. The abnormal loss will be:

$$€4.375 \times 100\ \text{units} = €437.50$$

6   The Process Account should balance on both sides:

DEBIT			PROCESS ACCOUNT		CREDIT
	UNITS	€		UNITS	€
Materials	1 000	2 000.00	Finished goods	700	3 062.50
Labour		1 000.00	Normal loss	200	0
Overheads		500.00	Abnormal loss	100	437.50
	1 000	3 500.00		1 000	3 500.00

7 The abnormal loss will be debited to the Abnormal Loss Account and the credit entry will be transferred as an expense in the income statement.

DEBIT			ABNORMAL LOSS ACCOUNT		CREDIT
	UNITS	€		UNITS	€
Process Account	100	437.50	Income statement	100	437.50

Where there are abnormal losses and scrap sales

Where losses can be sold for scrap sales then the normal and abnormal loss will both be sold.

Example 5.2.c

Using the information in Examples 5.2 and 5.2.b, the losses can now be sold for €2 per unit. Prepare the Process Account, the Normal Loss/Scrap Sales Account and the Abnormal Loss Account.

Solution to Example 5.2.c

1 The normal loss will be credited to the Process Account as 200 units and the scrap sales will be credited as €400 (200 units x €2).
2 The average cost per unit will now have to adjust to take account of the scrap sales. The input costs will be reduced by the amount of the scrap sales from the normal loss (see Example 5.2.a). Calculate the average cost per unit as follows:

$$\frac{\text{Input costs} - \text{scrap sales from normal loss}}{\text{Expected output}}$$

$$\frac{€2\ 000 + 1\ 000 + 500 - 400}{1\ 000\ \text{units} - 200\ \text{units}} = €3.875\ \text{per unit}$$

3 The abnormal loss will be credited to the Process Account as 100 units and will be valued at the average cost per unit:

$$100 \text{ units} \times €3.875 = €387.50$$

4 Value the finished goods at the average cost per unit:

$$700 \text{ units} \times €3.875 = €2\,712.50$$

This will be used to value the finished goods for insurance purposes and to formulate a pricing policy for the units.

5 The Process Account should balance on both sides:

DEBIT			PROCESS ACCOUNT		CREDIT
	UNITS	€		UNITS	€
Materials	1 000	2 000.00	Finished goods	700	2 712.50
Labour		1 000.00	Normal loss	200	400.00
Overheads		500.00	Abnormal loss	100	387.50
	1 000	3 500.00		1 000	3 500.00

6 Open up a Normal Loss/Scrap Sales Account. Transfer the normal loss from the Process Account to the debit side of the Normal Loss/Scrap Sales Account. On the credit side of this account show the receipt of the scrap sales from the normal loss into the Bank Account.

DEBIT			NORMAL LOSS/SCRAP SALES ACCOUNT		CREDIT
	UNITS	€		UNITS	€
Process Account	200	400	Bank Account	200	400

7 The abnormal loss will be debited to the Abnormal Loss Account and the corresponding credit entry will be transferred as an expense in the income statement.

DEBIT			ABNORMAL LOSS ACCOUNT		CREDIT
	UNITS	€		UNITS	€
Process Account	100	387.50	Income statement	100	387.50

Where there are abnormal gains

An abnormal gain occurs when actual losses are less than expected. This could result from an improvement in the production process or using better-quality raw materials.

Example 5.3

A manufacturing company produces units which go through one process. A total of 1 000 units are added at the start of the process. The cost of materials added to the process is €2 400. Labour costing €900 and overheads costing €300 are also added into the process. A normal loss of 10% of input is expected. Actual output to finished goods was 950 units. Losses cannot be sold for scrap. You are required to prepare the Process Account and Abnormal Gain Account.

Solution to Example 5.3

1 The normal loss is 10% of input, i.e., 100 units (10% x 1 000 units). The abnormal gain is calculated as follows:

	Units
Input	1 000
Less: Normal loss	(100)
Expected output	900
Less: Actual output	(950)
Abnormal gain	(50)

The abnormal gain will be debited in the Process Account and valued at the average cost per unit. The accounting treatment of the abnormal gain is similar to that of an abnormal loss, except that it is a gain in the income statement.

2 Calculate the average cost per unit as follows:

$$\frac{\text{Input costs}}{\text{Expected output}}$$

$$\frac{\text{€2 400 + 900 + 300}}{\text{1 000 units – 100 units}} \quad = \quad \text{€4 per unit}$$

3 Value the finished goods output at the average cost per unit:

$$\text{950 units x €4 = €3 800}$$

This will be used to value the finished goods for insurance purposes and to formulate a pricing policy for the units.

4 The abnormal gain will be valued at the average cost per unit:

$$\text{50 units x €4 = €200}$$

5 The normal loss will be valued at nil in the Process Account as the cost is being passed on to the customer in the average cost per unit.

6 The Process Account should balance on both sides:

DEBIT			PROCESS ACCOUNT	CREDIT		
	UNITS	€			UNITS	€
Materials	1 000	2 400	Finished goods		950	3 800
Labour		900	Normal loss		100	0
Overheads		300				
Abnormal gain	50	200				
	1 050	3 800			1 050	3 800

7   The abnormal gain will be credited to the Abnormal Gain Account and the debit entry will be transferred as a gain in the income statement.

DEBIT			ABNORMAL LOSS ACCOUNT	CREDIT		
	UNITS	€			UNITS	€
Income statement	50	200	Process Account		50	200

Where there are abnormal gains and a normal loss with scrap sales

Example 5.3.a

Using Example 5.3, the company can now sell losses for €2.25 per unit. You are required to prepare the Process Account, Normal Loss/Scrap Sales Account and Abnormal Gain Account.

Solution to Example 5.3.a

1   The abnormal gain as calculated in Example 5.3 is 50 units. The normal loss is 100 units and it can be sold for scrap and €225 recovered (100 units x €2.25). The abnormal gain will be debited to the Process Account and valued at the average cost per unit. The normal loss will be credited to the Process Account and valued at the scrap sales.

2   Calculate the average cost per unit as follows:

$$\frac{\text{Input costs} - \text{scrap sales from normal loss}}{\text{Expected output}}$$

$$\frac{€2\ 400 + 900 + 300 - 225}{1\ 000\ \text{units} - 100\ \text{units}} \quad = \quad €3.75\ \text{per unit}$$

3   Value the finished goods at the average cost per unit:

$$950\ \text{units} \times €3.75 = €3\ 562.50$$

This will be used to value the finished goods for insurance purposes and to formulate a pricing policy for the units.

4 The abnormal gain will be valued at the average cost per unit:

$$50 \text{ units x } €3.75 = €187.50$$

5 The Process Account should balance on both sides:

DEBIT		PROCESS ACCOUNT		CREDIT	
	UNITS	€		UNITS	€
Materials	1 000	2 400.00	Output: finished goods	950	3 562.50
Labour		900.00	Normal loss	100	225.00
Overheads		300.00			
Abnormal gain	50	187.50			
	1 050	3 787.50		1 050	3 787.50

6 The abnormal gain will be credited to the Abnormal Gain Account. The company has gained 50 units through efficiencies in its production process. The amount received from scrap sales will be less than expected:

	UNITS x SCRAP SALES	
Normal loss	100 X €2.25	€225.00
Abnormal gain	(50) X €2.25	(€112.50)
Reduction in scrap sales as a result of abnormal gain	50	€112.50

The reduction in scrap sales as a result of the abnormal gain will reduce the amount of the gain in the income statement:

	UNITS	
Gain expected	50 units x €3.75	€187.50
Reduction in scrap sales as a result of the abnormal gain	50 units x €2.25	(€112.50)
Actual gain – income statement		€75.00

DEBIT		ABNORMAL GAIN ACCOUNT		CREDIT	
	UNITS	€		UNITS	€
Normal Loss/Scrap Sales Account	50	112.50	Process Account	50	187.50
Income statement		75.00			
	50	187.50		50	187.50

7 The company will now receive only €112.50 from scrap sales on the normal loss:

DEBIT	NORMAL LOSS/SCRAP SALES ACCOUNT				CREDIT	
	UNITS	€		UNITS	€
Process Account	100	225.00	Abnormal Gain Account	50	112.50
			Bank Account	50	112.50
	100	225.00		100	225.00

Where there is closing work in progress – concept of equivalent units

In the previous examples we assumed that all units were fully processed at the end of the accounting period. The likelihood is that some units will be unfinished at the period end. This is called closing work in progress (WIP). We must place a value on closing WIP for inventory valuation and insurance purposes. The formula that we have been using to calculate the average cost per unit is:

$$\frac{\text{Input costs}}{\text{Number of units of output or expected output}}$$

When there is closing WIP and fully finished units, it is not appropriate to add them together and to call them the number of units of output. This is because the finished units are fully finished but the closing WIP is only partially finished. We would not be adding like with like. We need to equate the closing WIP to the equivalent of a fully finished unit, add it on to the fully finished units and then divide it into the input costs to calculate the average cost per unit.

Example 5.4

At the beginning of a process, a company inputs 1 500 units that have a cost of €1 300 attached to them. At the period end, 1 000 units are fully completed and there are 500 closing WIP units which are only 60% complete. You are required to prepare the Process Account.

Solution to Example 5.4

Calculate the total equivalent units by multiplying the closing WIP units by the percentage of completion and add on to the finished goods:

		TOTAL EQUIVALENT UNITS
Finished goods		1 000
Closing WIP	500 units x 60%	300
Total equivalent units		1 300

Now we can use the formula to calculate the average cost per unit:

$$\frac{\text{Input costs}}{\text{Number of units of output or total equivalent units}}$$

$$\frac{€1\ 300}{1\ 300\ \text{units}} \quad = \quad €1 \text{ per unit}$$

DEBIT	PROCESS ACCOUNT				CREDIT
	UNITS	€		UNITS	€
Input	1 500	1 300	Finished goods (w1)	1 000	1 000
			Closing WIP (w2)	500	300
	1 500	1 300		1 500	1 300

Workings

(w1) Value the finished goods at the average cost per unit:

$$1\ 000 \text{ units x } €1 = €1\ 000$$

(w2) Value the equivalent closing WIP units at the average cost per unit:

$$300 \text{ units x } €1 = €300$$

Where closing WIP has cost elements with different levels of completeness

In Example 5.4 the material, labour and overhead costs were totalled and called 'input costs'. Closing WIP was assumed to have had 60% of input costs added to it at the period end.

Closing WIP may have different percentages of materials, labour and overheads added. For example:

- Materials may all be added at the beginning of the process and so closing WIP may have 100% of materials added at the end of the period.
- Labour is usually added uniformly or evenly throughout the process. Staff working on the process turn up for work every day and do an eight-hour shift. If the closing WIP is 50% complete at the period end, then 50% of the labour cost will have been added to it.

- Overheads may be added uniformly throughout the process or at any time during the process.

Each question will be different so read it carefully to see when costs are added to closing WIP.

Where closing WIP has cost elements with different levels of completeness it is necessary to convert the closing WIP units into equivalent units for each element of cost – this is called a statement of equivalent units. Then calculate the average cost per unit.

Example 5.5

At the beginning of a process a company inputs 1 500 units. Input costs consist of: materials €3 000, labour €2 500 and overheads €625.

At the period end there are 1 000 units of finished goods and 500 units of closing WIP. The closing WIP is 50% complete at the period end. Materials are input at the beginning of the process and labour and overheads uniformly throughout the process. You are required to prepare a Process Account.

Solution to Example 5.5

(w1) It is necessary to calculate the closing WIP units as the equivalent of fully finished units for each cost element.

- Materials are added at the beginning of the process. Any closing WIP units at the period end are 100% complete as regards materials. The closing WIP units are:

$$100\% \times 500 \text{ units} = 500 \text{ units}$$

in respect of materials.

- Labour and overheads are added uniformly throughout the process. At the period end the closing WIP is 50% complete. Any closing WIP units at the period end are 50% complete as regards labour and overheads. The closing WIP units are:

$$50\% \times 500 \text{ units} = 250 \text{ units}$$

in respect of labour and overheads.

It is necessary to prepare a statement of equivalent units:

STATEMENT OF EQUIVALENT UNITS						
COST ELEMENT	€	FINISHED GOODS UNITS		EQUIVALENT CLOSING WIP UNITS (W1)	TOTAL EQUIVALENT UNITS	AVERAGE COST PER UNIT € (W2)
Materials	3 000	1 000	+	500 =	1 500	2.00
Labour	2 500	1 000	+	250 =	1 250	2.00
Overhead	625	1 000	+	250 =	1 250	0.50
						4.50

(w2) The average cost per unit is calculated by dividing the total cost by the total equivalent units, for each cost element:

Materials   €3 000/1 500 units =   €2.00
Labour   €2 500/1 250 units =   €2.00
Overheads   €625/1 250 units =   €0.50

Prepare the Process Account:

DEBIT			PROCESS ACCOUNT		CREDIT
	UNITS	€		**UNITS**	€
Materials	1 500	3 000	Finished goods (w3)	1 000	4 500
Labour		2 500	Closing WIP (w4)	500	1 625
Overheads		625			
	1 500	6 125		1 500	6 125

(w3) Value the finished goods at the average cost per unit:

1 000 units x €4.50 = €4 500

(w4) Value the closing WIP by multiplying the equivalent closing WIP units by the average cost for each cost element:

COST ELEMENT	EQUIVALENT CLOSING WIP UNITS (w1)		AVERAGE COST PER UNIT € (w2)		VALUE OF CLOSING WIP €
Materials	500	X	2.00	=	1 000
Labour	250	X	2.00	=	500
Overheads	250	X	0.50	=	125
					1 625

Check to ensure both sides of the Process Account are balanced.

Example 5.5.a

Use the information in Example 5.5 – but this time the materials are added at the beginning of the process, the labour is added uniformly throughout the process but the overheads are added at the end of the process. You are required to prepare the Process Account.

Solution to Example 5.5.a

(w1) It is necessary to calculate the closing WIP units as the equivalent of fully finished units for each cost element.

- Materials are added at the beginning of the process. Any closing WIP units at the period end are 100% complete as regards materials. The closing WIP units are:

$$100\% \times 500 \text{ units} = 500 \text{ units}$$

in respect of materials.

- Labour is added uniformly throughout the process. At the period end the closing WIP is 50% complete. Any closing WIP units at the period end are 50% complete as regards labour. The closing WIP units are:

$$50\% \times 500 \text{ units} = 250 \text{ units}$$

in respect of labour

- Overheads are only added into the process at the very end. As the process is only half complete at the period end, no overheads have been added to the closing WIP.

It is necessary to prepare a statement of equivalent units:

STATEMENT OF EQUIVALENT UNITS						
COST ELEMENT	€	FINISHED GOODS UNITS	EQUIVALENT CLOSING WIP UNITS (W1)		TOTAL EQUIVALENT UNITS	AVERAGE COST PER UNIT € (W2)
Materials	3 000	1 000 +	500	=	1 500	2.00
Labour	2 500	1 000 +	250	=	1 250	2.00
Overheads	625	1 000 +	0	=	1 000	0.625
						4.625

(w2) The average cost per unit is calculated by dividing the total cost by the total equivalent units, for each cost element:

Materials   €3 000/1 500 units =   €2.00
Labour   €2 500/1 250 units =   €2.00
Overheads   €625/1 000 units =   €0.625

Do not round the average cost per unit figure for overheads to two decimal places. If you do so the Process Account will not balance at the end of the question.

Prepare the Process Account:

DEBIT			PROCESS ACCOUNT		CREDIT
	UNITS	€		**UNITS**	€
Materials	1 500	3 000	Finished goods (w3)	1 000	4 625
Labour		2 500	Closing WIP (w4)	500	1 500
Overheads		625			
	1 500	6 125		1 500	6 125

(w3) Value the finished goods at the average cost per unit:

$$1\ 000 \text{ units} \times €4.625 = €4\ 625$$

(w4) Value the closing WIP by multiplying the equivalent closing WIP units by the average cost for each cost element:

COST ELEMENT	EQUIVALENT CLOSING WIP UNITS (w1)		AVERAGE COST PER UNIT € (w2)		VALUE OF CLOSING WIP €
Materials	500	X	2.00	=	1 000
Labour	250	X	2.00	=	500
Overheads	0	X	0.625	=	0
					1 500

Check to ensure that both sides of the Process Account are balanced.

Conversion costs

Labour and overheads are referred to as 'conversion costs'.

Where there are previous process costs

Units may go through a series of processes before they are completed. Consider a company which has two processes – Process A and Process B. As the units move from Process A (they must be fully finished before they leave Process A) they move into Process B. The costs of producing the units in Process A will become the input costs into Process B. We call this 'previous process costs'. In Process B more materials, labour and overheads may be added to complete the units. In the statement of equivalent units 'previous process costs' are treated as another cost element and are always assumed to be 100% complete for closing WIP. Otherwise they would be treated as incomplete units and would still be in Process A.

Example 5.6

A company manufactures a product which passes through two processes – A and B. The following information relates to Process B:

- 1 500 units input from Process A; previous process costs are €3 750
- Materials added in Process B €3 000
- Conversion costs added in Process B €3 125

At the period end there are 1 000 units of finished goods and 500 units of closing WIP. The closing WIP is 50% complete. Materials are input at the beginning of the process and conversion costs uniformly throughout the process. You are required to prepare a Process B Account.

Solution to Example 5.6

(w1) It is necessary to calculate the closing WIP units as the equivalent of fully finished units for each cost element.

- Previous process costs represent the costs of the 1 500 units which have been transferred from Process A to Process B. These units have been fully complete in Process A and are assumed to have been added in full to any closing WIP in Process B. Any WIP units at the period end are 100% complete as regards previous process costs. The closing WIP units are:

    100% x 500 units = 500 units

    in respect of previous process costs.

- Materials are added at the beginning of the process. Any closing WIP units at the period end are 100% complete as regards materials. The closing WIP units are:

    100% x 500 units = 500 units

    in respect of materials.

- Conversion costs are added uniformly throughout the process. At the period end the closing WIP is 50% complete. Any closing WIP units at the period end are 50% complete as regards conversion costs. The closing WIP units are:

    50% x 500 units = 250 units

    in respect of conversion costs.

STATEMENT OF EQUIVALENT UNITS					
COST ELEMENT	€	FINISHED GOODS UNITS	EQUIVALENT CLOSING WIP UNITS (w1)	TOTAL EQUIVALENT UNITS	AVERAGE COST PER UNIT € (w2)
Previous process costs	3 750	1 000 +	500 =	1 500	2.50
Materials	3 000	1 000 +	500 =	1 500	2.00
Conversion costs	3 125	1 000 +	250 =	1 250	2.50
					7.00

(w2) The average cost per unit is calculated by dividing the total cost by the total equivalent units, for each cost element:

Previous process costs	€3 750/1 500 units = €2.50
Materials	€3 000/1 500 units = €2.00
Conversion costs	€3 125/1 250 units = €2.50

Prepare the Process Account:

DEBIT		PROCESS ACCOUNT			CREDIT
	UNITS	€		UNITS	€
Previous process costs	1 500	3 750	Finished goods (w3)	1 000	7 000
Materials		3 000	Closing WIP (w4)	500	2 875
Conversion costs		3 125			
	1 500	9 875		1 500	9 875

(w3) Value the finished goods at the average cost per unit:

1 000 units x €7.00 = €7 000

(w4) Value the closing WIP by multiplying the equivalent closing WIP units by the average cost for each cost element:

COST ELEMENT	EQUIVALENT CLOSING WIP UNITS (w1)		AVERAGE COST PER UNIT € (w2)		VALUE OF CLOSING WIP €
Previous process costs	500	X	2.50	=	1 250
Materials	500	X	2.00	=	1 000
Conversion costs	250	X	2.50	=	625
					2 875

Check to ensure both sides of the Process Account are balanced.

Where there is opening WIP and closing WIP

So far we have looked at situations where there is closing WIP. Closing WIP at the end of one period becomes opening WIP at the beginning of the next period.

Opening WIP represents partially completed units brought forward from another accounting period. It will have values attached to it and may be split in its various cost elements – material, labour and overheads. Each of these costs may have different levels of completeness. In practice a process will have opening and closing WIP and the issue when this arises is how we value closing WIP where opening WIP exists.

Should we assume that opening WIP units are merged with units commenced during the current period? Thus the average cost per unit would include some of the previous period's costs. Should we assume instead that opening WIP units are the first units to be completed during the current period? Thus the average cost per unit will only include costs incurred during the current period.

There are two methods of accounting for opening WIP: (1) weighted average and (2) first in, first out (FIFO). To illustrate these two methods we will use the following example:

Example 5.7

A company produces a product which goes through three processes before it is fully complete. The following information is available for Process 2:

Opening WIP	500 Units	
	– Process 1 100% complete	€1 000
	– materials 100% complete	€2 400
	– labour 50% complete	€1 500
Fully finished units transferred from Process 1	1 600 units	€5 970
Fully finished units transferred to Process 3	2 700 units	
Closing WIP	400 units (75% complete)	
Costs added to Process 2: – materials – labour	1 000 units	€12 450 €8 000

Materials are added at the beginning of Process 2 and labour is added uniformly throughout the process. You are required to prepare a Process 2 Account.

(1) Weighted average

With this method it is assumed that opening WIP units carried forward from the previous accounting period are merged with units added in the current period. It is assumed that opening WIP is fully completed during the current period. The cost of the opening WIP and the current period's costs are added together and divided by the total equivalent units to form the average cost per unit. Closing WIP and finished units are valued at the average cost per unit.

Solution to Example 5.7 using weighted average

(w1) It is necessary to calculate the closing WIP units as the equivalent of fully finished units for each cost element.
   * It is assumed that any opening WIP will be fully completed during the current process so closing WIP will have had all their Process 1 costs added and will be 100% complete. Any closing WIP units at the period end are 100% complete as regards Process 1 costs. The closing WIP units are:
        100% x 400 units = 400 units
     in respect of Process 1 costs.

   * Materials are added at the beginning of the process. Any closing WIP units at the period end are 100% complete as regards materials. The closing WIP units are:
        100% x 400 units = 400 units
     in respect of materials.

   * Labour is added uniformly throughout the process. At the period end the closing WIP is 75% complete. Any closing WIP units at the period end are 75% complete as regards labour. The closing WIP units are:
        75% x 400 units = 300 units
     in respect of labour.

STATEMENT OF EQUIVALENT UNITS									
COST ELEMENT	OPENING WIP €	CURRENT COSTS €	TOTAL COSTS €	FINISHED GOODS UNITS		EQUIVALENT CLOSING WIP UNITS (W1)		TOTAL EQUIVALENT UNITS	AVERAGE COST PER UNIT €
Process 1	2 400	5 970	8 370	2 700	+	400	=	3 100	2.70
Materials	1 500	12 450	13 950	2 700	+	400	=	3 100	4.50
Labour	1 000	8 000	9 000	2 700	+	300	=	3 000	3.00
									10.20

Prepare the Process Account:

DEBIT		PROCESS 2 ACCOUNT		CREDIT	
	UNITS	€		UNITS	€
Opening WIP	500		Finished goods (w2)	2 700	27 540
– Process 1		1 000			
– materials		2 400			
– labour		1 500			
Process 1	1 600	5 970	Closing WIP (w3)	400	3 780
Costs added					
– materials	1 000	12 450			
– labour		8 000			
	3 100	31 320		3 100	31 320

(w2) Value the finished goods at the average cost per unit:

$$2\ 700 \text{ units} \times €10.20 = €27\ 540$$

(w3) Value the closing WIP by multiplying the equivalent closing WIP units by the average cost for each cost element:

COST ELEMENT	EQUIVALENT CLOSING WIP UNITS (w1)		AVERAGE COST PER UNIT €		VALUE OF CLOSING WIP €
Process 1	400	X	2.70	=	1 080
Materials	400	X	4.50	=	1 800
Labour	300	X	3.00	=	900
					3 780

Check to ensure both sides of the Process Account are balanced.

(2) FIFO

With this method it is assumed that opening WIP will be the first units to be completed in the current process, and then the units started in the period are completed. Units are completed on a first in, first out (FIFO) basis. Closing WIP arising will result only from units started in the current period and will not include any opening WIP units or opening WIP costs.

Finished goods units will be separated into units of opening WIP which are completed during the period and units started and completed during the period, i.e., the total units completed during the period minus the equivalent opening WIP units as fully finished units (see w1 below). Finished goods will be valued in two parts (see w3 below):

1   The value of the opening WIP which is completed in the current period.
2   The value of units started and finished in the current period. This is valued
    at the average cost per unit. The average cost per unit using the FIFO
    method is calculated by dividing the current period's costs by the current
    period's equivalent units.

Using the FIFO method it is assumed that closing WIP will only come from
units started during the period. So closing WIP will only include costs
incurred in the current period. Closing WIP units will be valued at the
average cost per unit (see w4 below). Any costs incurred in previous periods
are not carried forward in closing WIP.

Solution to Example 5.7 using FIFO

(w1)   It is necessary to calculate the equivalent units in opening WIP:
   * Process 1 is 100% complete for opening WIP units. The equivalent
     units are:

$$100\% \times 500 \text{ units} = 500 \text{ units}$$

   in respect of Process 1 costs.
   * Materials are 100% complete for opening WIP units. The equivalent
     units are:

$$100\% \times 500 \text{ units} = 500 \text{ units}$$

   in respect of materials.
   * Labour is 50% complete for opening WIP units. The equivalent units
     are:

$$50\% \times 500 \text{ units} = 250 \text{ units}$$

   in respect of labour.
   Then subtract them from the finished goods units to calculate the
   finished goods units less the equivalent opening WIP units:

	FINISHED GOODS UNITS		EQUIVALENT UNITS IN OPENING WIP		FINISHED GOODS UNITS LESS EQUIVALENT UNITS IN OPENING WIP
Process 1	1 600	–	500	=	1 100
Materials	1 600	–	500	=	1 100
Labour	1 600	–	250	=	1 350

(w2)   Calculate the closing WIP units as the equivalent of fully finished units
       for each cost element:
   * Any closing WIP units at the period end are 100% complete as
     regards Process 1 costs. The closing WIP units are:

$$100\% \times 400 \text{ units} = 400 \text{ units}$$

in respect of Process 1 costs.

- Materials are added at the beginning of the process. Any closing WIP units at the period end are 100% complete as regards materials. The closing WIP units are:

$$100\% \times 400 \text{ units} = 400 \text{ units}$$

in respect of materials.

- Labour is added uniformly throughout the process. At the period end the closing WIP is 75% complete. Any closing WIP units at the period end are 75% complete as regards labour. The closing WIP units are:

$$75\% \times 400 \text{ units} = 300 \text{ units}$$

in respect of labour.

STATEMENT OF EQUIVALENT UNITS							
COST ELEMENT	CURRENT COSTS €	FINISHED GOODS UNITS LESS EQUIVALENT UNITS IN OPENING WIP (w1)		EQUIVALENT CLOSING WIP UNITS (w2)		TOTAL EQUIVALENT UNITS	AVERAGE COST PER UNIT €
Process 1	5 970	1 100	+	400	=	1 500	3.9800
Materials	12 450	1 100	+	400	=	1 500	8.3000
Labour	8 000	1 350	+	300	=	1 650	4.8484
							17.1284

Prepare the Process Account:

DEBIT			PROCESS 2 ACCOUNT		CREDIT
	UNITS	€		UNITS	€
Opening WIP	500		Finished goods (w3)	2 700	24 953.34
– Process 1		1 000.00			
– materials		2 400.00			
– labour		1 500.00			
Process 1	1 600	5 970.00	Closing WIP (w4)	400	6 366.52
Costs added					
– materials	1 000	12 450.00			
– labour		8 000.00			
	3 100	31 320.00		3 100	31 319.86

(w3) Value the finished goods as follows:

		€
Opening WIP	– Process 1	1 000.00
	– materials	2 400.00
	– labour	1 500.00
Process 1	1 100 units x 3.98	4 378.00
Materials	1 100 units x 8.30	9 130.00
Labour	1 350 units x 4.8484	6 545.34
		24 953.34

(w4) Value the closing WIP by multiplying the equivalent closing WIP units by the average cost for each cost element:

COST ELEMENT	EQUIVALENT CLOSING WIP UNITS (w2)		AVERAGE COST PER UNIT €		VALUE OF CLOSING WIP €
Process 1	400	X	3.98	=	1 592.00
Materials	400	X	8.30	=	3 320.00
Labour	300	X	4.8484	=	1 454.52
					6 366.52

As you can see from the Process Account the accounts do not balance on both sides. There is a rounding difference as the average cost per unit was rounded to €4.8484 for labour. The difference is insignificant.

Weighted average method or FIFO method?

Each method will give a different inventory valuation but as you can see from Example 5.7 the differences are very small.

The problem with the weighted average method is that it may distort inventory valuation where process costs differ significantly from one period to the next. However, the weighted average method is a much easier method to use.

By-products

At the split-off point in the process, when individual products are distinguishable from each other, the main products are called 'joint products' and minor incidental products are called 'by-products'. *CIMA Official Terminology* defines by-products as follows:

A by-product is manufactured as an unavoidable result of the process. Although it has some sales value, its value is small in comparison to the main product.

By-products usually have a minor sales value. An example is sawdust arising from furniture making. The most common method of accounting for by-products is to deduct the net realisable value of the by-product from the total cost of production of the joint products.

Joint products

When two or more main products arise at the split-off point in a process they are referred to as 'joint products'. *CIMA Official Terminology* defines joint products as follows:

> Joint products are two or more separate products output from a common process, each having a sales value large enough to justify the treatment of the product as a main product.

Up until the split-off point the joint products are not distinguishable. At the split-off point processing costs must be allocated to joint products. These costs are referred to as joint costs and include materials, labour and overheads incurred in the process. After the split-off point it may be decided to process the joint products further and then sell them. This topic is further discussed in **Chapter 10: Relevant Costing and Decision-Making**.

Methods of allocating joint costs

Two methods that are used to allocate joint costs to joint products are:

1   Volume-based method – the joint costs are apportioned in proportion to volume, e.g., units of output, kilograms, litres, etc.
2   Sales value at the split-off point – the joint costs are apportioned in proportion to the relative sales value of the products.

These methods are illustrated in Example 5.8.

Example 5.8

A company makes three products, X, Y and Z, which are produced using a common process. Total joint costs are €8 000. The following information is available regarding the three products:

	KILOGRAMS	SELLING PRICE	SALES REVENUE
X	600	€12.50	€7 500
Y	1 200	€3.25	€3 900
Z	300	€15.00	€4 500

You are required to apportion the joint costs and calculate the profit and the profit as a percentage of sales for each product using:

a Volume-based method of apportioning joint costs
b Sales value at the split-off point method of apportioning joint costs

Solution to Example 5.8

a Volume-based method of apportioning joint costs

Apportion joint costs in proportion to the volume of each product:

	KILOGRAMS	APPORTIONMENT OF JOINT COSTS	JOINT COSTS ALLOCATION
X	600	600/2 100 x €8 000 =	€2 286
Y	1 200	1 200/2 100 x €8 000 =	€4 571
Z	300	300/2 100 x €8 000 =	€1 143
Total	2 100		€8 000

Profit is calculated as follows:

	SALES REVENUE €	LESS: JOINT COSTS €	PROFIT/(LOSS) €	PROFIT/(LOSS) AS A % OF SALES
X	7 500	(2 286)	5 214	69.5%
Y	3 900	(4 571)	(671)	(17.2%)
Z	4 500	(1 143)	3 357	74.6%
Total	15 900		7 900	49.7%

b Sales value at the split-off point method of apportioning joint costs

Apportion joint costs in proportion to the sales value of each product:

	SALES REVENUE	APPORTIONMENT OF JOINT COSTS	JOINT COSTS ALLOCATION
X	7 500	7 500/15 900 x €8 000 =	€3 774
Y	3 900	3 900/15 900 x €8 000 =	€1 962
Z	4 500	4 500/15 900 x €8 000 =	€2 264
Total	15 900		€8 000

Profit is calculated as follows:

	SALES REVENUE €	LESS: JOINT COSTS €	PROFIT/(LOSS) €	PROFIT/(LOSS) AS A % OF SALES
X	7 500	(3 774)	3 726	50%
Y	3 900	(1 962)	1 938	50%
Z	4 500	(2 264)	2 236	50%
	15 900		7 900	50%

Comparison of joint cost apportionment methods

The volume-based method allocates joint costs in proportion to volume. Product Y is allocated the largest share of the joint costs even though it generates the lowest sales revenue.

The sales value at the split-off point method allocates joint costs in proportion to sales revenue. Product X is allocated the largest share of the joint costs as it generates the highest sales revenue. The problem with this is that it is assumed that because a product earns a high proportion of revenue, it generates the highest proportion of joint costs. This may distort profits as it does not necessarily follow that because a product earns a high proportion of revenue, it is costly to produce. Revenue is influenced by demand and market forces. Using this method, a product earning a high proportion of revenue may show a modest profit, and an unprofitable product which earns a low revenue will be allocated a small amount of joint costs, thus showing a profit.

Chapter summary

At the beginning of this chapter the difference between process costing and job costing was explained. Process costing applies to the mass production of a single product while job costing is applied where a single task, product or service is charged to one customer. It would be uneconomical to cost each product individually in process costing so the average price per unit is used. The accounting treatment of process costs was illustrated in the Process Account.

Normal losses, abnormal losses and abnormal gains were defined and their accounting treatment illustrated. Where losses can be sold for scrap sales, the revenue generated must be accounted for in a Normal Loss/Scrap Sales Account.

A complication arises in process costing where there is closing work in progress which has varying degrees of completeness. A statement of equivalent units must be drawn up to equate closing WIP units to the equivalent of fully finished units.

Where there are opening and closing WIP units, the FIFO method or the weighted average method must be used. Both methods are illustrated in the chapter.

Finally, the accounting treatment of joint products and by-products which arise from the process were illustrated. There are two methods of allocating joint costs to joint products – the volume-based method and the sales value at the split-off point method, both of which were illustrated.

Test questions

Question 1*

A company produces whiskey which goes through three different processes before it is ready for sale. The following details relate to Process 1 for last month:

Materials	20 000 litres at a cost of €40 000
Conversion costs	€28 400
Output to Process 2	18 500 litres

Normal loss is estimated at 5% of materials input. There are no opening or closing inventories.

Required

a Prepare the Process 1 Account
b Calculate the average cost per unit
c Prepare workings to show the valuation of output to Process 2
d Prepare the Abnormal Loss or Abnormal Gain Account

Notes to students

1 You need to check to see if there is an abnormal loss or gain in this question. The first thing to do is to open the Process Account and put in all available information. Check to see if the units columns on both sides

balance. If the debit side is smaller there is an abnormal gain and if the credit side is smaller there is an abnormal loss.

2   Remember that conversion costs are the sum of labour and overhead costs.
3   As there is no mention of losses being sold we can assume that the normal loss is valued at nil.

* Based on question L7.1 in Alice Luby, *Cost and Management Accounting*, Gill & Macmillan, 1999.

Question 2

A company inputs 2 000 units into a process at a cost of €3 970. Normal loss is 10% of input and output to finished goods is 1 500 units. Losses are sold for scrap at €0.50 per unit. There is no opening or closing WIP.

Required

a   Prepare the Process Account
b   Calculate the average cost per unit
c   Prepare workings to show the valuation of output to finished goods
d   Prepare the Normal Loss/Scrap Sales Account
e   Prepare the Abnormal Loss Account

Notes to students

1   In this question losses, regardless of whether they are normal or abnormal, can be sold for scrap sales.
2   Transfer the normal loss from the Process Account to the debit side of the Normal Loss/Scrap Sales Account. The cash received from the sale of the normal loss is shown on the credit side of this account.
3   Transfer the abnormal loss to the debit side of the Abnormal Loss Account. The cash received from the sale of the abnormal loss is shown on the credit side. The balancing figure on the credit side will be transferred as an expense to the income statement.
4   There is no opening or closing WIP so the average cost per unit, taking into account scrap sales, is calculated as follows:

$$\frac{\text{Input costs} - \text{scrap sales from normal loss}}{\text{Expected output}}$$

Question 3

Butler Ltd manufactures fertilisers which pass through two processes before they are complete. The following information relates to the manufacture of the product in the period just ended:

	PROCESS 1	PROCESS 2
Materials	50 000 units valued at €53 250	Output from Process 1 forms the input into Process 2
Conversion costs	€20 000	€14 536
Normal loss	5% of input units	7% of input units
Scrap sales of losses	€0.80 per unit	€0.70 per unit
Output	46 000 units (to Process 2)	43 790 units (to finished goods)

There was no opening or closing WIP and units completed at the end of Process 2 are fully finished and ready for sale.

Required

Prepare the Process 1 Account and the Process 2 Account. Clearly show all workings.

Notes to students

1 There are two processes in this question. The output from Process 1 forms the input into Process 2.
2 Note that the normal loss % and scrap sales per unit changes in Process 2.
3 Check to see if there are any abnormal losses or gains.

For answers and additional test questions, see www.gillmacmillan.ie. Search for Management Accounting and click on the link in the right-hand column.

6 Budgetary Planning and Control

Learning outcomes of Chapter 6

At the end of this chapter, you will be able to:

- discuss the relationship between the mission statement, strategy and budget setting
- explain how budgeting forms part of the control process in a business
- explain budgeting terminology
- outline the stages in the budget process
- prepare budgets
- flex the budget at different levels of activity
- explain the terms incremental budgeting, zero-based budgeting, rolling budgets and activity-based budgeting
- discuss the benefits and drawbacks of budgeting
- discuss the theory of beyond budgeting

Introduction

CIMA Official Terminology defines a budget as 'a quantitative expression of a plan for a defined period of time'. It enables managers to control costs, revenues and profits by providing a yardstick with which to compare actual costs, revenues and profits. If actual results deviate from the budget, corrective action may be taken to bring results back in line with the original plan or budget.

In this chapter the relationship between the mission statement, strategy and budget-setting process will be discussed. Budgets as a control mechanism will be examined.

The preparation of budgets will be explained and illustrated with examples. The use of incremental budgeting, zero-based budgeting, rolling budgets, activity-based budgeting and the relationship between budgets and variance analysis will be examined. This chapter should be studied in conjunction with **Chapter 7: Standard Costing and Variance Analysis**. The benefits and drawbacks of budgeting will be discussed. Finally, the theory of beyond budgeting will be discussed and its relevance examined.

Relationship between the mission statement, strategy and budget setting

A mission statement is a published list of objectives and aspirations of a company. It is usually a number of lines of text in the company's annual accounts or on its website.

The mission statement for the Institute of Technology, Tallaght is:

Our mission
To provide learners with excellent flexible higher education opportunities. To provide programmes which reflect current and emerging knowledge … To offer accessible programmes, delivered in a professional manner, in a friendly and supportive environment.

To foster graduates ready to undertake the roles …

To be a major contributor to the social, cultural and economic life in South Dublin County …

CIMA Official Terminology states that strategy is 'a course of action, including the specification of resources required, to achieve a specific objective'. Ideally, the mission statement should drive the strategy of the company. Strategy is usually defined by time and organisations would outline their long-term, medium-term and short-term strategies.

For example, the mission statement of a retail company may state that it aspires to expand its number of outlets. The long-term strategy may be to have expanded its stores by 10 over the next five years. The medium-term strategy may be to have expanded its stores by five over the next two years and the short-term may be to open one new store in the next 12 months.

The timeframe of the strategy will depend on the organisation. For example, a government's new infrastructure strategy may extend over a 10-year period, whereas a retail company may have a strategy extending over a five-year period.

The long-range strategy (or, say, five-year plan) is then used to prepare the budget. If the company's plan is to open a new retail outlet in the next accounting period, the budget should be prepared with that in mind and sufficient funds should be made available to enable this to happen.

Budgets are used in all types of organisations, whether profit-making or non-profit-making, government departments, educational institutions, hospitals, etc. This chapter will concentrate on preparing budgets in a manufacturing organisation which is profit-making. Performance measurement in non-profit organisations is discussed in **Chapter 12: Performance Measurement and Issues in Accounting**.

Budgeting as part of the planning and control process in a business

If budgets are prepared for a 12-month period and this corresponds to the calendar year, then the budget preparation period usually begins the preceding September. The budget should be agreed and put into place by 1 January.

In **Chapter 7: Standard Costing and Variance Analysis**, it is explained that the budget is used as a control mechanism and each month the actual results are compared with the budget and the difference is called a variance. This is carried out in the monthly management accounts.

The management accountant usually carries out the variance analysis because they have the accounting expertise, but it is the responsibility of the manager who made the decision to incur the cost to explain why the variances have occurred. This acts as a motivation for managers to be more cost-efficient. This forms part of the concept of responsibility accounting, which is discussed in **Chapter 12: Performance Measurement and Issues in Accounting**.

Budgeting terminology

Throughout this chapter the following terms will be used:

(1) Budget period

CIMA Official Terminology defines the budget period as the 'period for which a budget is prepared and used, which may then be subdivided into control periods'. Control periods usually correspond to calendar months.

(2) Budget manual

CIMA Official Terminology defines the budget manual as a 'detailed set of guidelines and information about the budget process typically including a calendar of budgetary events, specimen budget forms, a statement of budgetary objectives and desired results, listing of budgetary activities and budget assumptions regarding, for example, inflation and interest rates'. The budget manual is prepared and distributed to those preparing budgets.

(3) Budget committee

The budget committee consists of departmental managers responsible for setting budgets, and members of the accounting department. It is usually chaired by the management accountant. In large organisations, a separate budgeting section within the accounting department may exist. The budget committee meets regularly during the budgeting process to agree deadlines, co-ordinate the preparation of the budget and discuss budget issues.

(4) Master budget

When all individual budgets for the various functions of the business, e.g., sales, production and purchases, have been agreed, they are summarised into the master budget, consisting of the cash budget, budgeted income statement and budgeted balance sheet.

(5) Budget slack

Budget slack involves building inefficiencies or padding into budgets by overestimating expenses or underestimating revenues.

Stages in the budget process

(1) Decide on the factor which limits activity

In a profit-making organisation, the limiting factor is usually the budgeted level of sales for the budget period. Once the level of sales has been estimated, this will determine the production budgets. The sales units and the sales revenue budgets are prepared. The limiting factor could also be production capacity, labour or cash constraints.

(2) Determine the production budgets

The production budget is driven by the sales budget. Once the level of sales required for the next accounting period is decided, the level of production required to fulfil the sales will be estimated. The production units budget is prepared.

(3) Communicate the budget guidelines

Guidelines on preparing the budget are communicated to those preparing budgets, using the budget manual and meetings of the budget committee. The budget committee should ensure that all managers are working towards the same set of objectives when preparing budgets.

(4) Prepare the master budget

The production budget drives all other budgets. Once the level of production units is estimated, this will determine the amount of materials, labour hours and production overheads required. The materials quantity and cost budgets, the labour hours and cost budgets, and the production overhead budgets are prepared.

All budgets are summarised into the master budget, consisting of the cash budget, budgeted income statement and budgeted balance sheet.

The types of budgets mentioned above are typical of a manufacturing organisation, but other budgets relevant to the business may be included in the master budget.

(5) Submit the master budget for agreement

The master budget is submitted to the board of directors for agreement. Usually revisions are required and the budget needs to go back to the budget committee and departmental managers.

(6) Final agreement of the master budget

Ideally, the budget should be agreed and should be uploaded into the management accounting system by the first day of the new accounting year.

(7) Use the budget for control purposes

The budget is used for control purposes and is compared with actual results in the monthly management accounts. The differences between the budget and actual results are investigated and explained by the person responsible for the decisions made.

Different types of budgets

The following diagram shows the typical budgets required to prepare the master budget in a manufacturing organisation. The sales budget will determine the level of manufacturing production in the business. This in turn will determine the direct labour budget, direct materials usage and purchases budget, and production overhead budget. These budgets are referred to as functional budgets. Once the functional budgets have been prepared, they are used to produce the master budget, which consists of the cash budget, budgeted income statement and budgeted balance sheet.

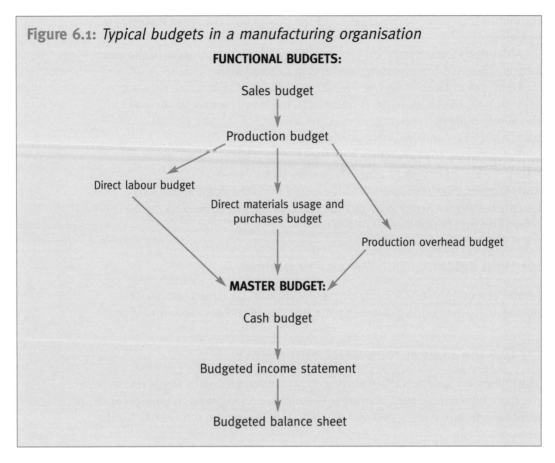

Figure 6.1: *Typical budgets in a manufacturing organisation*

FUNCTIONAL BUDGETS:

Sales budget

Production budget

Direct labour budget

Direct materials usage and purchases budget

Production overhead budget

MASTER BUDGET:

Cash budget

Budgeted income statement

Budgeted balance sheet

Preparation of budgets

The following example illustrates a number of the budgets discussed above and it shows how budgets are inter-linked and should be prepared in conjunction with each other.

Example 6.1*

Micro Components Ltd makes two types of CPU – the Basic and the Ultra. The Basic sells for €5 per unit and the Ultra for €7.50 per unit.

The following are the expected sales and inventory levels of the two products:

	BASIC UNITS	ULTRA UNITS
Sales	11 250	9 000
Opening inventory	1 000	1 875
Closing inventory	750	375

Standard costs are as follows:

Direct labour rate per hour	€7.00
Direct material per kg	€0.30

The standard labour hours required to produce a Basic unit is 0.5 hours. The standard labour hours required to produce an Ultra is 0.75 hours.

The standard kg of materials to produce a Basic unit is 2 kg, and the standard kg of materials to produce an Ultra unit is 3 kg.

The following amounts of inventory are expected and required:

	DIRECT MATERIALS (KG)
Opening inventory	45 000
Closing inventory	60 000

The standard fixed production overhead rate is €1.40 per labour hour.

Required

Prepare the following functional budgets for 2012:

a   Sales revenue budget (€)
b   Production budget (units)
c   Direct materials usage (kg) and purchases budgets (kg and €)
d   Direct labour budget (hours and €)
e   Fixed production overhead budget (€)
f   Production cost budget (€)

Notes

1   The standard labour hours and standard kg are mentioned in the question. Standard costing is discussed in **Chapter 7: Standard Costing and Variance Analysis**. The standard labour hours are the budgeted labour hours of one unit. Similarly, the standard kg is the budgeted kg of one unit.
2   The fixed production overhead is absorbed at €1.40 per labour hour. The company is using an absorption approach to budgeting. The fixed production overhead is absorbed into and treated as a product cost and included in the standard cost for each product. For a more detailed explanation of marginal and absorption costing see **Chapter 8: Marginal and Absorption Costing**.

* Based on Exhibit 16.5 in Alan Upchurch, *Cost Accounting Principles and Practice*, Financial Times/Prentice-Hall, 2002.

Solution to Example 6.1

a   Sales revenue budget (€)
    The sales budget is produced by multiplying the sales units by the sales price per unit:

	SALES UNITS x SALES PRICE PER UNIT	SALES REVENUE BUDGET €
Basic	11 250 units x €5	56 250
Ultra	9 000 units x €7.50	67 500
Sales budget		123 750

b   Production budget (units)
    The company needs to produce the required levels of inventory to meet sales demand and to take into account the desired levels of opening and closing inventory. This is calculated as follows:

	BASIC UNITS	ULTRA UNITS
Sales budget	11 250	9 000
Add: Closing inventory at the year end	750	375
Less: Opening inventory at the beginning of the year	(1 000)	(1 875)
Production required	11 000	7 500

c   Direct materials usage (kg) and purchases budgets (kg and €)
    In part (b) we estimated that 11 000 units of Basic and 7 500 units of Ultra need to be produced to meet the estimated sales. The quantity of materials required to produce these levels of inventory needs to be estimated, i.e., the direct materials usage budget.

Direct materials usage budget (kg)
The Basic requires 2 kg of materials to produce one finished unit and the Ultra requires 3 kg. Multiply the production units by the kg per unit:

	TOTAL DIRECT MATERIALS USAGE BUDGET (KG)
Production units x kg per unit: Basic 11 000 units x 2 kg	22 000
Ultra 7 500 units x 3 kg	22 500
Direct materials usage budget	44 500

Direct materials purchases budget (kg and €)

The direct materials purchases budget is driven by the direct materials usage budget. It should take into account the required opening inventory and expected closing inventory. Multiply the direct materials purchases quantity by the standard cost per kg:

	DIRECT MATERIALS (KG)
Direct materials usage budget	44 500
Add: Closing inventory at the year end	60 000
Less: Opening inventory at the beginning of the year	(45 000)
Direct material purchases (kg)	59 500
X	X
Standard cost per kg	€0.30
=	=
Direct materials purchases budget	€17 850

d   Direct labour budget (hours and €)

In part (b) we estimated that 11 000 units of Basic and 7 500 units of Ultra need to be produced to meet the estimated sales. The labour hours and cost required to produce these levels of inventory need to be estimated. Multiply the standard hours by the production budget for each product to calculate the direct labour hours required for production. Then multiply by the direct labour rate per hour:

	BASIC	ULTRA	TOTAL
Production budget (units)	11 000	7 500	
X	X	X	
Standard hours	0.5	0.75	
=	=	=	
Direct labour hours budget	5 500	5 625	11 125
X			X
Direct labour rate per hour			€7
=			=
Direct labour budget			€77 875

e   Fixed production overhead budget (€)

The standard fixed production overhead rate is €1.40 per labour hour. This is the overhead absorption rate (OAR), which is discussed in more detail in **Chapter 3: Product Costing – Overheads**. For the purpose of this example the OAR has previously been calculated at this rate. You should be aware that you may be required to calculate the OAR by dividing the budgeted fixed production overhead by the budgeted labour hours:

$$OAR = \frac{\text{Budgeted fixed production overhead}}{\text{Budgeted labour hours}}$$

The fixed production overhead budget is calculated by multiplying the number of budgeted labour hours by the OAR:

	BASIC	ULTRA	TOTAL
Budgeted labour hours	5 500	5 625	11 125
x	x	x	
OAR	€1.40	€1.40	
=	=	=	
Fixed production overhead budget	€7 700	€7 875	€15 575

f   Production cost budget (€)

The production cost budget lists all of the production costs involved in producing the budgeted units. Usually this budget is prepared from the standard cost budget. The standard cost is the budgeted cost of one unit. Once the standard cost is available, the budgeted cost is calculated by multiplying the standard cost by the budgeted units. Standard costing is discussed in **Chapter 7: Standard Costing and Variance Analysis**.

In Example 6.1, the standard cost for each product is:

		BASIC €	ULTRA €
Direct materials	Basic: 2 kg x €0.30	0.60	–
	Ultra: 3 kg x €0.30	–	0.90
Direct labour	Basic: 0.5 hrs x €7	3.50	–
	Ultra: 0.75 hrs x €7	–	5.25
Fixed production overhead	Basic: 0.5 hrs x €1.40	0.70	–
	Ultra: 0.75 hrs x €1.40	–	1.05
Standard production cost per unit (€)		4.80	7.20

The production cost budget is produced by multiplying the standard costs prepared above by the budgeted production. This was calculated in the production budget in part (b):

		BASIC €	ULTRA €
Direct materials	Basic: €0.60 x 11 000 units	6 600	–
	Ultra: €0.90 x 7 500 units	–	6 750
Direct labour	Basic: €3.50 x 11 000 units	38 500	–
	Ultra: €5.25 x 7 500 units	–	39 375
Fixed production overhead	Basic: €0.70 x 11 000 units	7 700	–
	Ultra: €1.05 x 7 500 units	–	7 875
Production cost budget		52 800	54 000

The production cost budget can be produced simply by multiplying the standard cost by the budgeted units as follows:

		BASIC €	ULTRA €
Basic	€4.80 x 11 000 units	52 800	–
Ultra	€7.20 x 7 500 units	–	54 000

Be careful, though – the production cost budget is not the sum of the direct materials purchases budget, direct labour budget and fixed production overhead budget. The production cost budget is the sum of the costs of production, and the direct materials purchases budget is the cost of the materials purchased for production, not the cost of the materials used in production.

Cash budget

Cash budgeting is an essential part of the budgeting process in a business. Unless the business has cash, it will suffer liquidity problems and will be unable to meet commitments such as paying staff and suppliers. A cash budget will highlight months when there may be insufficient funds available. Cash shortages can jeopardise the company's future plans or threaten the long-term survival of the company. If this is known in advance, bank loans and overdrafts can be negotiated with banks.

A cash budget will also highlight times when there will be surplus cash available. The interest received on a current account may be lower than a short-term investment. A cash budget will enable the accountant to plan short-term investment of surplus cash.

A cash budget may be prepared weekly, monthly, quarterly, annually, or as frequently as the business requires. It lists cash receipts from product sales, sales of assets, issues of shares, etc. It lists cash payments from materials purchases, labour costs, overheads costs, purchase of fixed assets, payment of dividends, etc. The opening cash balance at the beginning of the period is listed and the closing cash balance at the end of each month is calculated.

Budgeted income statement

The budgeted income statement records the estimated revenues, cost of sales and committed costs for the budget period. A budgeted profit or loss for the budget period is calculated. This will ensure the company will realise profits to secure long-term survival and growth.

Profit and cash are not the same. The cash budget records the cash transaction when it is estimated to be paid or received. The income statement records the transaction when it occurs or is committed. It is based on the accruals basis of accounting. For example, with sales the cash budget records the sales revenue when the cash is received; the income statement records the sales when the transactions take place, i.e., when the products are physically sold to the customer.

There are items which will only be recorded in the budgeted income statement and will not appear in the cash budget:

1   Profit or loss on the sale of a fixed asset. When an asset is sold, the cash received from the sale will appear as a receipt in the cash budget. If there was a profit or loss on the sale, this will only appear in the budgeted income statement.
3   Depreciation. *CIMA Official Terminology* states 'Depreciation is the systematic allocation of the depreciable amount of an asset over its useful life'. Depreciation does not represent a cash transaction and does not appear in the cash budget. It is recorded as an expense in the budgeted income statement.
4   Bad debts. Bad debts are trade receipts which are expected to be uncollectable. They are written off as an expense to the income statement or against a bad debt provision. They are not a cash item and do not appear in the cash budget.

Budgeted balance sheet

The final budget to be prepared is the budgeted balance sheet for 2012. It lists all assets, non-current and current, equity and liabilities at the end of the budget period.

Example 6.1.a

Micro Components Ltd wishes to prepare the master budget using the information calculated in Example 6.1.

The company wishes to prepare a cash budget on a quarterly basis and has summarised the budgeted sales receipts and payments prepared in Example 6.1 as follows:

2012 FINANCIAL YEAR					
€	QUARTER 1	QUARTER 2	QUARTER 3	QUARTER 4	TOTAL
Sales transactions	43 000	33 400	26 000	21 350	123 750
Direct materials purchase transactions	9 500	3 570	2 678	2 102	17 850
Direct labour costs	19 000	19 500	19 000	20 375	77 875
Fixed production overhead	1 400	2 180	4 361	7 634	15 575

Additional information regarding the cash budget:

- 10% of all sales are for cash, the remainder being credit sales received the following quarter. The amount received in Quarter 1 2012 for Quarter 4 2011 credit sales was €25 000.
- 75% of direct materials purchases are paid for in the quarter of purchase and the balance in the following quarter. The amount paid in Quarter 1 2012 for Quarter 4 2011 credit purchases was €1 500.
- Direct labour costs and fixed production overheads are paid in the quarter incurred.

The balance sheet as at 31 December 2011 was as follows:

ASSETS	€	€
Non-current assets:		
Machinery at cost		95 000
Premises at cost		150 000
		245 000
Current assets:		
Inventories: finished goods (Basic: 1 000 units and Ultra: 1 875 units)	18 300	
Inventories: raw materials (45 000 kg)	13 500	
Receivables (Quarter 4 2011 credit sales)	25 000	
Cash at bank	5 000	61 800
		306 800

EQUITY AND LIABILITIES	€	€
Equity:		
Share capital	15 000	
Retained earnings	290 300	305 300
Current liabilities:		
Payables for raw materials (Quarter 4 2011 credit purchases)		1 500
		306 800

Required

Prepare the master budget for 2012 consisting of:
(i)   Cash budget
(ii) Budgeted income statement
(iii) Budgeted balance sheet

Solution to Example 6.1.a

(i) Cash budget for 2012

	QUARTER 1	QUARTER 2	QUARTER 3	QUARTER 4	TOTAL
Receipts:					
Sales (w1)	29 300.00	42 040.00	32 660.00	25 535.00	129 535.00
Payments:					
Direct materials purchases (w2)	8 625.00	5 052.50	2 901.00	2 246.000	18 824.50
Direct labour	19 000.00	19 500.00	19 000.00	20 375.00	77 875.00
Fixed production overhead	1 400.00	2 180.00	4 361.00	7 634.00	15 575.00
	29 025.00	26 732.50	26 262.00	30 255.00	112 274.50
Net cash inflow/ (outflow)	275.00	15 307.50	6 398.00	(4 720.00)	17 260.50
Opening bank balance	5 000.00	5 275.00	20 582.50	26 980.50	5 000.00
Closing bank balance	5 275.00	20 582.50	26 980.50	22 260.50	22 260.50

Points to note

- Each quarter the payments are subtracted from the receipts to arrive at the net cash inflow (if receipts are greater than payments) or the net cash outflow (if receipts are less than payments).
- The opening bank balance is added to the net cash inflow/(outflow) to arrive at the closing bank balance.
- The closing bank balance at the end of Quarter 1 becomes the opening bank balance at the beginning of Quarter 2 and so on.
- The closing bank balance at the end of Quarter 4 should equal the closing bank balance in the Total column.

Workings

(w1) Sales receipts are calculated as follows:

	QUARTER 1	QUARTER 2	QUARTER 3	QUARTER 4
Sales transactions	43 000	33 400	26 000	21 350
Received as follows:				
10% for cash	4 300	3 340	2 600	2 135
90% on credit received the next quarter	25 000	38 700	30 060	23 400
Total sales receipts	29 300	42 040	32 660	25 535

(w2) Direct materials purchases

	QUARTER 1	QUARTER 2	QUARTER 3	QUARTER 4
Direct material purchase transactions	9 500	3 570	2 678	2 102
Paid as follows:				
75% for cash	7 125	2 677.50	2 008.50	1 576.50
25% on credit paid the next quarter	1 500	2 375.00	892.50	669.50
Total direct materials purchase transactions	8 625	5 052.50	2 901.00	2 246.00

(ii) Budgeted income statement as at 31 December 2012

	€	€
Sales revenue (w3)		123 750
Less: Cost of sales		
Opening inventory	18 300	
Cost of production (w4)	106 800	
Less: Closing inventory (w5)	(6 300)	(118 800)
Net profit		4 950

(w3) Sales revenue

In the income statement budget the sales recorded are the total of all of the sales transactions for the period, regardless of when the cash for sales was received:

	QUARTER 1	QUARTER 2	QUARTER 3	QUARTER 4	TOTAL
Sales transactions	43 000	33 400	26 000	21 350	123 750

(w4) Cost of production

In Example 6.1, part f: Production cost budget, it was calculated that the production cost of the Basic is €52 800 and the Ultra €54 000. The total production cost budget is €106 800.

(w5) Closing inventory

The company is budgeted to hold 750 units of Basic and 375 units of Ultra at the year end, valued at the standard cost:

		BASIC €	ULTRA €
Basic	€4.80 x 750 units	3 600	–
Ultra	€7.20 x 375 units	–	2 700

The standard cost was calculated in Example 6.1, part f.

The total budgeted cost of closing inventory is €6 300 (€3 600 + €2 700).

(iii) Budgeted balance sheet as at 31 December 2012

The budgeted balance sheet at the end of the year is as follows:

ASSETS	€	€
Non-current assets:		
Machinery at cost		95 000.00
Premises at cost		150 000.00
		245 000.00
Current assets:		
Inventories: finished goods (Basic: 750 units; Ultra: 375 units) (w5)	6 300.00	
Inventories: raw materials (60 000 kg) (w6)	18 000.00	
Receivables (Quarter 4 credit sales) (w7)	19 215.00	
Cash at bank (w8)	22 260.50	65 775.50
		310 775.50

EQUITY AND LIABILITIES	€	€
Equity:		
Share capital	15 000.00	
Retained earnings (w9)	295 250.00	310 250.00
Current liabilities:		
Payables for raw materials (Quarter 4 credit purchases) (w10)		525.50
		310 775.50

Workings

(w6) Inventories: raw materials

The company has budgeted for 60 000 kg of closing raw materials inventory. Raw materials are valued at €0.30 per kg. The value of closing raw materials inventory is:

$$€0.30 \times 60\ 000 \text{ kg} = €18\ 000$$

(w7) Receivables

90% of Quarter 4 sales are on credit and are outstanding at the end of the year. The amount is €19 215 (90% x €21 350).

(w8) Cash at bank

The budgeted closing bank balance was prepared in Example 6.1.a (i): Cash budget, and is €22 260.50.

(w9) Retained earnings

	€
Retained earnings at the end of last year	290 300
Budgeted net profit for this year	4 950
	295 250

(w10) *Payables*

25% of Quarter 4 purchases are on credit and are outstanding at the end of the year. The amount is €525.50 (25% x €2 102).

Fixed and flexible budgets

In Example 6.1 we produced fixed budgets based on budgeted sales. The budgets are used for control purposes and will be compared with actual results in the monthly management accounts. The difference between the budget and actual is a variance which can be favourable or adverse. This is discussed in more detail in **Chapter 7: Standard Costing and Variance Analysis**.

Consider if the budget was based on sales of 10 000 units of a product and this was compared with an actual result of only 8 000 units of actual sales. The company is not comparing like with like. It is comparing the budgeted sales revenue and costs of 10 000 units with the actual sales revenue and costs of 8 000 units. The resulting variances will provide very little meaningful information to management, as they will be the result of a difference in the sales volume and volume of units produced.

It would be more useful to managers if they could compare the budgeted sales revenue and costs of 8 000 units with the actual sales revenue and costs of 8 000 units. This is called flexing the budget and it is carried out at the end of the period.

A flexed budget will provide more information to enable managers to control costs. If, for example, the standard labour cost is €6 per unit and the actual labour cost to produce 8 000 units is €40 000, when the budget is flexed to 8 000 units, the flexed budgeted cost is €48 000; the resulting variance is €8 000 favourable. The variance may be due to a difference in the quantity of labour hours used or the rate per labour hour paid. It is not due to a difference in the volume of unit produced, so like is being compared with like.

Flexed budgets are used as part of a performance measurement system. Performance measurement is discussed in more detail in **Chapter 12: Performance Measurement and Issues in Accounting**.

Example 6.2

The following is a performance report for a company for the month of May:

	BUDGET	ACTUAL	VARIANCE
Sales (units)	12 000	10 000	
	€	€	€
Sales revenue	120 000	125 000	5 000 F
Less: Variable costs			
Materials	36 000	40 000	4 000 A
Labour	60 000	70 000	10 000 A
Variable overheads	6 000	5 000	1 000 F
	(102 000)	(115 000)	(13 000) A
Contribution	18 000	10 000	8 000 A
Less: Fixed costs	(10 000)	(8 000)	(2 000) F
Net profit	8 000	2 000	6 000 A

F = favourable variance   A = adverse variance

Required

Prepare a performance report using flexible budgeting and analyse the results. The performance report should show the original budget, flexed budget, actual results and a variance column which is the difference between the flexed budget and actual results.

Solution to Example 6.2

	ORIGINAL BUDGET	FLEXED BUDGET		ACTUAL	VARIANCE
Sales (units)	12 000	10 000		10 000	
	€	€		€	€
Sales revenue	120 000	100 000	(w1)	125 000	25 000 F
Less: Variable costs					
Materials	36 000	30 000	(w2)	40 000	10 000 A
Labour	60 000	50 000	(w3)	70 000	20 000 A
Variable overheads	6 000	5 000	(w4)	5 000	–
	(102 000)	(85 000)		(115 000)	(30 000) A
Contribution	18 000	15 000		10 000	5 000 A
Less: Fixed costs	(10 000)	(10 000)	(w5)	(8 000)	(2 000) F
Net profit	8 000	5 000		2 000	3 000 A

The actual number of units sold was 10 000 and the flexed budget is produced at this level of activity. If we had known that this was going to be the number of units sold, the original budget would have been prepared on that basis.

Workings

(w1) Sales revenue

$$\text{Standard selling price} = \frac{\text{Budgeted sales revenue}}{\text{Budgeted units}}$$

$$= \frac{\text{€120 000}}{\text{12 000 units}} = \text{€10 per unit}$$

Flex the budget to the actual level of sales:

Standard selling price x actual sales units
€10 x 10 000 units
€100 000

(w2) Materials

$$\text{Standard materials cost} = \frac{\text{Budgeted materials cost}}{\text{Budgeted units}}$$

$$= \frac{€36\ 000}{12\ 000\ \text{units}} = €3\ \text{per unit}$$

Flex the budget to the actual level of sales:

Standard materials cost x actual sales units
€3 x 10 000 units
€30 000

(w3) Labour

$$\text{Standard labour cost} = \frac{\text{Budgeted labour cost}}{\text{Budgeted units}}$$

$$= \frac{€60\ 000}{12\ 000\ \text{units}} = €5\ \text{per unit}$$

Flex the budget to the actual level of sales:

Standard labour cost x actual sales units
€5 x 10 000 units
€50 000

(w4) Variable overheads

$$\text{Standard variable overhead cost} = \frac{\text{Budgeted variable overhead cost}}{\text{Budgeted units}}$$

$$= \frac{€6\ 000}{12\ 000\ \text{units}} = €0.50\ \text{per unit}$$

Flex the budget to the actual level of sales:

Standard variable overhead cost x actual sales units
€0.50 x 10 000 units
€5 000

(w5) Fixed overheads
Fixed overheads are a fixed cost and they will remain the same regardless of the level of sales. The fixed overheads at the flexed budgeted level of sales remain at €10 000.

Analysis of results – students should attempt this part of the example after they have completed **Chapter 7: Standard Costing and Variance Analysis**.

Sales volume contribution variance

The company sold fewer units than originally anticipated. The difference between the original budgeted contribution, €18 000, and the flexed budget contribution, €15 000, is €3 000. This is the sales volume contribution variance, which is adverse.

Sales price variance

Even though fewer units have been sold than originally budgeted, the actual price per unit is more than the standard selling price. The actual selling price per unit is €12.50 per unit (€125 000/10 000 units) and the standard selling price is €10 (see working 1). The effect on profit is:

Actual sales: 10 000 units x €12.50	=	€125 000
Flexed sales: 10 000 units x €10	=	€100 000
Sales price variance		€25 000 F

Materials, labour and variable overheads

Materials and labour both have adverse variances, when the flexed budget and actual results are compared. This may be owing to a difference in the price per kilogram or labour hour, or the efficiency with which available materials and labour are used in production. There is no difference between the flexed budget and actual results for variable overheads.

Fixed overheads

The flexed fixed overheads are €10 000 and differ from the actual fixed overheads of €8 000, resulting in a favourable variance of €2 000.

Using the above analysis, a reconciliation statement can be produced which analyses the difference between the original budgeted profit and the actual profit. Further explanation of variance analysis will be given in **Chapter 7: Standard Costing and Variance Analysis**.

RECONCILIATION STATEMENT			
	€	€	€
Budgeted profit			8 000
Sales volume contribution variance			3 000 A
Flexed budgeted profit			5 000
Sales price variance			25 000 F
			30 000
Add: VARIANCES	FAVOURABLE	ADVERSE	
Materials	–	10 000	
Labour	–	20 000	
Fixed overhead	2 000	–	
	2 000	30 000	28 000 A
Actual profit			2 000

Incremental budgeting

CIMA Official Terminology states that incremental budgeting is a 'method of budgeting based on the previous budget or actual results, adjusting for known changes and inflation, for example'.

In practice this can mean that last year's budget is taken and increased by, for example, 2% to allow for inflation, or reduced during a period of deflation. This approach is simple and cuts down the time and effort involved in the budgeting process. Incremental budgets can be produced quickly using spreadsheets. Last year's budget is taken and 2% is added across all the variables.

The problem with this approach is that inefficiencies or slack built into the budget in previous years will never be addressed or may continue unnoticed over many years.

Zero-based budgeting

CIMA Official Terminology states that a zero-based budget is a 'method of budgeting that requires all costs to be specifically justified by the benefits expected'.

Zero-based budgeting is the opposite of incremental budgeting. The budget is built up from zero each year and no regard is given to what went before. The benefit is that it reduces inefficiencies which can go unnoticed in an incremental budget as all costs require careful thought and justification.

The drawback of zero-based budgeting is that it is very time-consuming and costly to implement. Managers may also see it as a threat to their authority as it reduces their discretionary spending.

Rolling budget

CIMA Official Terminology states that a rolling budget is a 'budget continuously updated by adding a further accounting period (month or quarter) when the earliest accounting period has expired'.

A rolling budget is particularly useful during periods of financial or commercial uncertainty when a company adopts an approach of 'wait and see' to see, for example, whether the European Central Bank (ECB) will increase or decrease interest rates. The company may only prepare a budget for any given 12-month period. The first three months are prepared in detail and the remaining nine months in less detail. During the first three months the ECB may reduce interest rates and the company can prepare the next three-month budget in detail, using updated interest rates, the next six months in less detail and add on a further three months as an estimate. The budget is rolled on every three months.

Activity-based budgeting

CIMA Official Terminology states that activity-based budgeting is a 'method of budgeting based on an activity framework and utilising cost driver data in the budget setting and variance feedback process'.

Activity-based budgeting (ABB) may be used by companies which have implemented activity-based costing (ABC). The demand for production and sales volume for the budget period is estimated. The company activities required to meet demand are estimated and the resources required to fulfil those activities are calculated. These resources form the activity-based budget.

Traditional budgeting prepares budgets by departments. ABB prepares budgets for each cost pool or activity. ABC is discussed in more detail in **Chapter 4: Activity-Based Costing**.

Benefits of budgeting

1. It provides a control mechanism, allowing managers to compare actual results against a benchmark to measure cost and revenues. Budgets form the basis of performance measurement reports. These reports can be used to measure managers' performance in controlling the costs and revenues in their departments. If actual costs are greater than budgeted costs, corrective action can be taken to avoid this continuing.
2. It facilitates the implementation of plans and strategies – long-term goals and objectives can be translated into short-term plans, ensuring their implementation through the budget process. Budgets ensure that all plans

are integrated and co-ordinated and that managers do not make decisions to the detriment of other departments.

3 Budgets are a communication tool – in the performance measurement report the actual results are compared against the budget and variances are calculated. This gives the readers of the performance measurement report, i.e., senior management, a snapshot of the performance of the company. This can motivate managers to achieve their budget goals as they will know that the performance report will be circulated around the company regularly.

Drawbacks of budgeting

1 Budgets are inflexible and not reactive – a fixed budget does not facilitate any unexpected change in circumstances. If an opportunity arises which has not been budgeted for, it may have to be passed over. This may be the case where a manager's performance is linked to the performance measurement report. They may pass over an opportunity, for example, to accept an order from a customer, if that order was not budgeted for as it may result in adverse cost variances and they may not achieve their budget targets and thus not earn their bonus.

2 Budgets can be time-consuming and costly to produce. Hope and Fraser (2003: 108–15) estimate that budgeting absorbs up to 30% of management time. Managers' time is spent attending budgetary meetings and drafting and redrafting budgets. The use of spreadsheets will assist with the preparation of budgets and when budgets need to be redrafted, but the budgeting process is lengthy and requires a large number of labour hours.

3 Budgets can quickly become outdated. If the budget covers a calendar year, by the time November or December comes around, the information in the budget may be 15 months old as the budget process will have started the previous September or October.

4 Budgets can create conflict between managers and staff if budget targets are unrealistic. Staff may consider these targets unachievable and may lose motivation as a result. Hope and Fraser (2003: 104–15) state that one published report says nine out of 10 finance people think the budget is cumbersome and unreliable.

5 Budgets, according to Hope and Fraser (1999: 16–21), were never designed to manage intangible assets such as patents, customer lists and computer software. They undermine their growth potential by directing management attention to short-term financial numbers, thus ignoring the key drivers of shareholder value.

Beyond budgeting

Hope and Fraser (2003: 108–15) state that budgeting as it is currently practised should be abolished. They say that companies have invested in IT networks, process engineering, a range of management tools, balanced scorecards and activity accounting but are unable to react to market conditions because budgets are hindering their progress. They state that budgets support the 'command and control' structure in organisations.

Budgets, Hope and Fraser write, are used as a benchmark to measure targets that can easily be manipulated. They state that budgets can lead to a breakdown in corporate ethics, where rigid demands force people to take unethical decisions. WorldCom, Enron and Barings Bank, companies that have failed, had tight budgetary control processes that funnelled information only to those with a 'need to know'.

Hope and Fraser point out that companies that wish to react quickly to market changes are the same ones that cling to budgeting. Budgets, they state, disempower the front line, discourage information-sharing and slow the response to market developments until it is too late.

The Beyond Budgeting Round Table (www.BBRT.org) was established in 1997 as a result of the dissatisfaction some companies felt with traditional budgeting. Since then more than 60 companies have joined the BBRT and they fund research into budgeting and alternatives. The three questions they ask are: is there an alternative to budgeting; is there a better management model; and if so, should it be implemented? The BBRT lists a number of companies that have been operating the beyond budgeting model for decades. They include:

- Japanese car manufacturer Toyota
- German retailer ALDI
- Swedish bank Svenska Handelsbanken
- Finnish telecommunications company Nokia

Hope and Fraser put forward alternatives to budgeting:

1 Instead of fixed annual targets, business units set longer-term goals based on benchmarks such as return on capital. Staff and management are rewarded on how well they compare with best-in-class industry benchmarks.
2 Managers have discretion in making decisions. As a result, they can react more quickly to changes in market conditions and they are more accountable for the profitability of their units. Employees need less supervision and therefore don't require expensive central services they might otherwise need.
3 Increased use of key performance indicators (KPIs) that are financial and non-financial. Hope and Fraser discuss a UK charity, Sight Savers International, that has begun to develop target ranges for its KPIs. Managers are free to devise ways of achieving results within these ranges.
4 Using rolling forecasts, typically each quarter, that help managers to reassess current action plans continually as market and economic conditions change.
5 Hope and Fraser (1999: 16–21) state that some businesses use value- and activity-based management, the balanced scorecard and process

management to support the business when budgets are abandoned. These systems aim to give more power to front-line people and to support management in evaluating results and trends.

Greenberg and Greenberg (2006: 41–5) state that budgets are not just about the numbers but also about communicating vital information within the organisation. They add that budgets provide a blueprint for effective, efficient interorganisational communication. They suggest that a better approach than abandoning budgets is to identify the problems with them and to fix them. If budgets promote a command and control environment, then more participation in budgeting should be encouraged. If the financial targets are no longer appropriate for the organisation, they should be expanded or changed. They state that companies should not be too hasty in abandoning budgets. Rather they should improve them.

In conclusion, the budget process appears to be going through a period of change. Abandoning budgets altogether would be a radical decision for most organisations. Budgets will still be required for financial planning in companies and will be sought by banks for loan applications. Perhaps a solution to the problems with budgeting is to address those problems as suggested by Greenberg and Greenberg, and fix the budgeting process.

Chapter summary

This chapter discussed the process of budgeting in a business. The relationship between the mission statement, strategy and budget process was explained. How budgeting forms part of the planning and control process in the business was discussed.

Budgeting terminology used in the chapter was explained. The different stages in the budget process were outlined and you were introduced to the preparation of functional budgets and master budgets.

The concept of flexing the budget was explained and how it is used in variance analysis. Incremental budgets, zero-based budgets, rolling budgets and activity-based budgeting terms were explained. The benefits and drawbacks of budgeting and the theory of beyond budgeting were discussed.

Test questions

Question 1*

O'Mahony's Ltd, a family business, has made a cream liqueur for the past 75 years. They are preparing their budgets for next year and estimate their sales per quarter as follows:

	BOTTLES
Quarter 1	25 000
Quarter 2	30 000
Quarter 3	27 000
Quarter 4	38 000

The inventory at the end of the previous year was 3 750 bottles. The company require closing inventory at the end of each quarter equal to 15% of the next quarter's sales.

Required

Prepare a production budget for the first three quarters of next year showing the number of bottles produced each quarter.

Note to students

Remember that the closing inventory at the end of one quarter equals the opening inventory at the beginning of the next quarter.

* Based on question E12.2 in W. Seal, R.H. Garrison and E. Noreen, *Management Accounting*, 2nd edition, McGraw Hill, 2006.

Question 2

Donnelly Ltd manufactures two types of tyres – the Phoenix and the Firehawk. The following are the expected sales and inventory levels of the two products:

	PHOENIX TYRES	FIREHAWK TYRES
Sales (tyres)	20 950	14 300
Opening inventory (tyres)	3 450	2 300
Closing inventory (tyres)	5 000	3 375

The standard direct materials cost per kg is €0.50. The Phoenix requires 5 kg of materials per tyre and the Firehawk requires 4 kg of materials per tyre.
   The following amounts of inventory are expected and are required:

	DIRECT MATERIALS KG
Opening inventory	20 500
Closing inventory	25 500

Required

Prepare a production budget (in units), a materials usage budget (in kg) and a purchases budget (in €).

Notes to students

1 This question is similar to Example 6.1 in this chapter.
2 Remember to calculate the production units first. Use this information to calculate the materials usage budget and, finally, the materials purchases budget.

Question 3*

Aoife has recently been made redundant and received a redundancy payment. She has always wanted to set up her own business and, as she is a keen cook, has decided to set up a stall selling fudge in a weekly farmers' market.

She is preparing a budget to ensure she has control over all the costs incurred over the next four months, after which she will decide whether to continue with the business or look for another full-time job. Aoife will invest €3 000 of her redundancy in the business bank account. She estimates the following:

	JANUARY	FEBRUARY	MARCH	APRIL
Sales (kg)	350	400	475	500
Material cost	€2 275	€2 200	€3 200	€2 500
Rent of stall	€200	€200	€200	€200
Transport costs	€100	€100	€100	€100

The budgeted selling price is €8 per kg. Aoife expects to sell 80% of her product for cash on the stall and hopes to negotiate the sale of the remainder of her product in a local café. She expects to allow one month's credit on the café sales.

Aoife initially expects to hire and pay for specialised machinery at a cost of €25 per month. She intends to purchase second-hand equipment for €2 000 at the beginning of January. Payment is not due until the following month.

Materials purchased will be paid for in the month following purchase. Aoife pays for the hire of the stall and transport costs where they are incurred.

Aoife will lodge her redundancy payment into the business bank account to help set up the business.

Required

a Prepare a cash budget for the four months, January, February, March and April, and in total
b Explain why there is a difference between cash and profit

Notes to students

1 The cash budget will record receipts and payments when the cash is estimated to be received or paid.
2 Remember to produce a cash budget for each individual month and also have a total column.

* Based on question 8.6 in Catherine Growthorpe, *Management Accounting*, 1st edition, South-Western Cengage Learning, 2008.

For answers and additional test questions, see www.gillmacmillan.ie. Search for Management Accounting and click on the link in the right-hand column.

7 Standard Costing and Variance Analysis

Learning outcomes of Chapter 7

At the end of this chapter, you will be able to:

- explain how a standard costing system operates
- explain how standards are set
- carry out variance analysis on materials, labour, variable production overheads, fixed production overheads and sales
- discuss the reasons for the occurrence of variances
- reconcile budgeted and actual profits using variance analysis
- reconcile flexed budgeted and actual costs using variance analysis
- provide variance analysis in a marginal and absorption costing system
- provide further analysis on fixed production overheads in an absorption costing system
- calculate idle time variances
- discuss the advantages and disadvantages of standard costing
- discuss the role of standard costing in the 21st century

Introduction

To survive, businesses need to be able to assess how they are performing. This is usually done monthly but can be more or less frequent, depending on the nature of the business. Performance is usually measured in the form of a set of monthly management accounts. Actual results such as labour, materials and overhead costs, along with sales revenue, are measured against budgeted costs and revenues. The budget would have been set out at the beginning of the financial period. Actual costs and revenues are gathered from the management accounts for the period under review. Actual results are compared with the budget and an analysis of the variances is carried out.

Example 7.1

The following information relates to Tiger Ltd for the month of May:

	BUDGET	ACTUAL
Sales (units)	25 000	25 000
Sales revenue	€5 000 000	€5 250 000
Materials	€2 000 000	€2 167 000
Labour	€1 350 000	€1 332 000

As the management accountant in Tiger Ltd you are required to prepare the management accounts for the month of May.

Solution to Example 7.1

Management accounts for the month of May:

	BUDGET €	ACTUAL €	VARIANCE €
Sales	5 000 000	5 250 000	250 000 F
Less: Variable costs			
Materials	2 000 000	2 167 000	167 000 A
Labour	1 350 000	1 332 000	18 000 F
	(3 350 000)	(3 499 000)	(149 000) A
Profit	1 650 000	1 751 000	101 000 F

Points to note

- With costs a favourable variance occurs when the budgeted cost is greater than the actual cost.
- A favourable (F) cost variance indicates that less was spent on costs than was budgeted.
- An adverse (A) cost variance indicates that more was spent on costs than was budgeted.
- With revenues and profits a favourable variance occurs when the actual revenue or profit is greater than the budgeted revenue or profit.
- A favourable (F) revenue or profit variance indicates that more was received in revenue or profit than was budgeted.
- An adverse (A) revenue or profit variance indicates that less was received in revenue or profit than was budgeted.

The management accounts are to be sent to the various managers with responsibility for costs and revenues and they would justify any favourable and adverse variances. This would be attached as a narrative to the management accounts and would assist the users of the accounts (e.g., managing director) in decision-making. It also makes the accounts more transparent and is an incentive for managers to be cost-conscious.

However, the information presented in the management accounts in Example 7.1 is limited. The user of the accounts would not know, for example, whether the materials variance of €167 000 adverse was due to an increase in the actual price per unit/litre/kilogram, or whether it was due to the material usage per finished unit being less efficient than the standard set.

Further analysis of the variances can be carried out, which will enable managers to make more efficient decisions. To do this the budget must be broken down into standard costs and revenues. For the purposes of this chapter when we discuss a standard costing system, we are referring to costs and revenues.

Standard costs

Standard costs are the budgeted or expected costs of producing a single unit. They are the costs that should have been incurred or achieved under efficient working conditions. Standard costing is suited to organisations whose activities consist of a series of common or repetitive tasks, e.g., manufacturing.

What is a standard cost system?

A standard cost system is a method of setting cost targets and evaluating performance. The actual cost outcomes are measured against standards and the results, i.e., variances, are investigated. This system is a means of helping managers with decision-making and control.

Drury (2008) notes that since its introduction in the early 1900s standard costing has flourished and is now one of the most widely used management accounting techniques.

A standard cost system is likened to a cybernetic control system where outcomes of the system provide feedback into the system to allow corrective action to take place. A simple example of this is an air-conditioning unit in which upper and lower temperature parameters are set. When the temperature goes above the upper parameter the air-conditioning unit starts. When the temperature falls below the lower parameter the air-conditioning unit stops. In the standard cost system the standards are set, e.g., the standard selling price per unit, and compared with the actual selling price per unit achieved. The difference or variance is fed back to the manager responsible and corrective action is taken.

Example 7.1.a

Upon investigation, further information is available for Example 7.1:

	BUDGET	ACTUAL
Materials (kg)	100 000	98 500
Labour (hours)	75 000	72 000

Required

As management accountant you are required to prepare:

a   The standard materials cost per kilogram
b   The standard labour cost per hour
c   The standard kilograms of material required per unit
d   The standard labour hours per unit
e   The standard sales price per unit
f   A standard cost card
g   The actual materials cost per kilogram
h   The actual labour cost per hour
i   The actual selling price per unit

Solution to Example 7.1.a

a   Standard materials cost per kilogram:

$$\frac{\text{Budgeted materials cost}}{\text{Budgeted kilograms}} \quad \frac{€2\ 000\ 000}{100\ 000\ \text{kilograms}} = \quad €20 \text{ per kilogram}$$

b   Standard labour cost per hour:

$$\frac{\text{Budgeted labour cost}}{\text{Budgeted hours}} \quad \frac{€1\ 350\ 000}{75\ 000\ \text{hours}} = \quad €18 \text{ per hour}$$

c   Standard kilograms of material required per unit:

$$\frac{\text{Budgeted kilograms material}}{\text{Budgeted units}} \quad \frac{100\ 000\ \text{kilograms}}{25\ 000\ \text{units}} = 4 \text{ kilograms per unit}$$

d   Standard labour hours per unit:

$$\frac{\text{Budgeted labour hours}}{\text{Budgeted units}} \quad \frac{75\ 000\ \text{hours}}{25\ 000\ \text{units}} = 3 \text{ hours per unit}$$

e   Standard sales price per unit:

$$\frac{\text{Budgeted sales revenue}}{\text{Budgeted units}} \quad \frac{€5\ 000\ 000}{25\ 000\ \text{units}} = €200 \text{ per unit}$$

f   Standard cost card for Tiger Ltd:

		€
Standard sales		200
Less: Variable costs		
Materials	4 kg x €20	80
Labour	3 hrs x €18	54
Standard profit		66

g   Actual materials cost per kilogram:

$$\frac{\text{Actual materials cost}}{\text{Actual kilograms}} \quad \frac{€2\ 167\ 000}{98\ 500\ \text{kilograms}} \quad = \quad €22 \text{ per kilogram}$$

h   Actual labour cost per hour:

$$\frac{\text{Actual labour cost}}{\text{Actual labour hours}} \quad \frac{€1\ 332\ 000}{72\ 000\ \text{hours}} \quad = \quad €18.50 \text{ per labour hour}$$

i   Actual selling price per unit:

$$\frac{\text{Actual sales revenue}}{\text{Actual sales units}} \quad \frac{€5\ 250\ 000}{25\ 000\ \text{units}} \quad = \quad €210 \text{ per unit sold}$$

How are standards set?

Standards are the budgeted or expected costs and revenues of producing a single unit. In Example 7.1.a we calculated the standard sales, materials and labour costs per unit, but we also calculated the standard hours and kilograms required to produce one unit.

In a business, the standards need to be set before the financial period. The standard hours may be set by measuring the average time it takes to produce a unit. The standard kilograms may be set by measuring the average kilograms it takes to produce a unit.

Standard costs and revenues will usually be influenced by the economy or market, and will need to be adjusted periodically. There are three types of standards:

(1) Basic standards

These have been developed over a long period and remain largely unchanged. They are the basic standard on which industries can base their own standard.

(2) Ideal standards

These are standards against which actual results would be compared in an ideal environment, i.e., an environment where machines never break down, staff are never sick or suppliers never fail to deliver. As they are ideal and generally unattainable they are rarely used in practice. They may be used in businesses which are implementing total quality management and are aiming to maximise efficiency and minimise defects.

(3) Attainable standards

These are the most commonly used standards. They are the most realistic targets to achieve because they take into account the fact that machines break down, suppliers fail to deliver and so on. Attainable standards should provide a challenge for the business and should not be so low that they are too easily attained. They may be decided upon by looking at the standards of similar businesses in the same industry which are achieving outcomes to which the business aspires. Since attainable standards are realistic, they are an acceptable method of inventory and product valuation during the financial period.

Variance analysis

Variance analysis is carried out on the differences between actual results and standard results and is published in the monthly management accounts. The management accountant usually carries out the variance analysis because they have the accounting expertise, but it is the responsibility of the manager who made the decision to incur the cost to explain why the variances have occurred. This acts as a motivation for managers to be more cost-efficient.

Examples of variances

Materials variances

Referring to the solution to Example 7.1, the materials total variance is €167 000 adverse. This variance can be analysed further into (i) a materials price variance and (ii) a materials usage variance.

(i) Materials price variance

By analysing the materials total variance further we can determine how much of the €167 000 adverse variance was due to the purchasing manager buying materials which were at a higher or lower cost than the standard set.

We analyse the difference between the standard price per kilogram and the actual price per kilogram and multiply it by the actual quantity, or in this case the actual kilograms purchased:

(standard price per kilogram – actual price per kilogram)
x actual kilograms purchased

Or, we can abbreviate the formula as follows:

(SP – AP) x AQ

where:

SP: standard price
AP: actual price
AQ: actual quantity, e.g., kilograms, litres, units

Example 7.1.b

Calculate the materials price variance using the information in the solution to Example 7.1.a.

Solution to Example 7.1.b

(standard price per kilogram – actual price per kilogram)
x actual kilograms purchased

(20 – 22) x 98 500 = 197 000 A

This variance is adverse because the actual price per kilogram was higher than the standard price per kilogram.

Possible reasons for an adverse materials price variance are:

- a price increase due to a change in market conditions
- loss of bulk discounts due to buying smaller quantities
- using more expensive suppliers

Sometimes the actual price per kilogram may be less than the standard price per kilogram, thus resulting in a favourable variance.

Possible reasons for a favourable materials price variance are:

- a price decrease due to a change in market conditions
- discounts received as a result of bulk buying
- changing to cheaper suppliers

However, the purchasing department must weigh up buying cheaper raw materials against risking poorer quality and, as a result, more wastage during the manufacturing process. On the one hand there will be a favourable materials price variance, but on the other hand there will be an adverse materials usage variance.

(ii) Materials usage variance

By analysing the materials total variance further we can determine how much of the €167 000 adverse variance was due to the fact that the manufacturing process was less efficient or more efficient in the usage of raw materials than the standard set.

We analyse the difference between the quantity of raw materials we should have used had the standard been applied and the actual quantity of raw materials used. The result is multiplied by the standard price:

((standard quantity x actual units produced) – actual quantity) x standard price

Or, we can abbreviate the formula as follows:

((SQ x Act Units) – AQ) x SP

where:

SQ:	standard quantity, e.g., kilograms, litres, units
Act Units:	actual units
AQ:	actual quantity, e.g., kilograms, litres, units
SP:	standard price

With the materials usage variance you will note that the standard price is used and not the actual price. We are analysing the usage of raw materials in this variance and we remove the inefficiencies attached to the actual price by using the standard price. The inefficiencies of the actual price are analysed in the materials price variance.

Example 7.1.c

Calculate the materials usage variance using the information in the solution to Example 7.1.a.

Solution to Example 7.1.c

((standard quantity x actual units produced) – actual quantity) x standard price

((4 kilograms x 25 000 units) – 98 500 kilograms) x €20

= (100 000 kilograms – 98 500 kilograms) x €20

= 30 000 F

This variance is favourable because the actual quantity of raw materials used to produce the actual units was less than the standard quantity that would have been used to produce the actual units, had the standard been applied.

Possible reasons for a favourable materials usage variance are:

- more highly trained staff working in manufacturing, who make fewer mistakes
- better-quality raw materials leading to less wastage
- implementation of quality control procedures leading to less wastage

Sometimes, an adverse materials usage variance may occur. The reasons for this could be:

- less experienced staff working in manufacturing, who make more mistakes
- use of more inferior-quality raw materials leading to more wastage
- failure to implement quality control procedure leading to more wastage

Summary of the materials variance

Example 7.1.b	Materials price variance	€197 000	A
Example 7.1.c	Materials usage variance	€30 000	F
Example 7.1	Materials total variance	€167 000	A

Points to note

- The materials total variance can be analysed into the materials price and usage variances.
- There is a link between the materials price and materials usage variances. This is possibly due to higher-quality raw materials being purchased, thus an adverse materials price variance, resulting in less wastage of raw materials, thus a favourable materials usage variance.
- In this example there is only one raw material. Where there are two or more raw materials, separate materials price and usage variances should be calculated.

Labour variances

Referring to the solution to Example 7.1, the labour total variance is €18 000 favourable. This variance can be analysed further into a (iii) labour rate variance and a (iv) labour efficiency variance.

(iii) Labour rate variance

By analysing the labour total variance further we can determine how much of the €18 000 favourable variance was due to the fact that the manufacturing manager paid a higher or lower labour rate per hour than the standard set.

We analyse the difference between the standard rate per hour and the actual rate per hour and multiply it by the actual hours.

(standard rate per hour – actual rate per hour) x actual hours used

Or, we can abbreviate the formula as follows:

(SR – AR) x AH

where:

SR:	standard rate
AR:	actual rate
AH:	actual hours used

Example 7.1.d

Calculate the labour rate variance using the information in the solution to Example 7.1.a.

Solution to Example 7.1.d

(standard rate per hour – actual rate per hour) x actual hours used

$$(18 - 18.50) \times 72\ 000 = 36\ 000\ \text{A}$$

This variance is adverse because the actual rate per hour was higher than the standard rate per hour.

Possible reasons for an adverse labour rate variance are:

- the standard rate per hour was not adjusted for a national wage increase
- the use of higher-paid, more expensive staff than was budgeted for
- the payment of overtime was not budgeted for

Sometimes the actual rate per hour may be less than the standard rate per hour, thus resulting in a favourable variance.

Possible reasons for a favourable labour rate variance are:

- the use of lower-paid, less experienced staff than was budgeted for
- the work was carried out in normal hours and not overtime as budgeted for

(iv) Labour efficiency variance

By analysing the labour total variance further we can determine how much of the €18 000 favourable variance was due to the fact that the labour force was less efficient or more efficient in the usage of labour hours than the standard set.

We analyse the difference between the labour hours we should have used, had the standard been applied, with the actual labour hours used. The result is multiplied by the standard rate per hour:

((standard hours x actual units) – actual hours) x standard rate per hour

Or, we can abbreviate the formula as follows:

((SH x Act Units) – AH) x SR

where:

SH:	standard hours
Act Units:	actual units
AH:	actual hours
SR:	standard rate per hour

Example 7.1.e

Calculate the labour efficiency variance using the information in the solution to Example 7.1.a.

Solution to Example 7.1.e

((standard hours x actual units produced) – actual hours) x standard rate per hour

$$((3 \text{ hours} \times 25\,000 \text{ units}) - 72\,000 \text{ hours}) \times €18$$
$$= (75\,000 \text{ hours} - 72\,000 \text{ hours}) \times €18$$
$$= 54\,000 \text{ F}$$

This variance is favourable because the actual hours used to produce the actual units were less than the standard hours that would have been used to produce the actual units, had the standard been applied.

Possible reasons for a favourable labour efficiency variance are:

- more highly trained staff working in manufacturing, leading to efficient work practices and less reworked units
- implementation of new technology leading to an increase in productivity

Sometimes an adverse labour efficiency variance may occur. The reasons for this could be:

- less experienced staff working in manufacturing, who are less efficient
- implementation of new technology or training which initially slows down productivity
- machine breakdowns or bottlenecks in production which slow down productivity

Summary of the labour variance

Example 7.1.d	Labour rate variance	€36 000	A
Example 7.1.e	Labour efficiency variance	€54 000	F
Example 7.1	Labour total variance	€18 000	F

Points to note

- The labour total variance can be analysed into the labour rate and efficiency variances.
- There is a link between the labour rate and labour efficiency. This is possibly due to a higher-quality grade of labour being used, thus an adverse labour rate variance, resulting in more efficient use of labour hours, thus a favourable labour efficiency variance.
- In this example there is only one grade of labour. Where there are two or more labour grades, separate labour rate and efficiency variances should be calculated.

Sales variances

Referring to the solution to Example 7.1, the sales total variance is €250 000 favourable. Normally we analyse this variance into a (v) sales price variance and a (vi) sales volume variance. However, with Example 7.1 the actual sales units and the budgeted sales units are the same, so the sales total variance can only be due to a difference in the actual price and standard price per unit. Later in the chapter we will look at the sales volume variance.

(v) Sales price variance

The sales price variance analyses the difference in the actual sales price per unit and the standard sales price per unit, and is multiplied by the number of units sold, i.e., sales volume:

(actual sales price per unit – standard sales price per unit) x actual sales volume

Or, we can abbreviate the formula as follows:

(AP – SP) x AV

where:

AP:	actual sales price
SP:	standard sales price
AV:	actual sales volume

Example 7.1.f

Calculate the sales price variance using the information in the solution to Example 7.1.a.

Solution to Example 7.1.f

(actual sales price – standard sales price) x actual sales volume

(210 – 200) x 25 000 units = 250 000 F

This variance is favourable because the actual selling price per unit was higher than the standard selling price per unit.

Possible reasons for a favourable sales price variance are:

- reduced competition in the market leading to an increase in the selling price
- sometimes the standard selling price per unit may be higher than the actual selling price per unit, thus resulting in an adverse variance

Possible reasons for an adverse sales price variance include:

- increased competition in the market leading to a reduction in the selling price

Reconciliation statement

After carrying out the variance analysis on the monthly management accounts, a reconciliation statement should be drawn up. The reconciliation statement will analyse the differences between the budgeted profit and the actual profit for the month.

Example 7.1.g

Using the results from the previous examples, prepare the reconciliation statement, reconciling from budgeted profit to actual profit.

Solution to Example 7.1.g

	€	€	€
Budgeted profit			1 650 000
Sales price variance			250 000 F
			1 900 000
VARIANCES	**FAVOURABLE**	**ADVERSE**	
Material price		197 000	
Material usage	30 000		
Labour rate		36 000	
Labour efficiency	54 000		
	84 000 F	233 000 A	149 000 A
Actual profit			1 751 000

This is the layout we will use to reconcile the budget and actual profits. As we introduce more variances we can incorporate them into the layout.

What happens when the budget and actual sales units differ?

In Example 7.1 the budgeted sales units were 25 000 units and the actual sales units were 25 000. The sales total variance calculated in Example 7.1 was €250 000 favourable. We analysed the sales price as €250 000 favourable in Example 7.1.f. We could have ascertained, even without calculating the sales price variance, that it was €250 000 favourable. This is because the budget and actual sales units are the same. There is no difference in sales volume so no sales volume variance is necessary.

When the budget and actual sales units differ, a further sales variance – the sales volume variance – is necessary. The formula for the sales volume variance will depend on whether the company is using a standard marginal costing system or a standard absorption costing system.

Standard marginal costing

In a marginal costing system fixed production overhead is treated as a period cost and decisions are based on contribution rather than profits. For a more detailed discussion of marginal costing, refer to Chapter 8.

When using a standard marginal costing system, care must be taken with the treatment of the fixed production overhead variance and the sales volume variance.

Fixed production overhead is treated as a period cost and is not absorbed into the product costs. There is only one variance necessary for fixed production overhead and it is called the fixed production overhead expenditure variance. The formula is:

Budgeted fixed production overhead cost – actual fixed production overhead cost

The sales volume variance is based on contribution rather than profit. In a standard marginal costing system we call it the sales volume *contribution* variance. The formula is:

(actual sales volume – budgeted sales volume) x standard contribution

In Example 7.2 the sales volume contribution variance and fixed overhead variance will be introduced and discussed in more detail.

Example 7.2

A company uses a marginal costing system and has produced the following production information for the month of May:

	BUDGET	ACTUAL
Sales units	16 000	16 400
Materials used (kg)	32 000	33 000
Labour hours used (hours)	24 000	25 600
Fixed production overhead (€)	60 000	59 200

The management accountant provided the following information:

	STANDARD €	ACTUAL €
Sales price	25.00	25.40
Material price (per kg)	2.00	1.85
Labour rate (per hour)	9.00	8.80

Required

You are required to prepare the management accounts for the month of May as follows:

a   Prepare statements showing the budgeted profit and actual profit
b   Calculate the standard selling price, variable costs and contribution
c   Calculate the following variances:
   (i)   Sales price
   (ii)   Sales volume contribution
   (iii)   Materials price
   (iv)   Materials usage
   (v)   Labour rate
   (vi)   Labour efficiency
   (vii)   Fixed production overhead expenditure
d   Using the results calculated in parts (a) and (b), reconcile the budgeted profit and the actual profit for the month of May

Solution to Example 7.2

a   Prepare statements showing the budgeted profit and actual profit

BUDGETED PROFIT		€	€
Sales	16 000 units x €25		400 000
Less: Variable costs			
Materials	32 000 kg x €2	64 000	
Labour	24 000 hrs x €9	216 000	(280 000)
Contribution			120 000
Less: Fixed production overhead			(60 000)
Budgeted profit			60 000

ACTUAL PROFIT		€	€
Sales	16 400 units x €25.40		416 560
Less: Variable costs			
Materials	33 000 kg x €1.85	61 050	
Labour	25 600 hrs x €8.80	225 280	(286 330)
Contribution			130 230
Less: Fixed production overhead			(59 200)
Actual profit			71 030

b Calculate the standard selling price, variable costs and contribution

The standard selling price, variable costs and contribution mean the budgeted selling price, variable costs and contribution per unit.

There are several ways of working out the standard sales, costs and contribution. We are already given the standard selling price, which is €25 per unit. Alternatively, we could have divided the budgeted sales by the budgeted units:

$$\frac{\text{Budgeted sales}}{\text{Budgeted units}} \quad \frac{€400\ 000}{16\ 000} \quad = \quad €25 \text{ per unit}$$

We now need to work out the standard variable costs. We can do this by dividing the budgeted variable costs, which consist of materials and labour, by the budgeted units:

$$\frac{\text{Budgeted variable costs}}{\text{Budgeted units}} \quad \frac{€280\ 000}{16\ 000} \quad = \quad €17.50 \text{ per unit}$$

The standard contribution is:

Standard selling price – standard variable costs

€25 – €17.50 = €7.50 per unit

c Calculate the following variances:

(i) Sales price

(actual sales price – standard sales price) x actual sales volume

(25.40 – 25.00) x 16 400 = 6 560 F

(ii) Sales volume contribution

In Example 7.1 we carried out variance analysis on sales. However, the actual sales volume and budgeted sales volume were the same quantity, so only the sales price variance needed to be calculated.

In Example 7.2 a marginal costing system is in operation and the actual sales volume and budgeted sales volume are different. The sales total variance analyses the influence that the sales function has on the difference between the actual contribution and the budgeted contribution. The difference may be due to a difference in the sales price per unit or the volume of units sold. However, the sales manager is responsible for the sales price and the units sold, not the manufacturing costs. For this reason, the actual contribution is calculated as the actual sales less the standard costs. The formula for the sales total variance is:

((actual sales – (standard costs x actual units) – budgeted contribution

In this example the sales total variance is:

((actual sales – (standard costs x actual units) – budgeted contribution

((416 560 – (17.50 x 16 400) – 120 000 = 9 560 F

If the sales total variance is €9 560 F and the sales price variance is €6 560 favourable, we can ascertain that the sales volume contribution variance is €3 000 favourable (€9 560 F less €6 560 F).

We can deduce the sales volume contribution variance in this example but it is important to be able to calculate it as follows.

Sales volume contribution variance

The sales volume contribution variance analyses the difference in the actual sales volume and the budgeted sales volume and multiplies it by the standard contribution:

(actual sales volume – budgeted sales volume) x standard contribution

Or, we can abbreviate the formula as follows:

(AV – BV) x stand contrib
where:

AV: actual sales volume
BV: budgeted sales volume
Stand contrib: standard contribution

The sales volume contribution variance in Example 7.2 is:

(actual sales volume – budgeted sales volume) x standard contribution

(16 400 – 16 000) x 7.50 = 3 000 F

Possible reasons for a favourable sales volume variance:

- increase in demand in the market, the company is a product leader
- reduction in competition

The sales price variance and volume variance should not be looked at in isolation because an increase or decrease in price may affect the sales volume. This will depend on market conditions, the economy, competitors' prices and the product life cycle. The sales price and volume variances will help the sales manager make decisions about the sales price in the particular economic climate in which they are operating.

(iii) Materials price variance

The formula for the materials price variance is:

(standard price per kilogram – actual price per kilogram)
x actual kilograms purchased

(2 – 1.85) x 33 000 kg = 4 950 F

(iv) Materials usage variance:

((standard quantity x actual units produced) – actual quantity) x standard price

The standard quantity is not given in this question but we can easily work it out as we are given the budgeted material quantity, which is 32 000 kg. The standard quantity is:

$$\frac{\text{Budgeted quantity}}{\text{Budgeted units}} \quad \frac{32\ 000\ kg}{16\ 000\ units} = 2\ kg\ per\ unit$$

The materials usage variance is:

((2 kg x 16 400 units) – 33 000 kg) x €2 = 400 A

(v) Labour rate variance

The formula for the labour rate variance is:

(standard rate per hour – actual rate per hour) x actual hours used

(9 – 8.80) x 25 600 hours = 5 120 F

(vi) Labour efficiency variance

The formula for the labour efficiency variance is:

((standard hours x actual units) – actual hours) x standard rate per hour

The standard hours are not given in this question but we can easily work out the figure as we are given the budgeted labour hours figure, which is 24 000 hours. The standard hours figure is:

$$\frac{\text{Budgeted hours}}{\text{Budgeted units}} \quad \frac{24\ 000\ hrs}{16\ 000\ units} = 1.5\ hrs\ per\ unit$$

The labour efficiency variance is:

((1.5 hrs x 16 400 units) – 25 600 hrs) x €9 = 9 000 A

(vii) Fixed production overhead expenditure variance

In marginal costing, fixed production overhead expenditure is treated as a period cost and is written off in full against profit in the period in which it is incurred. In other words, it is not absorbed into product costs.

The fixed production overhead expenditure variance will analyse the difference between the fixed production overhead budgeted and the actual fixed production overhead incurred.

The formula is:

Budgeted fixed production overhead cost – actual fixed production overhead cost

In Example 7.2 the variance is calculated as:

€60 000 – €59 200 = 800 F

Fixed production overheads such as supervisors' salaries or rent on the factory are usually fixed in the short term. This variance on its own does not provide the user of the accounts with much information. A variance will indicate to the user that further investigation into each element of fixed production overhead costs must be carried out to provide any meaningful information.

d Reconciliation statement

	€	€	€
Budgeted profit			60 000
Sales volume contribution variance			3 000 F
Flexed budgeted profit			63 000
Sales price variance			6 560 F
			69 560
VARIANCES	**FAVOURABLE**	**ADVERSE**	
Materials price	4 950		
Materials usage		400	
Labour rate	5 120		
Labour efficiency		9 000	
Fixed overhead expenditure	800		
	10 870	9 400	1 470 F
Actual profit			71 030

The sales volume contribution variance is added to the budgeted profit to calculate the flexed budgeted profit. For further discussion on flexing the budget, see Chapter 6.

Standard absorption costing

Under the absorption costing system, fixed production overhead is treated as a product cost and included in the manufacturing costs of the product. For a more detailed discussion of absorption costing refer to Chapter 8.

Fixed production overhead can be absorbed into the manufacturing costs of the product using the number of units produced. The more units of output we produce, the more fixed production overhead will be absorbed into costs.

The 'units of output' method is one way of absorbing fixed production overhead into product costs. There are five different methods of overhead absorption and these are discussed in more detail in Chapter 3. The five different methods are:

1 Units of output
2 Machine hours
3 Labour hours
4 Direct labour cost %
5 Direct material cost %

We will have to analyse the fixed production overhead in terms of volume, in this case units of output, as well as expenditure. The fixed production overhead variances are:

(i) Fixed production overhead volume variance is:

> (actual units of production – budgeted units of production)
> x standard fixed overhead rate per unit

The fixed production overhead volume variance will have to be adapted depending on which method of absorption you are using. In Example 7.3 we will be using a 'units of output' method to absorb fixed production overheads.

(ii) Fixed production overhead expenditure variance is as before:

> Budgeted fixed production overhead – actual fixed production overhead

In a standard absorption costing system the sales volume variance will be based on profit, not on contribution. We will refer to it as the sales volume *profit* variance. The sales price variance is not affected by the absorption system and remains the same.
    The sales volume profit variance is:

> (actual sales volume – budgeted sales volume) x standard profit

In Example 7.3 we will use a standard absorption costing system and we will also introduce variable overheads.

Example 7.3

A company uses an absorption costing system and has produced the following production information for the month of June:

	BUDGET	ACTUAL
Sales units	2 500	2 450
Production units	2 500	2 700
Materials used (kg)	5 000	5 300
Labour hours used (hours)	1 250	1 485
Fixed production overhead (€)	5 000	5 150
Fixed administration overhead (€)	1 500	1 550

The management accountant provided the following information:

	STANDARD €	ACTUAL €
Sales price (per unit)	10.00	11.00
Material price (per kg)	0.50	0.60
Labour rate (per hour)	4.00	3.80

The standard labour hours per unit are 0.5 hours. The standard kilograms per unit are 2 kilograms. The fixed production overhead is absorbed using the 'units of output' method.

There is no opening or closing work in progress.

Required

You are required to prepare the management accounts for the month of June as follows:

a Prepare statements showing the budgeted profit, standard profit and actual profit
b Calculate the following variances:
   (i)   Sales price
   (ii) Sales volume profit
   (iii) Materials price
   (iv) Materials usage
   (v)   Labour rate
   (vi) Labour efficiency
   (vii) Fixed production overhead expenditure
   (viii)Fixed production overhead volume
   (ix) Fixed administration expenditure
c Using the results calculated in parts (a) and (b), reconcile the budgeted profit and the actual profit for the month of June

Solution to Example 7.3

a Prepare statements showing the budgeted profit, standard profit and actual profit

BUDGETED PROFIT			
		€	€
Sales	€10 x 2 500 units		25 000
Less: Variable costs			
Materials	€0.50 x 5 000 kg	2 500	
Labour	€4 x 1 250 hours	5 000	(7 500)
Less: Fixed production overhead			(5 000)
Less: Fixed administration overhead			(1 500)
Budgeted profit			11 000

The standard cost card will show the standard sales, costs and profit of one unit. It will not include any non-production costs such as administration costs. As we are using a standard absorption costing system, we need to work out the standard fixed production overhead absorption rate (OAR) as follows:

Standard fixed production overhead absorption rate (OAR):

$$\frac{\text{Budgeted fixed production overhead}}{\text{Budgeted units of output}}$$

$$\frac{\text{€5 000}}{\text{2 500 units}} = \text{€2 per unit}$$

STANDARD COST CARD		
		€
Sales		10
Less: Variable costs		
Materials	2 kg x €0.50	(1)
Labour	0.5 hrs x €4	(2)
Less: Fixed production overhead		(2)
Standard profit		5

The actual units produced were 2 700 units and only 2 450 units were sold; the balance is 250 units, which is the closing inventory. The closing inventory should be valued at the standard cost of production.

ACTUAL PROFIT		€	€
Sales	2 450 units x €11		26 950
Less: Variable costs			
Materials	5 300 kg x €0.60	3 180	
Labour	1 485 hrs x €3.80	5 643	
Less: Fixed production overhead		5 150	
		13 973	
Less: Closing inventory 250 units x €5		(1 250)	(12 723)
			14 227
Less: Fixed administration overheads			(1 550)
Actual profit			12 677

b Variance analysis

(i) Sales price variance

(actual sales price – standard sales price) x actual sales volume
(11 – 10) x 2 450 units = 2 450 F

(ii) Sales volume profit variance

(actual sales volume – budgeted sales volume) x standard profit
(2 450 – 2 500 units) x €5 = 250 A

(iii)Materials price variance

(standard price per kilogram – actual price per kilogram)
x actual kilograms purchased
(0.50 – 0.60) x 5 300 kg = 530 A

(iv) Materials usage variance

((standard quantity x actual units produced) – actual quantity) x standard price
((2 kg x 2 700 units) – 5 300 kg) x €0.50 = 50 F

(v) Labour rate variance

(standard rate per hour – actual rate per hour) x actual hours used
(4 – 3.80) x 1 485 hours = 297 F

(vi) Labour efficiency variance

((standard hours x actual units produced) – actual hours) x standard rate per hour
((0.50 hrs x 2 700 units) – 1 485 hrs) x €4 = 540 A

(vii) Fixed production overhead expenditure variance

Budgeted fixed production overhead – actual fixed production overhead
€5 000 – €5 150 = 150 A

(viii) Fixed production overhead volume variance

(actual units of production – budgeted units of production) x standard fixed
overhead rate per unit
(2 700 units – 2 500 units) x €2 = 400 F

At this point it is important to understand what the fixed production overhead variances actually mean.

In Example 7.3, during the month of June fixed production overhead of €5 400 (€2 x 2 700 units) was absorbed into production costs. The actual fixed production overhead incurred was €5 150. The difference between the fixed production overhead absorbed (€5 400) and the actual fixed production overhead incurred (€5 150) is €250. This means that fixed production overhead was over-absorbed by €250 in June. The over-absorption may be due to the following:

1 The expenditure variance of €150 A arises from actual fixed production overhead (€5 150) being different from budgeted fixed production overhead (€5 000).
2 The volume variance of €400 F arises from actual production volume differing from budgeted production volume.

(ix) Fixed administration overhead expenditure variance

The fixed administration overhead is a non-production overhead and the variance is calculated by deducting the actual fixed administration overhead from the budgeted fixed administration overhead, as follows:

Budgeted fixed administration overhead − actual fixed administration overhead
€1 500 − €1 550 = 50 A

Investigation of why this adverse variance has occurred should take place. Actual administration overheads could have increased for a variety of reasons such as recruitment of new staff, new technology costs, training costs, etc.

c Reconciliation statement

	€	€	€
Budgeted profit			11 000
Sales volume profit variance			250 A
Flexed budgeted profit			10 750
Sales price variance			2 450 F
			13 200
VARIANCES	**FAVOURABLE**	**ADVERSE**	
Materials price		530	
Materials usage	50		
Labour rate	297		
Labour efficiency		540	
Fixed production overhead expenditure		150	
Fixed production overhead volume	400		
Fixed administration overhead		50	
	747	1 270	523 A
Actual profit			12 677

Further analysis of the fixed production overhead volume variance

In a standard absorption costing system, the fixed production overhead volume variance can be analysed further into (1) the fixed production overhead volume efficiency variance and (2) the fixed production overhead volume capacity variance. However, it must be noted that this is possible only where the fixed production overhead is absorbed on a 'labour hour' or 'machine hour' basis. In Example 7.4 we will analyse the fixed production overhead volume variance further using the 'labour hour' method of overhead absorption.

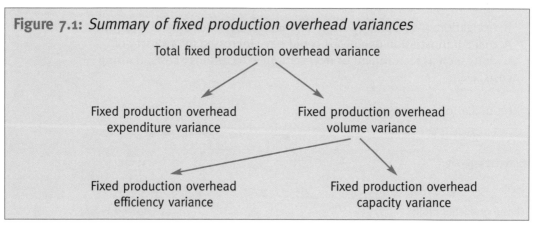

Figure 7.1: *Summary of fixed production overhead variances*

Total fixed production overhead variance

Fixed production overhead expenditure variance

Fixed production overhead volume variance

Fixed production overhead efficiency variance

Fixed production overhead capacity variance

Example 7.4

The following information about labour and fixed production overhead has been provided by the management accountant of a company:

	STANDARD QUANTITY	STANDARD PRICE	STANDARD COST PER UNIT
Labour	5 hours	€5	€25
Fixed production overhead	5 hours	€15	€75
Standard cost			€100

The company is budgeted to produce 600 units. Fixed production overhead is absorbed on a labour hour basis.

The actual results for the month of November are as follows:

		ACTUAL COST
Labour	2 300 hours @ €4.80	€11 040
Fixed production overhead		€60 000
Total actual cost		€71 040

The actual production was 450 units during November.

Required

a   Prepare a statement showing the budgeted cost for the month of
    November
b   Calculate the following variances:
    (i)   Labour rate variance
    (ii) Labour efficiency variance
    (iii) Fixed production overhead expenditure variance
    (iv) Fixed production overhead volume variance
    (v)   Analyse the fixed production overhead volume variance into the fixed
          production overhead capacity and efficiency variances
c   Reconcile the flexed budgeted cost and actual costs using the variances
    calculated in part (b) above

Solution to Example 7.4

a   Prepare a statement showing the budgeted cost for the month of
    November

		BUDGETED COST
		€
Labour	€25 x 600 units	15 000
Fixed production overhead	€75 x 600 units	45 000
Budgeted cost		60 000

b   Variance analysis

(i) Labour rate variance

(standard rate per hour – actual rate per hour) x actual hours used
(5 – 4.80) x 2 300 hours = 460 F

(ii) Labour efficiency variance

((standard hours x actual units) – actual hours) x standard rate per hour
((5 hrs x 450 units) – 2 300 hrs) x €5 = 250 A

(iii) Fixed production overhead expenditure variance

Budgeted fixed production overhead – actual fixed production overhead
(€75 x 600 units) – €60 000 = 15 000 A

(iv) Fixed production overhead volume variance

(actual units of production – budgeted units of production)
x standard fixed overhead rate per unit
(450 units – 600 units) x €75 = 11 250 A

(v) Fixed production overhead capacity and efficiency variances

The volume variance of €11 250 A arises from actual production differing from budgeted production. The fixed production overhead volume variance can be as a result of:

- fixed overhead efficiency variance – where labour efficiency is greater or less than the standard level of efficiency, or
- fixed overhead capacity variance – where the actual hours worked were greater or less than the original budgeted labour hours

The variances are calculated as follows:

Fixed production overhead efficiency variance:

((standard hours x actual units produced) – actual hours)
x standard fixed production overhead rate per hour
((5 hours x 450 units) – 2 300 hours) x €15 = 750 A

The fixed production overhead efficiency variance is €750 A. This means that had the standard labour hours been applied to production, we would have expected 2 250 hours (5 hours x 450 units) to have been worked. However, 450 units were produced in 2 300 hours, less units in more labour hours than had been expected.

Labour efficiency is less than expected, resulting in the adverse fixed production overhead efficiency variance of €750 A. The reasons for this adverse variance would be the same as for an adverse labour efficiency variance, since both variances use labour hours as their measure of efficiency.

Fixed production overhead capacity variance:

(actual labour hours – budgeted labour hours)
x standard fixed production overhead rate per hour
((2 300 hours – (5 hours x 600 units) x €15 = 10 500 A

The fixed production overhead capacity variance is €10 500 A. This means that the company budgeted for 3 000 labour hours (5 hours x 600 units) but actually used only 2 300 labour hours. In other words the company worked at a lower capacity than planned. This could be as a result of machines breaking down, bottlenecks in production or training of new staff.

Summary of fixed production overhead volume variances:

	€
Fixed production overhead efficiency variance	750 A
Fixed production overhead capacity variance	10 500 A
Fixed production overhead volume variance	11 250 A

c Reconcile the flexed budgeted cost and actual costs using the variances calculated in part (b) above

In this example the actual and budgeted units are different. Usually the sales volume variance would adjust the budgeted profit to the actual level of activity. This is why we have a line in the reconciliation statements in Examples 7.2 and 7.3 called 'flexed budgeted profit'. For a more detailed discussion on why we flex the budget see Chapter 6. In Example 7.4 there are no sales, so the budgeted cost must be 'flexed' to the actual level of activity. This is done by multiplying the standard cost by the actual units produced. The flexed budgeted cost is €45 000 (€100 x 450 units).

In Example 7.3 we reconciled the budgeted profit to the actual profit. We did this by adding the variances on to the budgeted profit.

In Example 7.4 we are asked to reconcile the flexed budgeted cost to the actual cost. To do this we must deduct the variances from the flexed budgeted cost.

RECONCILIATION STATEMENT			
	€	€	€
Flexed budgeted cost			45 000
VARIANCES	FAVOURABLE	ADVERSE	
Labour rate	460		
Labour efficiency		250	
Fixed production overhead expenditure		15 000	
Fixed production overhead volume		11 250	
	460	26 500	26 040 A
Actual cost			71 040

Variable production overhead variances

Variable production overhead costs vary with the level of activity. Examples would include fuel costs for the running of machinery. If the machine did not run, no fuel costs would be incurred. Variable production overheads differ from fixed production overheads because fixed production overheads will be incurred regardless of the level of activity. An example of a fixed production overhead is the rent on a factory. The rent will be incurred regardless of the level of activity.

Variable production overheads will be absorbed into product costs using one of the five overhead absorption methods, as mentioned earlier for the absorption of fixed overheads:

1 Units of output
2 Machine hours
3 Labour hours
4 Direct labour cost %
5 Direct material cost %

Usually variable production overhead is absorbed on the basis of 'machine hours' or 'labour hours'.

Example 7.5 will analyse the variable production overhead variance and discuss the reasons for the variances.

Example 7.5

A company operates a standard costing system and provides you with the following standard information regarding variable production overhead.

Variable production overhead	€10 per direct labour hour
Direct labour	6 hrs @ €7.50 per hour

The following information relates to September:

Variable production overhead	€224 000
Direct labour	24 300 hrs valued at €340 200
Units produced	3 600 units

The variable production overhead is absorbed on a direct labour hour basis.

Required

Calculate the following variances:

a Variable production overhead expenditure variance
b Variable production overhead efficiency variance

Solution to Example 7.5

a Variable production overhead expenditure variance
   In Example 7.5 the variable production overhead is absorbed into
   production costs using a direct labour hour method. The standard which
   has been set is that €10 should be added into each product for every one
   labour hour incurred. This variance compares the actual labour hours at
   the standard variable production overhead cost per hour with the actual
   variable production overhead cost incurred. The formula is as follows:

   (actual labour hours x standard variable production overhead rate per hour)
   – actual variable production overhead cost

(24 300 hrs x €10) – €224 000 = 19 000 F

With this variance we are comparing the standard variable production overhead rate at the actual hours with the actual variable production overhead rate at the actual hours. The standard variable production overhead rate was set at €10 per labour hour, but the actual variable overhead rate was €9.22 per labour hour (€224 000/24 300 labour hours). The favourable variance can only be due to the fact that the actual expenditure on variable production overhead per labour hour has decreased from the standard variable production overhead per labour hour.

b   Variable production overhead efficiency variance
This variance compares the standard labour hours multiplied by the actual units produced with the actual labour hours incurred, all at the standard variable production overhead rate per hour. The formula is as follows:

((standard labour hours x actual units produced) – actual labour hours)
x standard variable production overhead rate per hour

((6 hrs x 3 600 units) – 24 300 hrs) x €10 = 27 000 A

The standard was set at six labour hours to produce one unit, instead it took 6.75 labour hours (24 300 labour hours/3 600 units). As more labour hours were required, more variable production overhead was absorbed into product costs.

As we are using direct labour hours to absorb the variable production overhead into product costs, the reasons for an adverse variable production overhead efficiency variance are the same as for an adverse labour efficiency variance.

Summary of variable production overhead variances:

	€
Variable production overhead expenditure	19 000 F
Variable production overhead efficiency	27 000 A
Total variable production overhead	8 000 A

Idle-time variances

Idle time occurs when staff are on contract and there is no work for them to carry out. This may be due to a failure of the supplier to deliver materials or a bottleneck in production.

The idle-time variance is calculated by multiplying the idle-time hours by the standard rate per hour. The formula is:

Idle-time hours x standard rate per hour

The standard rate per hour is used and not the actual rate per hour because we are analysing labour inefficiency. The difference between the actual rate per hour and the standard rate per hour are analysed in the labour rate variance. The idle-time variance is always adverse. It is highlighting inefficiency in the company.

When there is idle time, the labour rate and efficiency variances will be calculated as follows:

Labour rate variance:
(standard rate per hour – actual rate per hour) x actual hours paid

Note that the differences in labour rates are multiplied by the actual hours paid, not the actual hours worked. This is because we are analysing the rates of pay based on the total hours that we paid staff.

Labour efficiency variance:
((standard hours x actual units produced) – actual hours worked)
x standard rate per hour

Note that the actual units produced at the standard hours are compared with the actual hours worked, not the actual hours paid. This is because we are analysing the efficiency of staff during the hours in which they worked.

In Example 7.6 we will calculate the idle-time variance.

Example 7.6

The following information relates to labour hours and costs in a business for the month of December:

Actual hours worked	220 hours
Actual hours paid	250 hours
Actual rate per hour	€8.80
Actual units produced	100

The standard rate per hour is €8 and the standard hours are 2 hours per unit.

Required

Calculate the following:

a   Labour rate variance
b   Labour efficiency variance
c   Idle-time variance

Solution to Example 7.6

a   Calculate the labour rate variance

(standard rate per hour – actual rate per hour) x actual hours paid
(8 – 8.80) x 250 hours = 200 A

b Calculate the labour efficiency variance

((standard hours x actual units produced) – actual hours worked)
x standard rate per hour
((2 hours x 100 units) – 220 hours) x €8 = 160 A

c Calculate the idle-time variance
In this example, 250 hours were paid for but only 220 hours were actually worked. This results in 30 hours (250 hours less 220 hours) of idle time.

Idle-time hours x standard rate per hour
30 hours x €8 = 240 A

Summary of labour variances:

	€
Labour rate variance	200 A
Labour efficiency variance	160 A
Idle-time variance	240 A
Labour total variance	600 A

Where there is idle time the variable production overhead variances will be based on actual labour hours worked not on actual labour hours paid.

Advantages of standard costing

1 Once standards have been set, they can be used to calculate the budget. This in turn will reduce the time and effort in preparing budgets because standards are available and budgeted costs and revenues can be based on them.
2 Standards can be used as a control mechanism in the business. Variance analysis is carried out on the standards costs against the actual results. Variances will be highlighted and corrective action taken where necessary.
3 Standards can be used as a motivational device in the business. If staff and managers know the standards which they have to attain, it can motivate them to achieve these standards, assuming the standards are realistic and attainable.
4 Standards can be used to value inventory during the accounting period when actual costs are not available.
5 Standards can be used in decision-making in the business. If the management accountant is involved in a decision, they can use standards to assess the impact of the decision on the finances of the company.

Disadvantages of standard costing

1 Setting standards and carrying out variance analysis can be a time-consuming and expensive exercise unless the results are meaningful and fully understood by managers.
2 Standards may be incorrect and may not be updated. Where the same variances occur each period, this may be owing to the standards being incorrect or out of date.
3 Variance analysis may be carried out too long after the period end, and there may be a significant time lag between the variance calculation and corrective action taking place.
4 Variance analysis is not a worthwhile exercise when no corrective action is taken where appropriate.
5 Variances should only be investigated where the benefits exceed the cost of the investigation.
6 In recent years, the cost structure has altered. More costs are becoming fixed whereas previously they were variable. For example, labour costs are increasingly fixed as staff are given contracts, whereas previously labour was a variable cost. Given that standard costing is a control mechanism suited to the control of direct and variable costs but not fixed or indirect costs, its usefulness has been questioned.
7 Variance analysis may not be a worthwhile exercise where budgets are imposed rather than negotiated. If the budgets are not achievable or negotiated with the staff involved, the variances may be meaningless.
8 Setting standards creates a climate of setting out to achieve only that standard. Once the target is achieved, staff may not be motivated to beat the target.

Summary of variances

Materials price variance

(standard price per kilogram – actual price per kilogram)
x actual kilograms purchased

Materials usage variance

((standard quantity x actual units produced) – actual quantity) x standard price

Labour rate variance

(standard rate per hour – actual rate per hour) x actual hours used

Labour efficiency variance

((standard hours x actual units) – actual hours) x standard rate per hour

Sales price variance

(actual sales price per unit – standard sales price per unit) x actual sales volume

Fixed production overhead expenditure variance

Budgeted fixed production overhead cost – actual fixed production overhead cost

Fixed administration overhead variance

Budgeted fixed administration overhead – actual fixed administration overhead

Variable production overhead expenditure variance (where variable production overheads are absorbed on a labour hour basis)

(actual labour hours x standard variable production overhead rate per hour) – actual variable production overhead cost

Note: if variable production overheads are absorbed on a machine hour basis, swap labour hours for machine hours in the formula.

Variable production overhead efficiency variance (where variable production overheads are absorbed on a labour hour basis)

((standard labour hours x actual units produced) – actual labour hours) x standard variable production overhead rate per hour

Note: if variable production overheads are absorbed on a machine hour basis, swap labour hours for machine hours in the formula.

Where idle time occurs, the labour variances and variable production overhead variances are as follows:

Labour rate variance (where there is idle time)

(standard rate per hour – actual rate per hour) **x actual hours paid**

Labour efficiency variance (where there is idle time)

((standard hours x actual units produced) – **actual hours worked**) x standard rate per hour

Idle-time variance

Idle-time hours x standard rate per hour

Variable production overhead expenditure

(**actual labour hours worked** x standard variable production overhead rate per hour) – actual variable production overhead cost

Variable production overhead efficiency

((standard labour hours x actual units produced) – **actual labour hours worked**) x standard variable production overhead rate per hour

---

In a standard marginal costing system:

Sales volume contribution variance

(actual sales volume – budgeted sales volume) x standard contribution

> In a standard absorption costing system:
> Sales volume profit variance
>
> > (actual sales volume – budgeted sales volume) x standard profit
>
> Fixed production overhead volume variance
>
> > (actual units of production – budgeted units of production)
> > x standard fixed overhead rate per unit
>
> Fixed production overhead efficiency variance
>
> > ((standard hours x actual units produced) – actual hours)
> > x standard fixed production overhead rate per hour
>
> Fixed production overhead capacity variance
>
> > (actual labour hours – budgeted labour hours)
> > x standard fixed production overhead rate per hour

Inter-relationship between the labour and materials variances

The labour and materials variances are essentially the same variances, just with some of the terminology changed. For example:

Materials price variance

> (standard *price* per *kilogram* – actual *price* per *kilogram*)
> x actual *kilograms* purchased

The labour rate variance is the same. Instead of price we use rate, and instead of kilograms we use hours:

Labour rate variance

> (standard *rate* per *hour* – actual *rate* per *hour*) x actual *hours* paid

The same applies for the materials usage and labour efficiency variances:

Materials usage variance

> ((standard *quantity* x actual units produced) – actual *quantity*) x standard *price*

Again, instead of price we use rate, and instead of quantity we use hours:

Labour efficiency variance

> ((standard *hours* x actual units) – actual *hours*) x standard *rate* per hour

The role of standard costing in the 21st century

Standard costing has traditionally been an important control mechanism in businesses. It was developed during the industrial age when labour and materials were the most significant costs in a business and when competition was national, not global.

In the 21st century, the global economy and Internet age have resulted in more international competition. The significance of labour and material costs has been overtaken by overhead costs. Performance is key, and businesses are looking to customers, staff and competitors to measure performance. Businesses need to be more reactive and adaptable. In this era, feedback on performance is required quickly and regularly. Businesses can no longer afford to wait until the management accounts have been prepared and variance analysis carried out to make decisions.

As a result, the role of standard costing in a business is in question. Businesses are implementing activity-based costing systems and scorecards to measure performance, systems which provide feedback quickly. It is up to businesses to decide how to measure their performance. Who knows whether standard costing will play the same role in a business in 20 years' time as it does today?

Chapter summary

This chapter began by examining the differences between budgeted costs, sales and profits and actual costs, sales and profits. Variance analysis was carried out on the differences and explanations were given for variances.

The chapter discussed how standards are set and the different types of standards used.

The chapter examined how fixed production overheads and sales are affected by marginal and absorption costing. Idle time was also discussed and calculated as a variance.

The chapter ended by examining the advantages and disadvantages of standard costing and its role in the 21st century.

Test questions

Question 1*

Andrews Ltd manufactures a single product called the Bracket. Each unit is budgeted to use 7.2 kg of raw material A, 4 kg of raw material B and 12 labour hours. The standard cost for each unit of Bracket is as follows:

	€
Direct materials:	
A: 7.2 kg @ €10	72
B: 4 kg @ 12.5	50
Direct labour:	
12 hrs @ €15	180
Standard cost:	302

In the month of May, 7 200 units of the Bracket were produced. The actual results were as follows:

	€
Direct materials:	
A: 5 040 kg @ €9.80	49 392
B: 3 240 kg @ 12.70	41 148
Direct labour:	
9 000 hrs @ €14	126 000
Total actual costs	216 540

Required

Calculate the following variances:

a   Material price for A and B
b   Material usage for A and B
c   Labour rate
d   Labour efficiency

Clearly show all workings.

Note to students

This is a straightforward question – only the variances are required. You are not required to do a reconciliation.

* Based on question 1, ATI Costing & Budgeting, Summer 2007.

Question 2

A company uses a standard costing system and has produced the following production information for a product during the month of February:

STANDARD/BUDGETED INFORMATION	
Direct materials	5 kg @ €15 per kg
Direct labour	3 hours @ €20 per hour
Sales price	€150 per unit
Sales and production units	4 000 units

ACTUAL INFORMATION	
Direct materials	21 000 kg @ €14.50 per kg
Direct labour	12 250 hours @ €22 per hour
Sales price	€155 per unit
Sales and production units	4 250 units

Required

a Prepare statements showing the budgeted and actual profit for February
b Calculate the following variances:
   (i) Sales price
   (ii) Sales volume
   (iii) Materials price
   (iv) Materials usage
   (v) Labour rate
   (vi) Labour efficiency

Clearly show all workings.

Notes to students

1 There is no reconciliation statement required for this question.
2 When calculating the standard profit which is required for the sales volume variance, divide the budgeted profit by the budgeted units.
3 There is no fixed production overhead in this question so we can calculate the sales volume variance using profit or contribution.

Question 3

A Ltd manufactures a single product called the Alpha. Budgeted annual sales and production are 48 000 units spread evenly throughout the year. The company's budgeted fixed production overhead is €720 000, spread evenly throughout the year. The company operates a standard marginal costing system.

As expected the budgeted production was actually produced in the month of May.

The standard cost for each unit of Alpha is as follows:

Direct materials	10 kg @ €5 per kg
Direct labour	5 hrs @ €8 per hour

In the month of May, the actual results were as follows:

Direct materials	42 000 kg	€199 500
Direct labour	22 000 hrs	€171 700
Fixed production overhead		€70 000

Required

a   Prepare statements showing the total budgeted costs and total actual costs of the Alpha for May
b   Calculate the following variances:
   (i)   Material price
   (ii) Material usage
   (iii) Labour rate
   (iv) Labour efficiency
   (v)   Fixed production overhead expenditure
c   Prepare a reconciliation statement which reconciles the total budgeted cost to the total actual cost using the answers from (b) above
d   Discuss possible reasons for the following variances:
   (i)   Material price
   (ii) Labour efficiency

Notes to students

1   Budgeted and actual production units are the same, so there is no need to flex the budget.
2   Budgeted units are 48 000 per annum and spread evenly throughout the year. This means that budgeted units are 4 000 units per month (48 000 units divided by 12 months).
3   The budgeted production, i.e., 4 000 units, was actually produced in May. Therefore, the actual production is also 4 000 units.
4   Budgeted fixed production overhead is €720 000 per annum and is spread evenly throughout the year. Therefore budgeted fixed production overhead is €60 000 per month (€720 000 divided by 12 months).
5   There is no sales information in this question, so we reconcile from the total budgeted cost to the total actual cost.
6   We reconcile from total budgeted cost to total actual cost by deducting the variances from budgeted cost.

For answers and additional test questions, see www.gillmacmillan.ie. Search for Management Accounting and click on the link in the right-hand column.

8 Marginal and Absorption Costing

Learning outcomes of Chapter 8

At the end of this chapter, you will be able to:

- distinguish between marginal and absorption costing
- explain when to use marginal and absorption costing
- explain the term 'contribution' and its importance in marginal costing
- discuss the accounting treatment of fixed production overhead in marginal and absorption costing
- calculate profits or losses for a period using marginal and absorption costing
- discuss the accounting treatment of selling and distribution overheads and administration expenses
- reconcile marginal and absorption profits and losses for a period
- discuss the reasons for the use of, and problems with using, marginal and absorption costing

Introduction

In Chapter 3 we discussed the traditional approach to costing products called absorption costing. Absorption costing is required for external financial accounting purposes whereas marginal or variable costing can only be used for internal accounts.

The difference between the two approaches is the accounting treatment of fixed production overhead. In the marginal approach, fixed production overhead is treated as a period cost and is written off against profit for the period in which it is incurred, in the marginal costing statement. In the absorption approach, fixed production overhead is treated as a product cost and is included in the inventory valuation, in the absorption costing statement.

Note that in this chapter the income statement is referred to as either the marginal costing statement or the absorption costing statement depending on which approach is being used.

In this chapter we will show how these two approaches differ. We will calculate profits and losses under the two approaches and discuss the arguments for and against each of their uses. Finally we will discuss how decision-making in an organisation will be affected by the costing approach taken.

Concept of marginal costing

In marginal or variable costing inventory is valued at the sum of:

Direct materials

+

Direct labour

+

Direct expenses

+

Variable production overhead costs

That is, all the variable production costs incurred in producing the product. Marginal costing is used for internally costing products and services. It is also used for measuring profitability and short-term decision-making. It focuses on cost behaviour and draws attention to the effect on contribution that an additional product sold will have.

Contribution

CIMA Official Terminology defines the term 'contribution' as 'sales value – variable cost of sales'. This can be interpreted as contribution being sales less any variable cost that has been incurred in bringing the product to a saleable state. Variable costs include variable production costs and variable selling and distribution overheads.

Contribution is used by managers to assess the likely effect on profits of higher or lower sales demand or the effect of increasing or reducing sales prices.

Fixed production overhead – marginal costing

IAS 2 (Ch 20:s2.2.1 pg 1293) states: 'fixed production overheads are indirect costs that remain relatively constant over a wide range of production, such as building and equipment maintenance and depreciation, and factory management and administration expenses'.

Fixed costs by their nature remain the same regardless of whether a unit is made. They represent the costs incurred to have the capacity to make products.

Fixed costs are not included in contribution. Consider a decision which needs to be made about the acceptance of a job which will be worked on in the next three months. The cost of the job is unaffected by the fixed costs, such as rent on the factory. Rent will need to be paid regardless of whether the job is accepted. If a decision is based on forecasted profit of the job the profits should not include any fixed costs. The decision should be based on contribution, i.e., sales less variable cost of sales. In Chapter 9 we will use cost volume profit analysis to make short-term decisions using contribution.

Any short-term decision to be made such as whether to produce a new product, to accept a job, to reduce production, etc. should be based on contribution. Fixed costs are treated as period costs and are written off against the profit in the marginal costing statement for the period.

Selling and distribution overheads

Selling and distribution overheads can be both variable and fixed. Variable selling and distribution overheads vary with the level of sales, e.g., sales commission paid to salespersons. Variable selling and distribution overheads are deducted from sales to calculate contribution in the marginal costing statement. They are deducted from gross profit in the absorption costing statement.

Fixed selling and distribution overheads do not vary with the level of sales, e.g., a salesperson's basic salary, and they should be treated as a period cost and written off against profit in the marginal and absorption costing statements.

Administration expenses

Fixed administration expenses should also be treated as a period cost and are written off against profit in the marginal and absorption costing statements.

When preparing a marginal costing statement the following layout should be used:

Sales
Less: Variable production cost of sales
Variable production costs (direct materials + direct labour + variable production overhead)
Less: Variable selling and distribution overhead
Equals: Contribution
Less: Fixed costs
Production overhead
Selling and distribution overhead
Administrative expenses
Equals: Marginal profit/(loss)

Reasons for the use of marginal costing

1   Marginal costing is useful for short-term decision-making as fixed costs are irrelevant in the short term. It is used in cost volume profit analysis to ascertain useful short-term information.
2   Marginal costing is used for regular profit reporting within the company. Regular reporting using marginal costing is very helpful to management, as the contribution reported will tie to the sales level achieved each month.
3   Where profit is used to assess a manager's performance, then marginal costing should be used. Otherwise managers could distort profit figures by inflating closing inventory in one accounting period to defer fixed production overheads into the next accounting period, thus making their profit statements in the current period look good.
4   Marginal costing is a simpler approach to use. It doesn't involve the calculation of overhead absorption rates.

Problems with using marginal costing

1   Not all direct costs are variable costs. Consider staff that are on contract and who work in production. Their costs are a direct cost yet they are fixed as they are on contract. Any decision based on contribution would not capture these fixed costs and would not provide a complete picture of all of the direct costs of production.
2   Marginal costing treats fixed production overheads as a period cost and does not include them in inventory valuation. Marginal costing does not give sufficient importance to fixed production overheads. If fixed production overheads did not exist then production would not be able to take place.

Example 8.1

A company produces a single product and has the following unit cost structure:

VARIABLE COSTS	€ UNIT
Direct materials	10
Direct labour	5
Variable production overhead	3
Variable selling and distribution overhead	1

Variable selling and distribution overhead varies with the units sold.

Budgeted fixed costs for the year are as follows:

	€
Fixed production overhead	30 000
Fixed selling and distribution overhead	10 000
Fixed administration expenses	5 000

Fixed production overhead costs are absorbed into the cost of production at a unit rate based on normal activity of 6 000 units per year.

There is no opening inventory at the beginning of the year, 6 000 units are produced during the year and 5 000 units are sold during the year. The selling price is €30 per unit. Actual costs and revenues are as per budget.

Required

Prepare a profit and loss statement for the year using marginal costing.

Solution to Example 8.1

MARGINAL COSTING STATEMENT			
	UNITS	**€**	**€**
Sales (w1)	5 000		150 000
Less: Variable production cost of sales			
Opening inventory (w2)	0	0	
Production (w2)	6 000	108 000	
Less: Closing inventory (w2)	1 000	(18 000)	(90 000)
			60 000
Less: Variable selling & distribution overhead (w3)			(5 000)
Contribution			55 000
Less: Fixed costs			
Production overhead (w4)			(30 000)
Selling and distribution overhead (w5)			(10 000)
Administration expenses (w6)			(5 000)
Marginal profit			10 000

Workings

(w1) Sales revenue is calculated:

Sales units x selling price per unit

5 000 units x €30 = €150 000

(w2) All inventories are calculated at the variable cost of production:

	€ per unit
Direct materials	10
Direct labour	5
Variable production overhead	3
Variable cost of production	18

Be careful not to include the variable selling and distribution overhead in the variable cost of production. This varies with the level of units sold, not the level of units produced, and is calculated separately. Production inventory is valued at:

Production inventory units x variable cost of production

6 000 units x €18 = €108 000

To calculate the value of closing inventory it is necessary to ascertain the closing inventory units. This is calculated as follows:

	UNITS
Opening inventory	0
Plus: Inventory produced	6 000
Less: Inventory sold	(5 000)
Closing inventory	1 000

Closing inventory is valued at:

Closing inventory units x marginal cost of production

1 000 units x €18 = €18 000

Opening inventory is valued at:

Opening inventory units x variable cost of production

0 units x €18 = €0

(w3) Calculate the variable selling and distribution overhead
Variable selling and distribution overhead varies with the number of units sold:

Units sold x variable selling and distribution overhead per unit

5 000 x €1 = €5 000

(w4) Fixed production overhead
In the marginal costing statement fixed production overhead is treated as a period cost and is written off against profit.

(w5) In both the marginal and absorption costing statements fixed selling and distribution overhead is treated as a period cost and is written off against profit.

(w6) In both the marginal and absorption costing statements fixed administration expenses are treated as a period cost and are written off against profit.

Concept of absorption costing

In absorption costing inventory is valued at the sum of:

Direct materials

+

Direct labour

+

Direct expenses

+

Variable production overhead costs

+

Fixed production overhead absorbed

That is, inventories are valued at their full production cost. When preparing a set of published accounts IAS 2 requires absorption costing. Users of accounts need to be sure the accounts have been prepared under generally accepted accounting practice.

Fixed production overhead – absorption costing

Fixed production overhead is treated as a product cost and is carried forward into subsequent accounting periods in closing inventory. IAS 2 (Ch 20:s2.2.1 pg 1293) states that product costs should include overhead costs apportioned using a 'systematic allocation of fixed and variable production overheads that are incurred in converting materials into finished goods'.

Fixed production overhead needs to be absorbed into product costs using a fixed overhead absorption method outlined in Chapter 3. IAS 2 (Ch 20:s2.2.1 pg 1293) states 'the allocation of fixed production overheads is to be based on the normal capacity of the facilities'. Normal capacity is defined as 'the production expected to be achieved on average over a number of periods or seasons under normal circumstances'. When calculating fixed production overhead absorption rates in this chapter we will use normal capacity as the absorption method.

The fixed production overhead absorption rate (OAR) will be calculated as follows:

$$\frac{\text{Budgeted fixed production overhead}}{\text{Normal capacity}}$$

Under- or over-absorption of fixed production overhead

In Chapter 3 we discussed the reasons for using budgeted information to calculate the OAR and that it may lead to under-absorbed or over-absorbed overhead. Under-absorbed or over-absorbed overhead means actual production volumes and/or actual production expenditure are different from the budgeted amounts. This area was discussed in detail in **Chapter 7: Standard Costing and Variance Analysis** (see fixed production overhead volume variance and fixed production overhead expenditure variance).

Example 8.2

Budgeted fixed production overhead is €100 000 per annum and overhead absorption rates are based on normal activity of 50 000 units per annum. The actual number of units produced was 55 000 units and actual costs incurred were as per budget.

Required

Calculate the amount of under- or over-absorption of fixed production overhead. Explain if the amount of under- or over-absorption is a result of a fixed production overhead expenditure variance (expenditure effect) and/or a fixed production overhead volume variance (volume effect).

Solution to Example 8.2

The fixed production OAR is calculated as follows:

$$\frac{\text{Budgeted fixed production overhead}}{\text{Normal activity}}$$

$$\text{OAR} = \frac{€100\ 000}{50\ 000\ \text{units}} = €2\ \text{per unit}$$

Calculate the under-absorbed or over-absorbed overhead:

	€
Fixed production overhead absorbed:	
OAR x actual units produced	
€ 2 x 55 000 units	110 000
Actual fixed production overhead	(100 000)
Over-absorbed overhead	10 000

In this example fixed production overhead is over-absorbed, too much overhead was included in the absorption costing statement and the profit will need to be increased to correct this.

The amount over-absorbed could be due to fixed production overhead volume variance:

(actual units of production – budgeted units of production)
x standard fixed overhead rate per unit

(55 000 units – 50 000 units) x €2 = 10 000 F

See **Chapter 7: Standard Costing and Variance Analysis** for a more detailed explanation of this variance.

Example 8.3

Budgeted fixed production overhead is €40 000 per annum and overhead absorption rates are based on normal activity of 20 000 units per annum. The actual number of units produced was 18 000 units and the actual fixed production overhead was €42 000.

Required

Calculate the amount of under- or over-absorption of fixed production overhead. Explain if the amount of under- or over-absorption is a result of a fixed production overhead expenditure variance (expenditure effect) and/or a fixed production overhead volume variance (volume effect).

Solution to Example 8.3

The fixed production OAR is calculated as follows:

$$\frac{\text{Budgeted fixed production overhead}}{\text{Normal activity}}$$

$$\text{OAR} = \frac{€40\ 000}{20\ 000\ \text{units}} = €2 \text{ per unit}$$

Calculate the under-absorbed or over-absorbed overhead:

	€
Fixed production overhead absorbed:	
OAR x actual units produced	
€ 2 x 18 000 units	36 000
Actual fixed production overhead	(42 000)
Under-absorbed overhead	(6 000)

In this example fixed production overhead is under-absorbed, too little overhead was included in the absorption costing statement and the profit will need to be reduced to correct this.

The amount under-absorbed could be due to fixed production overhead volume variance:

(actual units of production – budgeted units of production)
x standard fixed overhead rate per unit

(18 000 units – 20 000 units) x €2 = 4 000 A

and fixed production overhead expenditure variance:

Budgeted fixed production overhead – actual fixed production overhead

€40 000 – €42 000 = 2 000 A

The overall fixed production overhead variance is 6 000 A:

(4 000 A + 2 000 A)

See **Chapter 7: Standard Costing and Variance Analysis** for a more detailed explanation of these variances.

When preparing an absorption costing statement the following layout should be used:

Sales
Less: Production cost of sales Production costs (direct materials + direct labour + variable production overhead + fixed production overhead absorbed)
Equals: Gross profit
Less: Variable selling and distribution overhead Fixed selling and distribution overhead Fixed administrative expenses Adjust for under- or over-absorbed overhead
Equals: Absorption profit/(loss)

Reasons for the use of absorption costing

1   Absorption costing represents the full cost of producing a product. Without fixed production overheads the product would not be able to be produced.
2   Absorption costing is required for inventory valuation under IAS 2 when publishing accounts.
3   In the long term all costs are variable, e.g., rent on the factory may be fixed for a year but it will increase or decrease over a five-year period. Any long-term decisions made should use absorption costing.
4   If production is built up in one accounting period for sale in another, absorption costing should be used. If not, fixed production overheads will be written off against profit in the period of production and not matched against revenues which will happen in another accounting period. This will distort profits and affect decision-making.

Problems with absorption costing

1   The allocation of fixed production overheads to product costs is on an arbitrary basis, usually based on normal capacity. If budgeted and fixed capacity differ, this can have a distorting effect on product costs and pricing decisions and could result in the decision to drop profitable products. This problem is overcome with the use of activity-based costing (see Chapter 4).
2   If absorption costing was used in a period where demand fell, then inflated profits would be reported in the period as unsold inventory would be carried forward to the next period as closing inventory, along with fixed production overhead absorbed. If the inventory was perishable and could not be sold subsequently, then a large write-off of inventory would have to take place and profits be reduced, thus distorting profits from one period to another. This would not occur in a marginal approach as fixed production overheads are treated as a period cost and are written off against profit as they occur.
3   Absorption costing does not distinguish between fixed costs and variable costs. It would not be suitable for use in conjunction with cost volume profit analysis (see Chapter 9).

Example 8.4

Using the information in Example 8.1, prepare a profit and loss statement for the year using absorption costing.

Solution to Example 8.4

ABSORPTION COSTING STATEMENT			
	UNITS	€	€
Sales (w1)	5 000		150 000
Less: Production cost of sales			
Opening inventory (w7)	0	0	
Production (w7)	6 000	138 000	
Less: Closing inventory (w7)	1 000	(23 000)	(115 000)
Gross profit			35 000
Less: Variable selling and distribution overhead (w3)			(5 000)
Less: Fixed costs			
Selling and distribution overhead (w5)			(10 000)
Administration expenses (w6)			(5 000)
			15 000
Under-/over-absorbed overhead (w9)			0
Absorption profit			15 000

Workings

Workings 1–6 are listed under Example 8.1.

(w7) All inventories are calculated at the absorption cost of production:

	€ per unit
Direct materials	10
Direct labour	5
Variable production overhead	3
Fixed production OAR (w8)	5
Absorption cost of production	23

Opening inventory is valued at:

Opening inventory units x absorption cost of production

$$0 \times €23 = €0$$

Production inventory is valued at:

Production inventory units x absorption cost of production

$$6\ 000 \text{ units} \times €23 = €138\ 000$$

Closing inventory is valued at:

Closing inventory units x absorption cost of production

1 000 units x €23 = €23 000

(w8) Fixed production OAR is based on normal capacity:

$$OAR = \frac{\text{Budgeted fixed production overhead}}{\text{Normal capacity}}$$

$$OAR = \frac{€30\ 000}{6\ 000\ \text{units}} = €5 \text{ per unit produced}$$

Be careful not to include the variable selling and distribution overhead in the variable cost of production.

(w9) Check for under-absorption or over-absorption of fixed production overhead. In this example actual fixed production costs are known. The under-/over-absorption is calculated as follows:

	€
Fixed production overhead absorbed:	
OAR x actual units produced	
€ 5 x 6 000 units	30 000
Actual fixed production overhead	(30 000)
Under-absorbed or over-absorbed overhead	0

In this example the normal capacity level upon which the OAR was based was the same as the actual production level, i.e., they are both 6 000 units. There is no under-absorbed or over-absorbed overhead in this example.

Reconciling marginal and absorption profits

It is possible to reconcile the absorption profit with the marginal profit. The difference in profit between the two approaches is a result of the accounting treatment of fixed production overhead. In the absorption approach the fixed production overhead is carried forward in closing inventory into the next accounting period. In the marginal approach closing inventories are unaffected by fixed production overhead as it is treated as a period cost. As a general rule the relationship between the absorption and marginal profits can be summarised as follows:

(1) Production equals sales

There is no change in inventory levels and absorption profit equals marginal profit.

(2) Production is greater than sales

Closing inventory levels will increase and absorption profit will be greater than marginal profit.

(3) Production is less than sales

Closing inventory levels will decrease and absorption profit will be less than marginal profit.

Consider the profits calculated in Examples 8.1 and 8.4:

	€
Solution 8.1 marginal profit	10 000
Solution 8.4 absorption profit	15 000

In this example absorption profit is €5 000 greater than marginal profit. This is because production exceeds sales by 1 000 units. There is no opening inventory. In the absorption statement €5 000 (OAR €5 x 1 000 units of closing inventory) of the fixed production overhead is deferred and is carried forward in closing inventory to the next accounting period. Under marginal costing all of the fixed production overhead has been treated as a period cost and written off against profit. As a result, the profit under marginal costing is €5 000 lower than it is under absorption costing.

Example 8.5

Prepare a reconciliation statement, reconciling your answers from Examples 8.1 and 8.4.

Solution to Example 8.5

	€
Absorption profit	15 000
Add: Fixed production overhead included in opening inventory OAR x opening inventory units €5 x 0 units	0
Less: Fixed production overhead included in closing inventory OAR x closing inventory units €5 x 1 000 units	(5 000)
Marginal profit	10 000

Preparing statements for two or more accounting periods

In questions the student may be asked to prepare marginal and absorption costing statements for two or more accounting periods. In this case the profit statements are prepared in columnar format.

Example 8.6

A company makes a single product. The following data are available for periods 1 and 2:

	PERIOD 1	PERIOD 2
Sales (units)	1 000	800
Production (units)	1 000	1 000

Fixed production overhead cost is €6 000 in each period and is absorbed based on normal activity of 1 000 units.

Other information is as follows:

	€
Variable production cost per unit	15.00
Selling price per unit	27.50

There are no opening inventories at the beginning of period 1.

Required

a   Prepare a marginal costing statement for period 1 and period 2 in columnar format
b   Prepare an absorption costing statement for period 1 and period 2 in columnar format
c   Reconcile your answers to (a) and (b) above
d   Comment on the results obtained in each period

Solution to Example 8.6

(a) Marginal costing statement

	PERIOD 1			PERIOD 2		
	UNITS	€	€	UNITS	€	€
Sales (w1)	1 000		27 500	800		22 000
Less: Variable production cost of sales						
Opening inventory (w2)	0	0		0	0	
Production (w2)	1 000	15 000		1 000	15 000	
Less: Closing inventory (w2)	0	0	(15 000)	200	(3 000)	(12 000)
Contribution			12 500			10 000
Less: Fixed costs						
Production overhead (w3)			(6 000)			(6 000)
Marginal profit			6 500			4 000

(b) Absorption costing statement

	PERIOD 1			PERIOD 2		
	UNITS	€	€	UNITS	€	€
Sales (w1)	1 000		27 500	800		22 000
Less: Production cost of sales						
Opening inventory (w4)	0	0		0	0	
Production (w4)	1 000	21 000		1 000	21 000	
Less: Closing inventory (w4)	0	0	(21 000)	200	(4 200)	(16 800)
Gross profit			6 500			5 200
Under-/over-absorbed overhead (w6)			0			0
Absorption profit			6 500			5 200

Workings

(w1) Sales revenue is calculated:

Sales units x selling price per unit

Period 1: 1 000 units x €27.50 = €27 500

Period 2: 800 units x €27.50 = €22 000

(w2) All inventories are calculated at the variable cost of production, which is €15 per unit.
Production inventory is valued at:

Production inventory units x variable cost of production

Period 1: 1 000 units x €15 = €15 000

Period 2: 1 000 units x €15 = €15 000

To calculate the value of closing inventory it is necessary to ascertain the closing inventory units. This is calculated as follows:

	PERIOD 1 UNITS	PERIOD 2 UNITS
Opening inventory	0	0
Plus: Inventory produced	1 000	1 000
Less: Inventory sold	(1 000)	(800)
Closing inventory	0	200

Closing inventory is valued at:

Closing inventory units x marginal cost of production

Period 1:   0 units x €15 = €0

Period 2: 200 units x €15 = €3 000

Opening inventory is valued at:

Opening inventory units x variable cost of production

Period 1: 0 units x €15 = €0

Period 2: 0 units x €15 = €0

(w3) Fixed production overhead

In the marginal statement fixed production overhead is treated as a period cost and is written off against profit.

(w4) All inventories are calculated at the absorption cost of production:

	€ per unit
Variable production cost	15.00
Fixed production OAR (w5)	6.00
Absorption cost of production	21.00

Production inventory is valued at:

Production inventory units x absorption cost of production

Period 1: 1 000 units x €21 = €21 000

Period 2: 1 000 units x €21 = €21 000

Closing inventory is valued at:

Closing inventory units x absorption cost of production

Period 1: 0 units x €21 = €0

Period 2: 200 units x €21 = €4 200

Opening inventory is valued at:

Opening inventory units x absorption cost of production

Period 1: 0 units x €21 = €0

Period 2: 0 units x €21 = €0

In this question there is no selling and distribution overhead or administration expenses, so they are left out of the costing statement.

(w5) Fixed production OAR is based on normal capacity:

$$\text{OAR} = \frac{€6\ 000}{1\ 000\ \text{units}} = €6 \text{ per unit produced}$$

(w6) Check for under-absorption or over-absorption of fixed production overhead:

	PERIOD 1 €	PERIOD 2 €
Fixed production overhead absorbed: OAR x actual units produced		
Period 1: €6 x 1 000 units	6 000	–
Period 2: €6 x 1 000 units	–	6 000
Actual fixed production overhead	(6 000)	(6 000)
Under- or over-absorbed overhead	0	0

In this example the normal capacity level upon which the OAR was based was the same as the actual production level, i.e., they are both 1 000 units, for both periods. There is no under- or over-absorbed overhead in this example. The actual and budgeted expenditure on fixed production overhead were equal.

(c) Reconciliation statement

	PERIOD 1 €	PERIOD 2 €
Absorption profit	6 500	5 200
Add: Fixed production overhead included in opening inventory OAR x opening inventory units		
Period 1: €6 x 0 units	0	–
Period 2: €6 x 0 units	–	0
Less: Fixed production overhead included in closing inventory OAR x closing inventory units		
Period 1: €6 x 0 units	0	–
Period 2: €6 x 200 units	–	(1 200)
Marginal profit	6 500	4 000

(d) Comment on the results obtained in each period

In period 1 production units equal sales units and there is no opening or closing inventory. The fixed production overhead of €6 000 is written off as a period cost in the marginal statement and €6 000 (OAR €6 x 1 000 units) of fixed production overhead is absorbed into product costs in the absorption statement, which becomes part of that period's cost of sales. Marginal and absorption profits are equal.

In period 2 production units exceed sales units and there are 200 units of closing inventory. The fixed production overhead of €6 000 is written off as a period cost in the marginal statement, but only €4 800 (OAR €6 x 800 units) of fixed production overhead is absorbed into product costs in the absorption statement. The remainder, €1 200 (OAR €6 x 200 units), of fixed production overhead is deferred in closing inventory, this cost has been excluded from cost of sales. As a result, in the marginal costing statement the profit for period 2 is €1 200 lower than it is under the absorption costing statement:

Fixed production overhead written off in marginal costing statement	€6 000
Fixed production overhead charged to cost of sales in absorption costing statement	€4 800
Difference	€1 200

Chapter summary

In this chapter we compared marginal and absorption costing approaches. In a marginal costing approach fixed production overhead is treated as a period cost. In an absorption costing approach it is treated as a product cost and is used to value inventory. IAS 2 states that absorption costing must be used for inventory valuation in published accounts. Marginal costing is used only for internal accounts and for short-term decision-making.

The main differences between marginal and absorption costing can be summarised as follows:

	MARGINAL COSTING	ABSORPTION COSTING
Regulated by:	Not regulated	IAS 2 Inventories
Used for:	Internal reporting and decision-making	External reporting
Uses the term 'contribution':	Yes	No
Treatment of fixed production overhead:	Treats as a period cost	Treats as a product cost
Used in cost volume profit analysis:	Yes	No
Need to check for under-absorbed or over-absorbed overhead:	No	Yes

The chapter illustrated inventory valuation and profit calculation under the two approaches. The reasons for using the two approaches were discussed along with the problems with each approach. The marginal costing approach is used again in **Chapter 9: Cost Volume Profit Analysis**.

Test questions

Question 1*

Burkes Ltd sells a single product and has the following standard costs:

	€
Direct materials	45
Direct labour	35
Variable production overhead	15
Fixed production overhead (OAR)	5
	100

There is no opening inventory at the beginning of April. Fixed production overhead is absorbed based on budgeted production levels of 2 000 units per month.

Fixed costs are assumed to be incurred evenly throughout the year. A mark-up of 20% is added to the full standard cost to calculate selling price.

During the months of April and May the following sales and production levels were recorded:

	APRIL	MAY
Sales (units)	600	1 000
Production (units)	900	700

Required

a Prepare a marginal costing statement for the months of April and May
b Prepare an absorption costing statement for the months of April and May
c Explain the differences in the reported profits

Notes to students

1 The question mentions standard costs. Standard cost is the budgeted cost of one unit. Standard costing is discussed further in Chapter 7.
2 The selling price is calculated by adding a profit mark-up of 20% on to the full cost. This is an example of full cost plus pricing where all variable and

fixed production costs are included in the product price. In this question the full cost plus approach to calculating the selling price is applied to the marginal and absorption costing approach.

3 There are no selling and distribution overheads or administration expenses in this question, so they can be left out of the answer.

4 Check to see if there is any under-absorbed or over-absorbed overhead. Is it due to a volume effect (are the actual units produced different to the budgeted production units upon which the OAR is based?) and/or an expenditure effect (is there a difference between the actual fixed production overhead and the budgeted fixed production overhead?)?

* Based on question 7 in ATI Costing & Budgeting, Summer 2007.

Question 2

Blue Skies Ltd produces a single product and has the following budgeted costs and selling price:

	€
Selling price per unit	40
Direct materials per unit	8
Direct labour per unit	7
Variable production overhead per unit	5

Budgeted fixed production overhead expenditure is €24 000 per month. Budgeted production and sales were 10 000 units. Actual production was 9 600 units and actual sales were 9 400 units. There was no opening inventory. The actual costs incurred were as per budget and the actual sales price was as per budget.

Required

a Prepare profit statements for the month using:
  (i) marginal costing
  (ii) absorption costing
b Reconcile the differences between the absorption profit and marginal profit which you have calculated in your answer to (a) above

Notes to students

1 When calculating the OAR we normally divide the budgeted fixed production overhead by the normal capacity. There is no mention of normal capacity in this question so divide by the budgeted capacity.

2 Remember when valuing inventories that actual production and sales units should be used – not budgeted.

Question 3*

Cois Tine Ltd makes and sells heaters. The selling price is €15 per unit and the following are unit costs:

	€
Direct materials	3
Direct labour	2
Variable production overhead	3
Fixed production overhead (OAR)	4
	12

Variable selling and distribution costs are €1 per unit sold and fixed selling and distribution costs are €9 000 per annum.

Fixed production overhead (OAR) is based on normal production capacity of 4 000 units per annum. There is no opening inventory at the beginning of year 1.

Production and sales for years 1 and 2 were as follows:

	YEAR 1	YEAR 2
Production (units)	6 000	9 000
Sales (units)	4 000	9 000

Required

a Prepare operating statements for each year based on:
   (i)   marginal costing
   (ii) absorption costing
b Reconcile the absorption profit and marginal profit for each year

Notes to students

1 There are fixed and variable selling and distribution overheads in this question but no fixed administration expenses.
2 Fixed production overhead is based on normal capacity. To calculate the fixed production overhead for the marginal statement it will be necessary to reconstruct the budgeted fixed production overhead.

* Based on question 5 in CIMA, *P1 Management Acccounting – Performance Evaluation*, Kaplan Publishing Foulks Lynch, 2006, 16.

For answers and additional test questions, see www.gillmacmillan.ie. Search for Management Accounting and click on the link in the right-hand column.

9 Cost Volume Profit Analysis

Learning outcomes of Chapter 9

At the end of this chapter, you will be able to:

- explain how changes in volume affect contribution and profit
- using formulae, calculate the break-even point, margin of safety, contribution sales ratio and units required to earn a profit
- calculate the degree of operating leverage at a particular level of sales and explain its importance in predicting profits
- apply cost volume profit (CVP) analysis to different scenarios
- construct break-even, contribution and profit-volume graphs
- discuss the benefits of using graphs to illustrate cost volume profit information
- apply CVP analysis in a sales mix
- separate semi-variable costs using the high-low method
- discuss the assumptions of cost volume analysis

Introduction

Businesses are continually evolving – new products are introduced and old products removed, costs go up and down and profits increase and fall. As a result, a business needs to make decisions such as increasing or decreasing a product's selling price. There is a relationship between costs, the number or volume of units sold and the profit made. This is called cost volume profit (CVP) analysis or break-even analysis. It is a very simple approach taken to short-term decisions, usually those within a year, that if costs change or the volume of units sold changes then the profits will also change.

A marginal costing approach is taken in this chapter. Marginal costing was discussed in Chapter 8. The decision being considered in the examples and questions in this chapter are all short-term decisions, i.e., they will affect the profits of the next 12 months. As they are short-term decisions they are unaffected by fixed costs – as these are fixed in the short term – so the decisions will be based on contribution.

The formula approach to cost volume profit analysis will be illustrated along with the graphic approach. Calculating the break-even point where products are sold in a constant sales mix will be illustrated, as will the separation of semi-variable costs.

The benefits of using graphs will be explained and the underlying theories of using cost volume profit analysis will be discussed.

Cost volume profit analysis

In **Chapter 8: Marginal and Absorption Costing**, the use of short-term decision-making was discussed. Decisions are based on contribution rather than profit as profit includes fixed costs which are irrelevant in the short term. The marginal approach calculates profit using the following layout:

Sales
Less: Variable costs
Contribution
Less: Fixed costs
Profit/(loss)

Contribution is the amount left over after variable costs have been deducted from sales. It is the amount that 'contributes' towards fixed costs. Anything left over after fixed costs have been deducted from sales is profit. If contribution does not 'contribute' or cover fixed costs then there is a loss.

Sales, variable costs and contribution can be expressed in total or on a unit basis, whereas fixed costs are usually expressed on a total basis. This is because fixed costs do not increase as volume increases but sales and variable costs do. Fixed costs and variable costs are discussed under cost behaviour in Chapter 1. Consider the following example which illustrates this point:

Example 9.1

A company produces a single product which has a selling price of €20 per unit and a variable cost of €10 per unit. The fixed costs for the period are €1 200. The company is unsure of the level of units to sell and is interested in estimating the profit at different levels of sales.

Required

Calculate the profit if the company were to sell 100 units and 200 units.

Solution to Example 9.1

The profit if 100 units were sold would be:

	TOTAL €	PER UNIT €
Sales €20 x 100 units	2 000	20
Less: Variable costs €10 x 100 units	(1 000)	(10)
Contribution	1 000	10
Less: Fixed costs	(1 200)	
Profit/(loss)	(200)	

The profit if 200 units were sold would be:

	TOTAL €	PER UNIT €
Sales €20 x 200 units	4 000	20
Less: Variable costs €10 x 200 units	(2 000)	(10)
Contribution	2 000	10
Less: Fixed costs	(1 200)	
Profit/(loss)	800	

If the company only sells 100 units, it will make a loss of €200. If it sells 200 units, it will make a profit of €800. Notice that the fixed costs remain the same regardless of whether 100 or 200 units are sold. The selling price per unit, variable costs per unit and contribution per unit remain constant.

It can be ascertained that for each additional unit sold, €10 in contribution will be made to cover fixed costs.

Break-even point using formula method

A company will need to know how many units it will need to sell to break even, i.e., where it makes neither a profit nor a loss. Anything it sells over and above the break-even point will result in a profit. Anything below will result in a loss. Break-even can also be described as the level of sales in units and revenue which covers all the costs.

Example 9.1.a

Using the information in Example 9.1, the break-even point is somewhere between 100 units, where a loss of €200 is made, and 200 units, where a profit of €800 is made. It was illustrated that for every additional unit sold a contribution of €10 per unit was made to cover fixed costs. If the company can generate enough contribution to cover the fixed costs it will break even.

Required

Calculate the break-even point in units and in sales revenue.

Solution to Example 9.1.a

The number of units to be sold to break even is calculated using the following formula:

$$\frac{\text{Total fixed costs}}{\text{Contribution per unit}}$$

$$\frac{€1\ 200}{€10} = 120 \text{ units}$$

This means that 120 units must be sold to break even.

The sales value at break-even point is calculated using the following formula:

$$\frac{\text{Total fixed costs}}{\text{Contribution per unit}} \quad \text{x} \quad \text{selling price per unit}$$

$$\frac{€1\ 200}{€10} \quad \text{x} \quad €20 = €2\ 400$$

This means that €2 400 of sales revenue must be made to break even.

The break-even point can also be calculated by using the marginal costing layout, slotting in the available information and working backwards to calculate the sales revenue and sales units at the break-even point:

		€
Sales	€20 x ??? units	?????
Less: Variable costs	€10 x ??? units	?????
Contribution	€10 x ??? units	?????
Less: Fixed costs		(1 200)
Profit/(loss)		0

The first step is to calculate the contribution. It can be assumed that at the break-even point the fixed costs and contribution will be equal:

		€
Sales	€20 x ??? units	?????
Less: Variable costs	€10 x ??? units	?????
Contribution	€10 x ??? units	1 200
Less: Fixed costs		(1 200)
Profit/(loss)		0

The next step is to calculate the number of units sold. If the contribution per unit is €10 and the total contribution at the level of sales is €1 200, then the number of units sold is calculated as follows:

$$\frac{\text{Total contribution}}{\text{Contribution per unit}}$$

$$\frac{€1\ 200}{€10} = 120 \text{ units}$$

		€
Sales	€20 x ??? units	?????
Less: Variable costs	€10 x ??? units	?????
Contribution	€10 x 120 units	1 200
Less: Fixed costs		(1 200)
Profit/(loss)		0

The last step is to work out the sales revenue at the break-even point. If 120 units are required to break even and the sales revenue is €20 per unit, the sales revenue at the break-even point is:

Break-even sales units x selling price per unit = break-even sales revenue

120 units x €20 = €2 400

		€
Sales	€20 x 120 units	2 400
Less: Variable costs	€10 x 120 units	(1 200)
Contribution	€10 x 120 units	1 200
Less: Fixed costs		(1 200)
Profit/(loss)		0

The break-even point is a very useful piece of information for the business. Once the break-even point has been reached, any additional unit sold above the break-even point will increase profit by the contribution per unit.

Example 9.1.b

Using the information in Example 9.1.a, calculate the additional profit if 121 units were to be sold.

Solution to Example 9.1.b

It is not necessary to calculate the total sales, total variable costs and total contribution to calculate the total profit as it is known that for every additional unit sold above the break-even point, €10 in contribution will be earned. If the company sells 121 units this is one unit above the break-even point, so an additional €10 in profit will be earned.

This is verified using the marginal costing layout and calculating the profit at 120 units and 121 units:

		120 UNITS €		121 UNITS €
Sales	€20 x 120 units	2 400	€20 x 121 units	2 420
Less: Variable costs	€10 x 120 units	(1 200)	€10 x 121 units	(1 210)
Contribution	€10 x 120 units	1 200	€10 x 121 units	1 210
Less: Fixed costs		(1 200)		(1 200)
Profit/(loss)		0		10

Profit increases from €0 to €10 when sales increase from 120 units to 121 units.

Contribution sales ratio

Contribution can be expressed as a percentage of sales:

$$\frac{\text{Contribution}}{\text{Sales}} \quad X \quad 100$$

The information used in the formula can be on a total basis or a unit basis. Consider the following example:

Example 9.2

A company sells 500 units of its product. The selling price is €12 per unit and variable costs are €4.80 per unit. The fixed costs are €1 080.

Required

Calculate the contribution to sales ratio.

Solution to Example 9.2

The contribution per unit, total contribution and profit of the company are:

		TOTAL €	PER UNIT €
Sales	€12.00 x 500 units	6 000	12.00
Less: Variable costs	€4.80 x 500 units	(2 400)	(4.80)
Contribution		3 600	7.20
Less: Fixed costs		(1 080)	
Profit/(loss)		2 520	

The contribution sales (C/S) ratio can be calculated using a unit basis or a total basis.

C/S ratio using a unit basis:

$$\frac{\text{Contribution per unit}}{\text{Sales price per unit}} \times 100$$

$$\frac{€7.20}{€12.00} \times 100 = 60\%$$

C/S ratio on a total basis:

$$\frac{\text{Total contribution}}{\text{Total sales}} \times 100$$

$$\frac{€3\ 600}{€6\ 000} \times 100 = 60\%$$

The results are the same, using the unit basis or total basis. The C/S ratio is 60%. This means that for every €1 increase in sales, contribution will increase by 60 cent (€1 x 60% = €0.60). Profit will also increase by 60 cent assuming that there are no changes in fixed costs. The C/S ratio can be used very quickly to calculate the effect on profit of an increase in sales.

Example 9.2.a

Using the information in Example 9.2, calculate the effect on profit if the company plans to increase sales by €1 200.

Solution to Example 9.2.a

If sales increase by €1 200 then profit will increase by €720 (sales €1 200 x 60% C/S ratio).

The revised sales are €7 200 (present sales €6 000 + increase in sales €1 200). If the selling price is €12 per unit then 600 units will be sold (€7 200/€12 per unit). This can be verified as follows:

		500 UNITS €		600 UNITS €
Sales	€12.00 x 500 units	6 000	€12.00 x 600 units	7 200
Less: Variable costs	€4.80 x 500 units	(2 400)	€4.80 x 600 units	(2 880)
Contribution	€7.20 x 500 units	3 600	€7.20 x 600 units	4 320
Less: Fixed costs		(1 080)		(1 080)
Profit/(loss)		2 520		3 240

Profit increases by €720 (€3 240 – €2 520) as sales increase by €1 200.

Break-even point – using contribution sales ratio

The break-even point in sales revenue can also be calculated using the C/S ratio. The formula is:

$$\frac{\text{Total fixed costs}}{\text{C/S ratio}}$$

Example 9.2.b

Using the information in Example 9.2.a, calculate the break-even sales revenue using the C/S ratio and the break-even sales units.

Solution to Example 9.2.b

The break-even sales revenue formula using the C/S ratio is:

$$\frac{\text{Total fixed costs}}{\text{C/S ratio}}$$

The break-even sales revenue is calculated as follows:

$$\frac{€1\ 080}{60\%} = €1\ 800$$

If the selling price per unit is €12, the break-even sales units can be calculated by dividing the break-even sales revenue by the selling price per unit:

$$\frac{\text{Break-even sales revenue}}{\text{Selling price per unit}}$$

$$\frac{€1\ 800}{€12} = 150\ \text{units}$$

This can be verified as follows:

		TOTAL €	PER UNIT €
Sales	€12.00 x 150 units	1 800	12.00
Less: Variable costs	€4.80 x 150 units	(720)	(4.80)
Contribution		1 080	7.20
Less: Fixed costs		(1 080)	
Profit/(loss)		0	

If the company's sales revenue is €1 800 it will break even.

Margin of safety

The margin of safety is the difference between the budgeted (or actual) sales and the break-even sales. It indicates by how much sales can fall before a loss is incurred. It can be expressed in:

(i) Sales revenue

> Budgeted (or actual) sales revenue € – break-even sales revenue €
> = margin of safety (sales revenue €)

(ii) Sales units

> Budgeted (or actual) sales units – break-even sales units
> = margin of safety (sales units)

(iii) A percentage of budgeted sales

$$\frac{\text{Budgeted (or actual) sales revenue} - \text{break-even sales revenue}}{\text{Budgeted (or actual) sales revenue}} \times 100$$

Example 9.3

A company forecasts that it will sell 180 units next year. The selling price per unit is €20 and the variable cost per unit is €15. Fixed costs are €800.

Required

a Calculate the break-even point in sales units and sales revenue
b Calculate the margin of safety in sales revenue, sales units and a percentage of budgeted sales

Solution to Example 9.3

a Break-even point (sales units)

$$\frac{\text{Total fixed costs}}{\text{Contribution per unit}}$$

Sales – variable costs = contribution per unit

€20 – €15 = €5

$$\frac{€800}{€5} = 160 \text{ units}$$

This means that 160 units must be sold to break even.

Break-even point (sales revenue)

$$\frac{\text{Total fixed costs}}{\text{Contribution per unit}} \text{ x selling price per unit}$$

$$\frac{€800}{€5} \text{ x €20 = €3 200}$$

This means that €3 200 of sales revenue must be made to break even.

b Margin of safety (sales revenue)

Budgeted sales revenue € – break-even sales revenue €
= margin of safety (sales revenue €)

(180 units x €20) – €3 200 = €400

Margin of safety (sales units)

Budgeted sales units – break-even sales units =
margin of safety (sales units)

180 units – 160 units = 20 units

Margin of safety (%)

$$\frac{\text{Budgeted sales revenue} - \text{break-even sales revenue}}{\text{Budgeted sales revenue}} \text{ x 100}$$

$$\frac{(180 \text{ units x €20}) - €3 200}{(180 \text{ units x €20})} \text{ x 100 = 11.11\%}$$

This margin of safety means that at the budgeted level of sales and with the company's current prices and cost structure, a reduction in sales of €400, or a reduction in units of 20 units, or an 11.11% fall in sales would result in just breaking even.

Target profit

Cost volume profit analysis can be used to calculate how many units need to be sold to achieve a certain profit. The formula used is:

$$\frac{\text{Fixed costs + target profit}}{\text{Contribution per unit}} = \text{units required to achieve target profit}$$

Example 9.3.a

Using the information in Example 9.3, if the company wishes to make a profit of €1 000, how many units will it need to sell?

Solution to Example 9.3.a

Using the target profit formula:

$$\frac{\text{Fixed costs + target profit}}{\text{Contribution per unit}}$$

The units required to achieve the target profit are:

$$\frac{€800 + €1\ 000}{€5} = 360 \text{ units}$$

This can be verified as follows:

		TOTAL €	PER UNIT €
Sales	€20 x 360 units	7 200	20
Less: Variable costs	€15 x 360 units	(5 400)	(15)
Contribution		1 800	5
Less: Fixed costs		(800)	
Profit/(loss)		1 000	

Operating leverage

CIMA Official Terminology states that operating gearing or leverage is the 'relationship of fixed cost to total cost of an operating unit'.

Operating leverage is a measure of how sensitive profit is to a percentage change in sales. Fixed costs are easier to predict but they are difficult to reduce if volumes of production fall rapidly. If a company has a high degree of operating leverage and sales fall, then it is at risk of incurring losses, because it has a high level of fixed costs. Operating leverage is calculated using the following formula:

$$\frac{\text{Contribution}}{\text{Profit}} = \text{degree of operating leverage}$$

This information is used to access the impact on profit of a percentage increase in sales. By multiplying the degree of operating leverage by the percentage change in sales, it is possible to ascertain the percentage impact on profit. Operating leverage can be used to estimate quickly, without doing detailed calculations, what impact various percentage changes in sales will have on profits. Consider the following example:

Example 9.4

Consider the results of the following two companies:

	TURF €	BOG €
Sales	75 000	75 000
Less: Variable costs	(45 000)	(25 000)
Contribution	30 000	50 000
Less: Fixed costs	(25 000)	(45 000)
Profit/(loss)	5 000	5 000

Required

Calculate the degree of operating leverage of each company and calculate the percentage impact on profit of a 5% fall in sales.

Solution to Example 9.4

Even though both companies yield the same profit, Bog is much more highly leveraged than Turf, i.e., it has a higher level of fixed costs than Turf.

The degree of operating leverage is calculated using the following formula:

$$\frac{\text{Contribution}}{\text{Profit}} = \text{degree of operating leverage}$$

Turf: $\dfrac{€30\ 000}{€5\ 000} = 6$

Bog: $\dfrac{€50\ 000}{€5\ 000} = 10$

The degree of operating leverage for Bog is 10, which means that its profits grow 10 times as fast as its sales. Turf has an operating leverage of 6, this means that its profits grow 6 times as fast as its sales. Overall Bog's profits are more sensitive to changes in sales volume than Turf's.

If sales were to fall by 5%, profit for Bog would fall by 50%:

Degree of operating leverage x % change in sales
10 x 5% = 50%

If sales were to fall by 5%, profit for Turf would fall by 30%:

Degree of operating leverage x % change in sales
6 x 5% = 30%

A similar relationship would exist if sales were to increase. Then Bog would yield a much larger increase in profits than Turf.

Applying CVP analysis to different scenarios

Various concepts in CVP analysis have been introduced in the preceding examples. These concepts will be used to analyse the effect on profits of different scenarios using the basic information in Example 9.5.

Example 9.5

A company currently sells its product for €300 per unit and incurs €150 variable costs per unit. Fixed costs are €30 000 per year and the company sells 350 units. The management accountant has worked out the following:

		TOTAL €	PER UNIT €
Sales	€300 x 350 units	105 000	300
Less: Variable costs	€150 x 350 units	(52 500)	(150)
Contribution	€150 x 350 units	52 500	150
Less: Fixed costs		(30 000)	
Profit/(loss)		22 500	

C/S ratio:

$$\frac{\text{Contribution per unit}}{\text{Sales per unit}} \times 100$$

$$\frac{€150}{€300} \times 100 = 50\%$$

Scenario 1 – where fixed costs increase and sales volume increases

The company wishes to increase fixed costs by €6 000 and believes sales would increase by €15 000. Show the effect on profit if this were to happen.

The selling price per unit and variable cost per unit remain the same, fixed costs will increase by €6 000 and sales volume will increase by 50 units (€15 000/€300). A quick way is to work out the incremental effect on profit:

Multiply C/S ratio by increase in sales revenue:

	€
50% x €15 000 =	7 500
Less: Increase in fixed costs	(6 000)
Increased profit	1 500

This can be verified by comparing the profit if we sell 350 units at the current fixed cost level, with the profit if we sell 400 units at the increased fixed cost level:

		350 UNITS €		400 UNITS €
Sales	€300 x 350 units	105 000	€300 x 400 units	120 000
Less: Variable costs	€150 x 350 units	(52 500)	€150 x 400 units	(60 000)
Contribution	€150 x 350 units	52 500		60 000
Less: Fixed costs		(30 000)		(36 000)
Profit/(loss)		22 500		24 000

Profit increases by €1 500 (€24 000 – €22 500).

Scenario 2 – where variable costs increase and sales volume increases

Consider the original information in Example 9.5. In this scenario the company wishes to use better quality raw materials, which will increase the variable cost per unit by €15. It is hoped that this will have the effect of increasing sales volume by 200 units. Is this a wise decision for the company?

The selling price per unit and the fixed costs remain the same. Only the variable cost per unit and the sales volume are affected by this decision. The sales volume will increase by 200 units to a revised level of 550 units (350 units + 200 units). As fixed costs are unaffected, the decision will be based on contribution. The revised contribution per unit is:

	€
Original contribution per unit	150
Less: Increase in variable costs	(15)
Revised contribution per unit	135

Compare the revised total contribution with the original total contribution:

	€
Revised contribution €135 x 550 units	74 250
Less: Original contribution €150 x 350 units	(52 500)
Increased contribution	21 750

This can be verified as follows:

		350 UNITS €		550 UNITS €
Sales	€300 x 350 units	105 000	€300 x 550 units 1	65 000
Less: Variable costs	€150 x 350 units	(52 500)	€165 x 550 units	(90 750)
Contribution	€150 x 350 units	52 500	€135 x 550 units	74 250
Less: Fixed costs		(30 000)		(30 000)
Profit/(loss)		22 500		44 250

Contribution and profit increase by €21 750 so the company should go ahead and purchase the better quality raw materials.

Scenario 3 – where fixed costs increase, selling price per unit decreases and sales volume increases

Consider the original information in Example 9.5. In this scenario the company wishes to increase sales volume by 50 units by reducing the selling price per unit to €290 and by increasing the fixed costs by €6 000. Advise it on whether it should go ahead with this scenario.

Work out the incremental effect on profit. The revised contribution per unit is:

	€
Selling price per unit	290
Less: Variable costs per unit	(150)
Revised contribution per unit	140

The effect on profit if this decision goes ahead:

		€
Revised contribution	€140 x 400 units	56 000
Less: Original contribution	€150 x 350 units	(52 500)
Increased contribution		3 500
Less: Increase in fixed costs		(6 000)
Decrease in profit		(2 500)

This can be verified as follows:

		350 UNITS €		400 UNITS €
Sales	€300 x 350 units	105 000	€290 x 400 units	116 000
Less: Variable costs	€150 x 350 units	(52 500)	€150 x 400 units	(60 000)
Contribution	€150 x 350 units	52 500	€140 x 400 units	56 000
Less: Fixed costs		(30 000)		(36 000)
Profit/(loss)		22 500		20 000

Profit decreases by €2 500 (€20 000 – €22 500). It would initially appear that the decision to decrease the selling price by €10 would be a good idea as sales revenue increases and total contribution increases. However, with this decision fixed costs increase by €6 000 and the result is that profit decreases by €2 500.

For this decision to be worthwhile from a financial point of view, sales would need to increase to 418 units to match the original profit. This is worked out using the target profit formula:

$$\frac{\text{Fixed costs + target profit}}{\text{Contribution per unit}}$$

The units required to achieve the target profit are:

$$\frac{€36\ 000 + €22\ 500}{€140} = 418 \text{ units (to the nearest unit)}$$

This is verified as follows:

		TOTAL €
Contribution	€140 x 418 units	58 520
Less: Fixed costs		(36 000)
Profit/(loss)		22 520

Relevant range

In Scenario 3 we saw that as sales volume increased by 50 units the fixed costs increased by €6 000. Fixed costs are only fixed within a relevant range of output. If you exceed that range of output the fixed costs increase. *CIMA Official Terminology* defines relevant range as 'activity levels within which assumptions about cost behaviour in break-even analysis remain valid'. Fixed costs, variable costs per unit and selling price per unit are all deemed to be constant within the relevant range. If the results from any calculations made are outside of the relevant range, they may be incorrect.

Use of graphs in CVP analysis

Graphs may also be used to represent cost volume profit data. There are three common graphs used:

1 Break-even graph
2 Contribution graph
3 Profit/volume graph

Use Example 9.1 to construct these graphs:

A company produces a single product which has a selling price of €20 per unit and a variable cost of €10 per unit. The fixed costs for the period are €1 200. The budgeted sales are 150 units. Prepare a break-even graph.

Break-even graph

The following information is represented on the break-even graph:

a   Sales revenue line
b   Total costs line
c   Fixed costs line
d   Break-even point in units and €
e   Margin of safety in units and €
f   Profit and loss areas

Constructing a break-even graph

1   The horizontal (x) axis represents volume of units and the vertical (y) axis costs and revenues.
2   Draw the fixed costs line. It is a horizontal line and is parallel to the horizontal axis. Remember when drawing a line on a graph it needs to pass through two points of contact. The fixed costs are €1 200 regardless of whether zero units are sold or 100 units are sold. The fixed costs line will pass through zero units and €1 200, and 100 units and €1 200. Label the line 'Fixed costs'.
3   Draw the sales line. If no sales take place then sales revenue is zero, the first point of contact is zero units and zero €. For every one unit sold €20 of sales revenue is earned. Take any level of sales, e.g., if 100 units are sold, sales revenue will be €2 000 (€20 x 100 units). The second point of contact is 100 units and €2 000. Draw the sales line by placing a rule through these two points, extend the line out to the edge of the graph and label it 'Sales revenue'.
4   Draw the total costs line. Total costs are made up of variable costs and fixed costs. Pick two levels of sales and work out the total costs.
    For example, the total costs if zero units are sold will be:

	€
Variable costs (€10 x 0 units)	0
Fixed costs	1 200
Total costs	1 200

If 100 units are sold the total costs will be:

	€
Variable costs (€10 x 100 units)	1 000
Fixed costs	1 200
Total costs	2 200

The line will be drawn through these two points and extended to the edge of the graph and labelled 'Total costs'.

5 The point at which the total cost line and the sales revenue line intersect is the break-even point. At this point total sales revenue equals total costs. Extend a broken line from the intersection of the two lines down to the horizontal axis (120 units) and across to the vertical axis (€2 400). The break-even point was calculated earlier in the chapter in Example 9.1.a as 120 units and €2 400 in sales revenue. Label the intersection of the two lines as the 'Break-even point'.

6 The area to the right of the break-even point between the sales revenue line and total costs line is the profit area. The area to the left of the break-even point between the total costs line and sales revenue line is the loss area. Label the 'Profit' area and 'Loss' areas.

7 The margin of safety can also be shown on the graph. It is the difference between the budgeted sales (150 units) and break-even sales (120 units). Place a ruler on 150 units and extend a broken line up to the sales revenue line and extend over to the vertical axis. It should intersect the vertical axis at €3 000. Label these areas as 'Margin of safety'.

If the graph is drawn accurately it is possible to read information off the graph without doing detailed calculations. Try to read the following information from the graph:

a The total costs if 110 units are sold (answer: €2 300)
b The sales revenue if 90 units are sold (answer: €1 800)
c The fixed costs if 80 units are sold (answer €1 200)
d If 160 units are sold, will a profit or loss be made? (answer: profit)
e If 70 units are sold, will a profit or loss be made? (answer: loss)

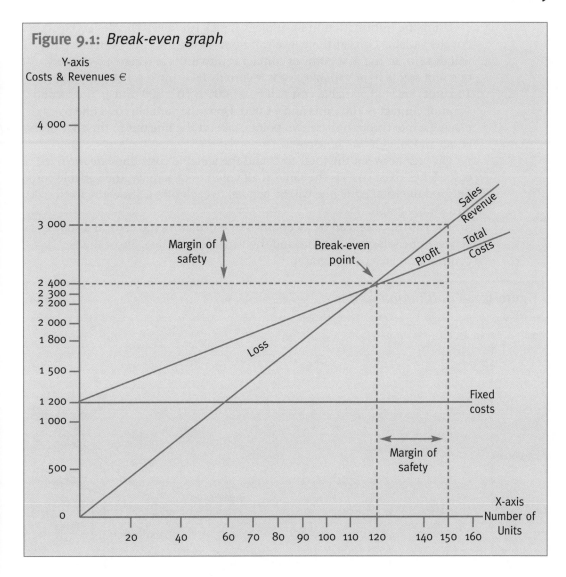

Figure 9.1: *Break-even graph*

Contribution graph

An alternative representation of cost volume profit information is illustrated in the contribution graph. This graph represents the same information as the break-even graph with the exception of fixed costs. It also shows the variable costs line.

Construction of the contribution graph

This graph is constructed in the same way as the break-even graph except for the fixed costs line. The fixed costs line is not shown and in its place the variable costs line is shown. To draw the variable costs line it is necessary to have two points of contact.

Using the information in Example 9.1, pick two levels of sales and work out the variable costs at these levels. If no units are sold then variable costs will be zero, so the first point of contact is zero units and zero €. For every one unit sold €10 of variable cost is incurred. Take any level of sales, e.g., if 100 units are sold, variable cost will be €1 000 (€10 x 100 units). The second point of contact is 100 units and €1 000. Draw the variable costs line by placing a rule through these two points, extend the line out to the edge of the graph and label it 'Variable costs'.

The area between the total costs and the variable costs lines are the fixed costs. Since fixed costs is the same at all volumes of activity, the variable costs line and the total costs line will be parallel to each other. Show the fixed costs area on the graph.

The contribution can be ascertained by calculating the vertical distance between the sales revenue line and the variable costs line. Show the contribution area on the graph.

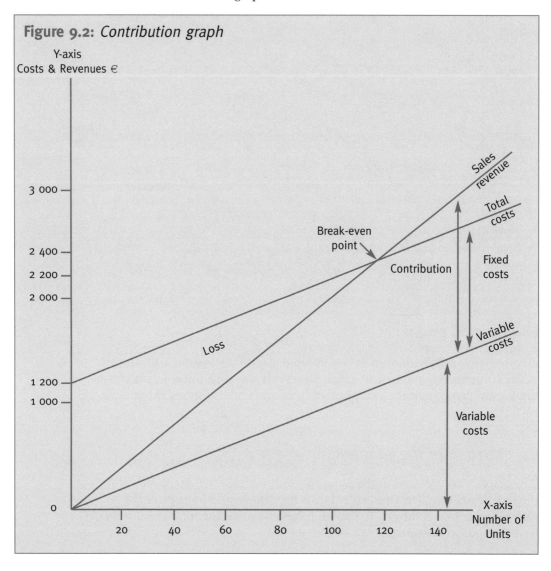

Figure 9.2: *Contribution graph*

Profit/volume graph

Neither the break-even graph nor the contribution graph show the profit or loss at different levels of output. The profit/volume graph shows the effect of changes of volume on profit.

Construction of profit/volume graph

The horizontal axis represents volume of units. The vertical axis above zero represents profit and the vertical axis below zero represents loss.

There is only one line plotted on this graph: the 'profit/loss' line. Using the information in Example 9.1, we need to plot the 'profit/loss' line using two points of contact. When units sold are zero there will be no sales revenue or variable costs, but there will be fixed costs. At zero units there will be a loss of €1 200, i.e., the fixed costs. The first point on the line will intersect zero units and –€1 200. Take any other level of sales, e.g., if we sell 130 units the profit will be:

		TOTAL €
Contribution	€10 x 130 units	1 300
Less: Fixed costs		(1 200)
Profit/(loss)		100

The second point on the line will intersect 130 units and €100. Draw the line through these two points and extend out towards the edge of the graph and label 'Profit/loss'.

The break-even point was calculated in Example 9.1.a as 120 units. Notice that the 'profit/loss' line intersects the X-axis at 120 units. At this point there is neither a profit nor a loss. It is the break-even point. Label the intersection of the two lines as the 'Break-even point'.

The area to the right of the break-even point between the horizontal axis and the 'profit/loss' line is the profit area. The area to the left of the break-even point between the horizontal axis and the 'profit/loss' line is the loss area. Label the 'Profit' area and 'Loss' area.

If the graph is drawn accurately it is possible to read information off the graph without doing detailed calculations. Try to read the following information from the graph:

a   The profit or loss if 80 units are sold (answer: loss of €400)
b   The profit or loss if 110 units are sold (answer: loss of €100)
c   The profit or loss if 140 units are sold (answer: profit of €200)

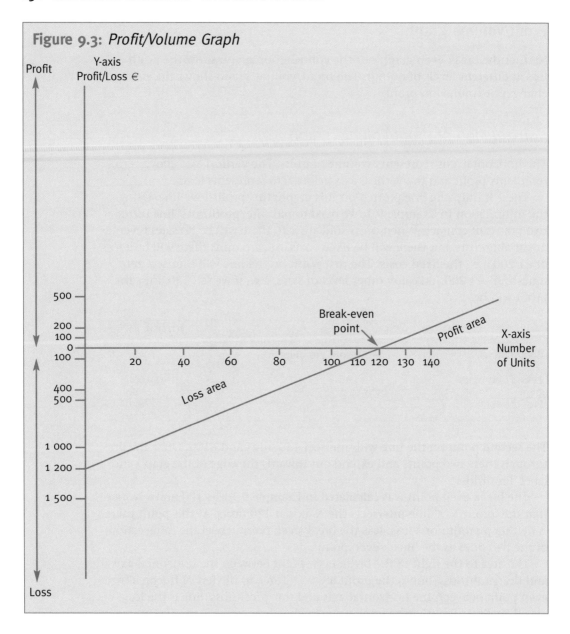

Figure 9.3: *Profit/Volume Graph*

Benefits of using graphs to illustrate cost volume profit information

1 Graphs are a visual representation of mathematical information and may be easier for non-accountants to use.

2 Information at different levels of activity can be read from the graph without doing detailed calculations. For example, in the profit/volume graph it is easy to read off the profit or loss at different levels of activity.

3 CVP analysis is done using spreadsheets and graphs can easily be produced using spreadsheet functions.

Cost volume profit analysis in a sales mix

Where a company sells a variety of products in a sales mix, CVP analysis can be applied.

(1) Individual break-even points

Individual break-even points can be established where products do not share fixed costs or where fixed costs can easily and fairly be split between products. The individual break-even points are then added together to give one overall break-even point for the company.

Example 9.6

A company sells three different types of wireless routers – Select, Selectpro and the Basic. The following financial information is available:

€ PER UNIT	SELECT	SELECTPRO	BASIC
Selling price	50.00	75.00	30.00
Less: Variable costs	(15.00)	(56.25)	(18.00)
Contribution per unit	35.00	18.75	12.00

	SELECT	SELECTPRO	BASIC	TOTAL
Fixed costs	€2 450	€1 250	€3 200	€6 900

Required

Calculate individual break-even points in sales revenue and an overall break-even point in sales revenue for the company.

Solution to Example 9.6

Calculate the C/S ratio for each product:

	SELECT	SELECTPRO	BASIC
$\dfrac{\text{Contribution}}{\text{Sales}} \times 100$	$\dfrac{35}{50} \times 100$	$\dfrac{18.75}{75} \times 100$	$\dfrac{12}{30} \times 100$
	=	=	=
C/S ratio	70%	25%	40%

Calculate the break-even point (sales revenue):

	SELECT	SELECTPRO	BASIC	OVERALL
Fixed costs	€2 450	€1 250	€3 200	
C/S ratio	70%	25%	40%	
	=	=	=	
Break-even point (sales revenue)	€3 500	€5 000	€8 000	€16 500

Fixed costs have already been allocated directly to products, and the break-even point (sales revenue) is calculated for each product. Individual break-even points (sales revenue) are added together to give an overall break-even point (sales revenue) of €16 500.

In reality this method is unlikely to be used as it is unusual for fixed costs to be apportioned directly to individual products.

(2) Overall break-even points

An overall break-even point can be established where it is not easy to apportion fixed costs over individual products or where fixed costs are not identifiable with individual products. A sales mix is established and a weighted average contribution in the current sales mix is calculated. A C/S ratio is established to work out the break-even point.

Example 9.7

A company sells three types of bulbs – Incandescent Spot, Halogen and Green CVL. The following financial information is available:

€ PER UNIT	INCANDESCENT SPOT	HALOGEN LAMP	GREEN CVL LAMP
Selling price	50.00	75.00	30.00
Less: Variable costs	(15.00)	(56.25)	(18.00)
Contribution per unit	35.00	18.75	12.00

The total fixed costs are €6 900 and they cannot be fairly allocated to individual products. The company plans to sell 300 units of the Incandescent Spot, 200 units of the Halogen and 100 units of the Green CVL.

Required

Calculate an overall break-even point (units and sales revenue) for the company. In your workings show the individual break-even points (units and sales revenue) for each product.

Solution to Example 9.7

The sales mix is:

	UNITS	SALES MIX
Incandescent Spot	300	3/6
Halogen	200	2/6
Green CVL	100	1/6
Total	600	

Work out the weighted average contribution per unit by multiplying the contribution per unit for each product by the sales mix:

€ PER UNIT	INCANDESCENT SPOT	HALOGEN LAMP	GREEN CVL LAMP
Contribution per unit €	35.00	18.75	12.00
x	x	x	x
Sales mix	3/6	2/6	1/6
=	=	=	=
Weighted average contribution per unit €	17.50	6.25	2.00

The overall weighted average contribution per unit is €25.75 (€17.50 + €6.25 + €2.00).

Next work out the break-even point (units):

	OVERALL
Fixed costs ⎯⎯⎯⎯⎯ Contribution per unit	€6 900 ⎯⎯⎯⎯ €25.75
=	=
Break-even point (units)	268 (to nearest whole unit)

In the current sales mix the break-even point is 268 units. To calculate the break-even point in sales revenue, it is necessary to allocate the 268 break-even units to the three products using the current sales mix, then multiply the units by the selling price per unit:

	SALES MIX		BREAK-EVEN UNITS		BREAK-EVEN UNITS IN CURRENT SALES MIX		SELLING PRICE PER UNIT €		BREAK-EVEN (SALES REVENUE) €
Incandescent Spot	3/6	x	268	=	134	x	50	=	6 700
Halogen Lamp	2/6	x	268	=	89	x	75	=	6 675
Green CVL Lamp	1/6	x	268	=	45	x	30	=	1 350
Total					268				14 725

The break-even sales revenue in the current sales mix is €14 725.

Separating semi-variable costs using the high-low method

To analyse semi-variable costs into the fixed cost element and variable cost per unit element, it is necessary to use the 'high-low method'. This method involves comparing the total costs at the highest and lowest levels of activity. The difference in costs is assumed to be caused by the variable cost element. The variable cost per unit is calculated by dividing the difference in costs by the difference in the levels of activity. Since the total cost is known, the variable cost per unit can be used to derive the fixed cost.

The high-low method is a very simple method to apply but assumes that fixed costs remain fixed at all levels of activity and that the variable cost per unit remains constant. The high-low method uses only two pairs of data and may result in inaccurate information. For more accurate analysis the scatter graph method or least-squares regression method should be used, as they incorporate all available pairs of data. For the purposes of simplicity the high-low method is used in this book.

Example 9.8

Total costs for the last five years along with levels of activity are listed below:

YEAR	LEVEL OF ACTIVITY, UNITS	TOTAL COSTS €
1	3 000	11 000
2	5 000	15 000
3	750	6 500
4	4 500	14 000
5	1 000	7 000

Required

a   Using the high-low method calculate the variable cost per unit and the total fixed costs

b   Use the information calculated in (a) to estimate the total cost if 6 000 units are produced

Solution to Example 9.8

a   Compare the total costs at the highest and lowest levels of activity:

YEAR	LEVEL OF ACTIVITY, UNITS	TOTAL COSTS €
2	5 000	15 000
3	750	6 500
Difference	4 250	8 500

As the level of activity has increased by 4 250 units total costs have increased by €8 500. Total costs include a fixed element, which is fixed regardless of the level of activity, and a variable cost per unit element, which varies with the level of activity.

Calculate the variable cost per unit by dividing the difference in total costs by the difference in units:

$$\frac{\text{Difference in total costs €}}{\text{Difference in units}} = \text{variable cost per unit €}$$

$$\frac{\text{€8 500}}{\text{4 250 units}} = \text{€2 per unit}$$

Calculate the fixed costs by deducting the variable costs from the total costs at any level of activity.

For example, choose year 5 where there were 1 000 units and total cost was €7 000:

	€
Total cost	7 000
Less: Variable cost (€2 x 1 000 units)	(2 000)
Fixed costs	5 000

The variable cost per unit is €2 and the fixed costs are €5 000.

b   Calculate the total cost if 6 000 units are produced:

	€
Variable cost (€2 x 6 000 units)	12 000
Fixed cost	5 000
Total cost	17 000

Assumptions of cost volume profit analysis

1 Assumes that selling price per unit and variable cost per unit are constant within the relevant range. In reality, as sales volumes increase, the unit selling price may fall as discounts are applied for bulk sells. If production volumes increase, variable costs per unit may fall as discounts may be received for bulk purchases.

2 Assumes that fixed costs are constant within the relevant range. This may be untrue if volumes of output increase. The production process may become more complex requiring investment in fixed costs, e.g., new machinery.

3 Assumes a single product is sold or if there is a sales mix that it is constant. In reality the sales mix may need to be changed at different volumes of sales to stimulate demand.

4 Applies to short-term decision-making since in the long term all costs are variable.

5 Assumes that production and sales are the same or there is no significant change in inventories during the period under review. In reality inventories fluctuate from period to period.

6 Assumes that costs can easily be analysed as fixed or variable. In reality semi-variable costs can be problematic to split into their fixed and variable elements, and unless they are, CVP analysis cannot be applied.

7 Assumes that decisions are based on quantitative information and ignores the role that qualitative information plays in decision-making.

Chapter summary

CVP analysis provides managers with a tool with which to maximise profitability. The trade-off between selling price, variable costs, fixed costs and sales volume is analysed and the most favourable combination is sought.

In this chapter concepts which allow managers to make better decisions were introduced, such as break-even point, margin of safety, the C/S ratio, target profit, operating leverage and sales mix.

The use of graphs to illustrate CVP data was demonstrated. The chapter concluded by discussing the assumptions on which CVP analysis is based.

Test questions

Question 1*

A company manufactures a USB cable, and had the following results for last year:

	TOTAL €	PER UNIT €
Sales	8 000	20
Less: Variable costs	(4 000)	(10)
Contribution	4 000	10
Less: Fixed costs	(2 400)	
Profit/(loss)	1 600	

Required

a Calculate the break-even point in units and sales revenue
b Calculate the contribution sales ratio
c Calculate the margin of safety in units and sales revenue
d How many units would need to be sold to achieve a target profit of
   €5 000?
e Using the original data, if sales increase by €4 000 next year and the
   selling price per unit, the variable cost per unit and fixed costs remain the
   same, calculate by how much the company's profit will increase
f Calculate the company's degree of operating leverage using the original
   data in the question
g Using your answer to (f), calculate the percentage impact on profit of a 7%
   increase in sales. Verify your answer by preparing a new profit and loss
   statement
h Using the original data, the company is considering an investment which
   will increase fixed costs by €2 000 but, as a result, the selling price per unit
   can be increased by €2 and sales will increase by 10%. Advise the company
   on whether this investment should take place

Notes to students

1 Operating leverage is a measure of how sensitive profit is to a percentage
   change in sales.
2 Calculate operating leverage by dividing contribution by profit.
3 Multiply the operating leverage by the percentage change in sales to assess
   the impact on profit.
4 Remember that you can verify that your figures are correct by slotting
   them into a profit and loss statement.

* Based on question E7.1 in W. Seal, R. H. Garrison and E. Noreen, *Management
Accounting*, 2nd edition, McGraw Hill, 2006.

Question 2*

A company produces and sells memory sticks which have the following selling price and variable cost:

	€
Selling price per unit	7.00
Less. Variable costs per unit	(3 50)
Contribution per unit	3.50

Fixed costs are €70 000 and the company currently sells 25 000 units.

Required

a   Calculate the company's current profit or loss
b   Calculate the break-even point in units and sales revenue
c   Calculate the contribution sales ratio
d   Using your answer to (c), calculate the effect on profit if the company increased its sales by €3 500 and the selling price per unit, the variable costs per unit and the fixed costs remained the same. Verify your answer by preparing a new profit and loss statement showing an increase in sales of €3 500
e   Calculate the company's degree of operating leverage using the original data in the question
f   Using your answer to (e), calculate the percentage impact on profit of a 10% decrease in sales. Verify your answer by preparing a new profit and loss statement

Notes to students

1   Contribution and sales are related and a percentage increase in one will result in a percentage increase in another.
2   You will need to use the contribution sales ratio in part (d) and also to verify your answer using a profit and loss statement.
3   Remember to answer all parts of the question to maximise your marks.

* Based on question L9.2 in Alice Luby, *Cost and Management Accounting*, Gill & Macmillan, 1999.

Question 3*

The management accountant at Molly O'Leary Chocolates Ltd is unsure of the level of production for the next accounting period and has produced two flexible budgets at two different levels of activity:

	FLEXED BUDGET A: 50 000 BOXES	FLEXED BUDGET B: 70 000 BOXES
Selling price per box of chocolates	€10	€10
Budgeted profit/(loss)	€50 000	€90 000

Required

Prepare the following calculations for the company:

a   The contribution per box of chocolates
b   The variable costs per box of chocolates and the fixed costs
c   The break-even point for the company in boxes of chocolates and sales revenue
d   A flexed budget if 60 000 boxes were to be sold

Notes to students

1   This question incorporates CVP analysis and flexible budgeting.
2   A flexible budget is prepared when a company is unsure of the level of activity for a forthcoming period and so prepares several budgets at different levels of activity. Flexible budgeting is discussed in **Chapter 6: Budgetary Planning and Control**.
3   The selling price per box, variable costs per box, contribution per box and total fixed costs will be the same at all levels of activity. It is easy then to prepare a flexible budget at 60 000 boxes.

* Based on question 6 in ATI Management Accounting, Summer 2008.

For answers and additional test questions, see www.gillmacmillan.ie. Search for Management Accounting and click on the link in the right-hand column.

10 Relevant Costing and Decision-Making

Learning outcomes of Chapter 10

At the end of this chapter, you will be able to:

- explain the meaning of relevance in management accounting
- discuss the use of marginal costing principles in decision-making
- explain the relevance of various costs such as fixed costs, past costs, committed costs, opportunity costs, depreciation and other non-cash items and variable costs in decision-making
- provide advice with supporting quantitative analysis for decisions that may need to be made
- discuss why absorption costing is not used when making short-term decisions
- discuss the use of qualitative information in decision-making

Introduction

In **Chapter 8: Marginal and Absorption Costing**, it was explained that management accountants use marginal costing principles when making decisions about businesses. Marginal costing assumes that all fixed costs, and fixed production overheads in particular, are fixed in the short-term and are irrelevant to any short-term decisions. In this chapter we will discuss the role of marginal costing principles in decision-making and we will see that in some situations fixed costs are relevant.

Terminology used in decision-making will be explained. The relevance of various costs such as fixed costs, past costs, committed costs, opportunity costs, depreciation and other non-cash items and variable costs will be explained in relation to their use in decision-making.

Examples of decisions that businesses may need to make will be examined and advice on the decision will be given along with the quantitative analysis.

Another concept introduced in this chapter will be a limiting factor approach. Businesses may need to make decisions where capacity constraints exist such as limited availability of materials, labour or machine hours. A limiting factor approach will be used to make the appropriate decision. Where products are produced using process costing a decision may need to be made on whether to sell the products at the split-off point or process them further and then sell. This concept will be explained using an example.

Decision-making using marginal costing information

Decisions can be based on financial accounting information, i.e., absorption costing, or management accounting information, i.e., marginal costing.

Marginal costing assumes that all fixed costs are fixed in the short term and are irrelevant to any short-term decisions. An example of a fixed cost is the rent on the factory or business. Usually a rental agreement is entered into for a year. The business is committed to paying the rent for the year. The rent will be paid regardless of any decisions the business makes, e.g., increasing production or hiring new equipment.

However, if as a result of a decision the company needs to invest in additional fixed costs, e.g., rent a new factory, then the increase in the fixed costs is relevant to the decision and should be included in the quantitative analysis.

If as a result of a decision the company will save on fixed costs, e.g., no longer renting an office, then the saving in the fixed costs is relevant to the decision and should be included in the quantitative analysis.

In general, the absorption of fixed overheads is irrelevant in decision-making. Absorption of fixed overheads is a method of allocating fixed overheads to products or departments using, for example, machine hours or labour hours. For a more detailed discussion of absorption costing see **Chapter 3: Production Costing – Overheads**. The actual fixed overheads will be paid by the company anyway so if a product is discontinued, the fixed overheads will still have to be paid and the absorption of fixed overheads is not relevant in decision-making.

Any short-term decision that the business needs to make will be based on contribution, not on profit. Contribution is sales less variable production costs. Contribution was discussed in **Chapter 8: Marginal and Absorption Costing**.

The meaning of relevance in decision-making

When making a decision about the future, e.g., producing more units, accepting a new contract or sub-contracting some work, the company needs to establish the costs and benefits involved in the decision and decide whether they are relevant to the decision. Should they be included in the decision quantitative analysis process? The decisions which we will consider in this chapter are assumed to be short-term decisions. In **Chapter 11: Capital Investment Decisions**, we will consider more long-term decisions. It is up to each business to determine what a short-term decision is and what a long-term decision is for it.

When deciding on whether a cost or revenue is relevant to the decision, the following question should be asked: if I go ahead with this decision will I incur this cost or revenue? If the answer is yes, then the cost is considered to be an avoidable cost or avoidable revenue and is relevant to the decision. If the answer is no, then the cost or revenue is considered to be unavoidable, it will be incurred regardless of the decision made, and it is irrelevant to the decision.

Since decisions will affect the future of the business, only future cash inflows and cash outflows will be considered in the decision. It is impossible to know future cash inflows and cash outflows with certainty, so in reality the figures included in decisions will have varying degrees of uncertainty attached to them. In the examples and questions in this chapter, we will assume that all future cash inflows and outflows are known with certainty.

Consider the relevance of the following costs:

(1) The relevance of past costs in decision-making

Decisions which a business will make are based on future costs relevant to that decision. Past costs or 'historic costs' are not relevant as they have already occurred or are already committed. Past costs are ignored in decision-making. Another name for a past cost is a 'sunk cost'.

Consider a new product that a business is thinking of producing. It requires the hire of a piece of equipment and the use of 1 000 kg of raw materials. The company has the raw materials in stock and they were purchased last year and they have no other use in the business. What are the relevant costs which the company needs to consider in its decision? The hire of equipment is relevant to the decision. If the new product didn't go ahead, the equipment would not be hired. The raw materials are irrelevant as the company has these in stock. The raw materials were purchased last year and are considered to be a past or sunk cost and are not relevant to the decision.

However, if the raw materials could be used elsewhere in the business but are used on the new product, the raw materials would be a relevant cost.

(2) The relevance of committed costs in decision-making

Committed costs such as a contract that has already been entered into or staff who are on contract and whom the company is committed to pay are considered to be irrelevant in decision-making. These costs will be paid regardless of any decisions made.

(3) The relevance of opportunity costs in decision-making

CIMA Official Terminology defines opportunity costs as 'the value of the benefit sacrificed when one course of action is chosen in preference to an alternative. The opportunity cost is represented by the foregone potential benefit from the best rejected course of action'.

Consider an example where a company has only 500 labour hours available in the month, and it cannot avail of any other labour. It can use the labour hours on Project A which would earn a contribution of €5 000, or Project B which would earn a contribution of €5 500. If the company chose to use the available labour for Project B, the opportunity cost is the loss of contribution on Project A, i.e., €5 000. Opportunity costs are relevant in decision-making.

(4) The relevance of depreciation and other non-cash items in decision-making

Depreciation is not a cash item but an adjustment in the financial accounts. It does not represent a future cash flow. Depreciation is treated as an expense in the income statement but it is not relevant to any future decisions the business will make.

(5) The relevance of variable costs in decision-making

Variable costs include materials, labour and variable overheads. Consider a new product the business is thinking of introducing. Are the variable costs, i.e., the materials, labour and variable overhead costs, relevant to the decision? In answering this question consider if the costs are a cash cost and if they will be incurred in the future. If the answer is yes, then the variable costs are relevant to the decision.

Perhaps the business has some materials already in stock which it could use in making the new product. Is this cost relevant? The answer is no, it is a sunk cost and while the stock can be used in making the new product, the cost of the stock has already been incurred and there is no future cash cost involved.

Maybe the stock already on hand will have to be replaced. Is this cost relevant to the decision? The answer is yes, the replacement cost is a future cash cost and is relevant to the decision.

Labour is a relevant cost only if the staff involved can be hired and laid off on a casual basis. If staff are on contract and they are available to work on the contract, they are considered to be a fixed cost and are not a relevant cost in the decision-making. The company will incur their cost regardless of the decision made.

Relevant costs are also called 'incremental costs' and 'avoidable costs'. While an attempt has been made in notes (1) to (5) above to cover all incremental costs the student may encounter, others may appear which are not covered above. If so, the student should consider only future costs or revenues or incremental costs or revenues and opportunity costs as being relevant in decision-making. Past costs, sunk costs, historic costs or committed costs are irrelevant in decision-making.

Types of decision

(1) Accepting or rejecting decisions

If the benefits of doing something outweigh the costs, then the decision should be to go ahead with it. Consider the following example which illustrates this point:

Example 10.1

Dara Murphy, a mother with two children, studied for a two-year certificate in accounting five years ago. Unfortunately, she had to leave the course after one year but she has been offered a place on a part-time course to complete the qualification. The course will involve lectures two nights a week for 24 weeks over the year. She is concerned about the costs involved but her boss has said that if she qualifies, she will receive a bonus of €3 000. From a financial point of view can you advise Dara on whether she should accept or reject the offer of the place on the course?

Dara has gathered the following information on the costs she believes will be incurred if she returns to studying:

Cost of the course for one year	€800
Cost of hiring a babysitter for two nights a week for 24 weeks	€1 250
Transport costs – Dara purchased an annual unlimited travel bus ticket earlier in the year	€750
Cost of a laptop bought last month for home use and study use	€500
Cost of software necessary for the course	€100
Cost of dinner for two nights a week for 24 weeks. Dara will not have time to go home for dinner and will have to eat out the nights of the course	€450
Cost of lunch for two days a week for 24 weeks. Dara usually eats out at lunchtime three days a week and brings her own lunch in the other two days	€300
Total costs	€4 150

Solution to Example 10.1

Initially from the figures that Dara has presented it does not look feasible from a financial perspective for her to return to studying as the costs involved, i.e., €4 150, are greater than the bonus, i.e., €3 000. However, upon closer inspection it is revealed that not all the costs listed are relevant to her decision. A detailed analysis of the costs reveals the following:

Cost of the course for one year	€800

This is a relevant cost. It will be incurred if Dara decides to go ahead with the course and it will be saved if she decides not to go ahead.

Cost of hiring a babysitter for two nights a week for 24 weeks	€1 250

This cost is relevant. Dara must include the cost of hiring a babysitter over the 24 weeks. If she didn't do the course then she wouldn't incur the cost. The cost is relevant to the decision.

Transport costs	€0

Dara purchased an annual unlimited travel bus ticket costing €750. She has already purchased the ticket so it is a sunk cost and she will not incur any additional costs if she needs to take additional bus journeys to go to her lectures. The transport costs are not relevant to her decision.

Cost of the laptop	€0

The laptop was bought last month and is therefore considered to be a sunk cost, as Dara has bought it regardless of the decision that she makes regarding the course.

Cost of software	€100

The cost of the software is a relevant cost and should be included in the decision. The software would not be purchased if Dara did not go ahead with the course.

Cost of dinner	€450

This cost of dinner is a relevant cost as Dara will not have time to go home and eat dinner on two nights per week for the duration of the course. This is a relevant cost and should be included in the decision.

Cost of lunch	€0

Dara eats out for lunch three days a week anyway, so there is no additional lunch cost involved if Dara decides to go ahead with the course.

Total incremental costs	€2 600
Bonus earned if Dara qualifies	€3 000
Net increase in income	€400

If only the relevant costs are taken into account in making the decision then Dara will have a net increase of €400 in her income in the year in which she qualifies. From a financial or quantitative point of view Dara should accept the place on the course. Of course the decision is based on the assumption that Dara will pass her exams and earn the bonus.

(2) Make or buy decisions

Example 10.2

Rapid Wheelies Ltd produces motorcycles and components for motorcycles. It produces a part called 'Inter-flow tube' or 'IFT' for short. An outside supplier has offered to produce the IFT for a price of €30 per tube. The budgeted production of the IFT is 5 000 tubes for the next accounting year.

The cost of producing the IFT in-house is as follows:

	€ per tube
Direct materials	10
Direct labour	12
Variable overheads	4
Fixed overhead absorbed	5
Depreciation of machinery	4
Total cost per tube	35

As management accountant you are required to make the decision to continue to make the IFT in-house or buy from an outside supplier. Prepare any necessary calculations to support your decision.

Solution to Example 10.2

Relevant costs of producing the IFT in-house:

Direct materials €10

The direct materials are a variable cost. If production of the IFT continues in-house, the direct materials costs will be incurred and if the IFT is bought from the outside supplier the direct material costs will be saved. Direct materials are relevant to the decision.

Direct labour €12

Direct labour is a variable cost. See direct materials for an explanation as to why they are relevant to the decision.

Variable overheads €4

Variable overheads are a variable cost. See direct materials for an explanation as to why they are relevant to the decision.

Fixed overhead absorbed €0

Fixed overhead absorbed is irrelevant in decision-making. Rapid Wheelies Ltd will continue to incur the fixed overhead upon which the fixed overhead absorbed is based regardless of whether the IFT is produced in-house or bought from an outside supplier.

Depreciation of machinery €0

Depreciation is irrelevant in decision-making. It is not a cash item and it will not be saved if Rapid Wheelies Ltd decides to buy the IFT from an outside supplier. If the machinery is used only for the production of the IFT and could be sold, any money received for its sale would be relevant to the decision. We are not told this information in the question, so we must assume that the machinery has other uses in the company.

Relevant costs of producing IFT in-house	€26
Cost of buying IFT from outside supplier	€30
Saving if IFT is produced in-house	€4
	x
	5 000 tubes
	=
Total saving if IFT is produced in-house	€20 000

Since it costs €4 less per tube to produce it in-house, Rapid Wheelies Ltd should continue to produce the IFT. This represents a saving of €20 000 over the next accounting year.

(3) Shut-down decisions

Example 10.3

A mobile phone company has four divisions (covering the four provinces in Ireland), which are all located in the Head Office building in Galway. Each division is considered to be a profit centre. Call centres engage in direct selling of mobile phone products to customers. The call centre for Munster is operating at a loss and the Head Office is considering closing it. The following budgeted information is available for Munster for the next accounting year:

	€ 000
Sales	150
Less: Variable cost of sales	(90)
Contribution	60
Less: Fixed costs	
Insurance costs	(7)
Office rent	(10)
Call centre staff salaries	(50)
Advertising costs	(5)
Profit/(loss)	(12)

Points to Note

1 Sales represent the revenue earned by direct sales made by the Munster division.
2 Insurance costs are fixed, relate to the entire building, and are split evenly among the four divisions. They will be paid regardless of whether the Munster division closes or not.
3 Office rent is fixed, relates to the entire building and is split evenly among the four divisions. If the Munster division is closed, the company will still have to pay the rent on the entire building.
4 All staff working in the Munster division are on short-term contracts and will be discharged if the division is closed.
5 Advertising costs represent direct advertising of each division and are avoidable if the division is closed.
6 Variable cost of sales refers to the cost of the mobile phone products on offer to customers. If the Munster division is closed, these costs will be avoided.

The following budgeted information is available concerning the company for the next accounting year. This includes all costs and revenues for the four provinces, including Munster:

	€ 000
Sales	5 000
Less: Variable cost of sales	(3 000)
Contribution	2 000
Less: Fixed costs	
Insurance costs	(28)
Office rent	(40)
Call centre staff salaries	(250)
Advertising costs	(30)
Profit/(loss)	1 652

Required

From a financial perspective calculate whether it would be in the interests of the Head Office to close the Munster division. Comment on your findings and discuss why each cost and revenue is relevant or irrelevant to the decision.

Solution to Example 10.3

Effect on Head Office budgeted profits if the Munster division is closed:

	€ 000
Loss of sales revenue in Munster division (note i)	(150)
Insurance costs (note ii)	–
Office rent (note iii)	–
Saving of call centre staff salaries (note iv)	50
Saving of advertising costs (note v)	5
Saving of variable costs of sales (note vi)	90
Decrease in budgeted profits of Head Office if Munster division is closed	(5)

Comment: The calculations show that the future profits of Head Office would decline by €5 000 if the Munster division were to close. Therefore, the Munster division should not be closed. Perhaps the company could consider a more equitable allocation of insurance costs and office rent to the four divisions.

Notes to students

1 The sales revenue in the Munster division is relevant to the decision as this revenue will be lost to the Head Office if Munster closes.
2 Insurance costs relate to the entire building and are split evenly among the four divisions. They are irrelevant to the decision as they will be paid regardless of whether the Munster division closes.
3 Office rent relates to the entire building and is split evenly amongst the four divisions. It is irrelevant to the decision as it will be paid regardless of whether the Munster division closes.
4 Call centre staff are on short-term contracts. They are a relevant cost as they will be discharged if the Munster division is closed and their salaries will be saved.
5 Advertising costs represent direct advertising of each division and are avoidable if the division is closed. Advertising costs are relevant to the decision.
6 Variable cost of sales refers to the cost of the mobile phone products on offer to customers. If the Munster division is closed, these costs will be avoided. Variable cost of sales is relevant to the decision.

(4) Limiting factor decisions

A limiting factor is 'anything which limits the activity of an entity. An entity seeks to optimise the benefits it obtains from the limiting factor', *CIMA Official Terminology*.

A limiting factor is a constraint which limits production and in most cases it will be raw materials, labour hours or machine hours. In the situations which we will consider we will assume that the capacity constraint is a short-term one which is unavoidable.

A company's objective is to maximise profit and since fixed costs are unavoidable in the short term, the company's objective is to maximise contribution. It makes sense that the products which have the highest contribution not just per unit but per limiting factory, e.g., per machine hour if that is the constraint, should be produced first, then the next product with the highest contribution per limiting factor and so on.

When preparing a production plan where there is a capacity constraint follow these steps:

1 Calculate the shortfall of the limiting factor
2 Calculate the contribution per unit of each product
3 Calculate the contribution per limiting factor of each product
4 Determine the production plan which will maximise the company's contribution and profit by ranking the products in order of production
5 Calculate the total contribution and profit using the production plan

Consider the following example:

Example 10.4

A company produces three products – X, Y and Z – and has the following contributions per unit and labour hours per unit:

	X	Y	Z
Contribution per unit	€248	€275	€413
Labour hours per unit	4	5.5	7

Labour is available for 15 000 hours only in a period. Fixed costs for the period are €500 000.

The maximum demand for the products is:

X	Y	Z
1 000	1 500	900

Required

a Calculate the shortfall in labour hours
b Determine the best production plan, assuming that the company wishes to maximise profit
c Calculate the profit that could be achieved from the plan in part (b) above

Solution to Example 10.4

a Calculate the shortfall in labour hours

	LABOUR HOURS PER UNIT x UNITS	TOTAL LABOUR HOURS REQUIRED
X	4 hours x 1 000 units =	4 000
Y	5.5 hours x 1 500 units =	8 250
Z	7 hours x 900 units =	6 300
	Total labour hours required	18 550
	Labour hours available	(15 000)
	Shortfall in labour hours	3 550

b   Determine the best production plan, assuming that the company wishes
to maximise profit
The contribution per unit is already available in this question. The next
step is to calculate the contribution per limiting factor, i.e., per labour
hour, and determine the best production plan by ranking the products in
order of priority:

	CONTRIBUTION PER UNIT €		LABOUR HOURS PER UNIT		CONTRIBUTION PER LABOUR HOUR €	RANK IN ORDER OF PRODUCTION
X	248	/	4	=	62	1st
Y	275	/	5.5	=	50	3rd
Z	413	/	7	=	59	2nd

c   Calculate the profit that could be achieved from the plan in part (b) above

	TOTAL LABOUR HOURS REQUIRED		LABOUR HOURS PER UNIT		UNITS PRODUCED UNDER PRODUCTION PLAN		CONTRIBUTION PER UNIT		TOTAL CONTRIBUTION €
X	4 000	/	4	=	1 000	X	248	=	248 000
Z	6 300	/	7	=	900	X	413	=	371 700
Y	4 700	/	5.5	=	855	X	275	=	235 125
	15 000						Total contribution		854 825
							Less: Fixed costs		(500 000)
							Profit		354 825

There are only 15 000 labour hours available. If X (4 000 hours) and Z
(6 300 hours) are to be produced this will leave only 4 700 hours to
produce Y.

A common error with limiting factor questions is that the student bases
the decision on the contribution per unit and not on the contribution per

limiting factor. If the decision is based on contribution per unit, the profit will not be maximised. Try it out and see.

This method can be used only where there is a single limiting factor. Where there are two or more constraints, then linear programming and simplex techniques are used. Only single constraints are covered in this book.

(5) Decisions on whether to sell at split-off point or process further and then sell

In **Chapter 5: Process Costing**, we looked at how a business values production units and closing inventory where products are produced using mass production. The company may have to make a decision to sell its products after it has completed the process, i.e., the split-off point, or further process them and then sell the products for a higher price. Joint costs are the costs incurred in the initial process. See **Chapter 5: Process Costing** for a more detailed discussion of joint costs in process costing.

If the incremental revenue earned from further processing covers the incremental costs incurred from further processing then, from a financial point of view, the product should be processed further. Consider the following example:

Example 10.5

A company produces three products – canoes, kayaks and dinghies – all of which are completed using a series of processes. Upon competition of the final process, i.e., the split-off point, the company can sell the products at this point or process them further by upgrading the finish and then selling the enhanced product. The following information is available:

	CANOE €	KAYAK €	DINGHY €
Sales revenue at split-off point	80 000	75 000	30 000
Sales revenue after further processing	100 000	110 000	70 000
Joint costs	25 000	30 000	5 000
Post-separation costs	25 000	10 000	25 000

Required

Which product or products should be sold at the split-off point and which product or products should be processed further? Show your computations which have helped you arrive at your decision.

Solution to Example 10.5

In arriving at the decision to sell the product or products at the split-off point or to process it or them further it is necessary to look at the incremental revenues and costs of further processing:

	CANOE €	KAYAK €	DINGHY €
Sales revenue at the split-off point	(80 000)	(75 000)	(30 000)
Sales revenue after further processing	100 000	110 000	70 000
Incremental sales revenue	20 000	35 000	40 000
Less: Incremental costs			
Post-separation costs	(25 000)	(10 000)	(25 000)
Incremental profit/(loss)	(5 000)	25 000	15 000

At the point when the decision to process further or not is being made, the joint costs have already been incurred. They are a sunk cost and are irrelevant to the decision.

From the calculations above it shows that the Kayak and Dinghy should be processed further as it will lead to an increase in profit for both these products. The Canoe should be sold at the split-off point as its profit will decrease if it is processed further.

It should be noted that the above figures are dependent on the joint costs allocation method chosen. We are not told which method was used to allocate the joint costs to the three products. We can only surmise that an alternative method could result in deciding to process the Canoe further. For a more detailed discussion on allocating joint costs, look at **Chapter 5: Process Costing**.

Why not use absorption costing when making short-term decisions?

Grahame Steven in 'Management Accounting – Decision Management' states that using marginal costing as a decision-making tool may oversimplify a business's situation. He states that businesses may have many opportunities available to them and if they accept one contract, it may affect their ability to accept another more profitable one in the future. In this situation it is appropriate to use profit, i.e., absorption costing, and not contribution as the deciding factor. Marginal costing, he states, is more safely applied to one-off orders.

Marginal costing is suitable only when making short-term decisions. Over the long term, fixed costs can become variable. If a decision is being made that will have consequences over the long term, it would be more appropriate to base it on profit, i.e., absorption costing. Consider rent, it is a fixed cost in the short term, but viewed over a number of years it is a variable cost, as it may increase or decrease.

Steven states that most companies operate in complex, dynamic environments and are under pressure to achieve objectives over the long term and short term. Decisions to accept or reject projects should be made with caution. The marginal costing approach can be used but all information available to the business should be used in the decision.

Qualitative information

In the examples used above, we decided on a course of action using the quantitative or financial information in the question. This adopts a very simplistic approach to decision-making. Businesses operate in a complex and dynamic environment and it is unlikely that decisions can be made in isolation and solely on financial information.

Other relevant information, i.e., qualitative information, should be considered when making decisions. For example, if we decide to accept a new contract but this involves our staff working overtime, we should consider whether they are willing to work overtime, or whether they will be able to fulfil their other tasks if they are feeling tired. If not, how will this influence our decision? If we reject a contract purely on financial grounds, are we closing off the offer of future more lucrative contracts? If so how will this influence our decision?

Qualitative factors are difficult to measure as they are subjective and different values can be attributed to them depending on who is measuring them. When making decisions, the management accountant should try to put a measurable value on qualitative factors to eliminate the subjectivity. His or her decision should be based on both the qualitative and the quantitative factors.

Chapter summary

In this chapter, relevant costing and its importance in decision-making was explained. The difference between short-term and long-term decisions was explained. You learnt that short-term decisions should be based on marginal costing principles.

Different types of decisions were examined using examples. There is one common theme in all the examples – only future costs that differ between alternatives are relevant in decision-making. All other costs are unavoidable or irrelevant. Costs which are irrelevant are not affected by a decision. They will be incurred regardless of the course of action taken. A decision to go ahead with a course of action will be taken where the relevant revenues are greater than the relevant costs.

Not all decisions can be made purely on consideration of financial or quantitative information. In making a decision the management accountant should consider non-financial or qualitative information.

The decisions being made in this chapter are short-term decisions. It is up to the business to decide on what is short term and what is long term for it. It should be noted that in the long term all costs are variable and thus avoidable.

Test questions

Question 1*

Copper Kettles Ltd makes and sells 1 000 kettles per month. Its variable costs are €10 per kettle and its selling price is €13.50 per kettle. The company incurs fixed costs of €1 000 per month.

The company has spare capacity and is considering accepting a once-off order from a customer for 500 kettles. It will sell the kettles for €12.50 each and its variable costs will remain the same. If Copper Kettles accepts the order, its fixed costs will increase by €500 per month.

Required

a From a financial perspective should Copper Kettles accept the order?
b Discuss any qualitative factors that Copper Kettles should consider before making its decision

Notes to students

1 Base your decision on the additional or incremental costs and revenues incurred if the company accepts the order.
2 Existing fixed costs and additional fixed costs are mentioned. Consider which, if any, are relevant to the decision.
3 In part (b) you are asked to discuss any qualitative factors that should be considered by the company in making its decision. There is very limited information in the question about Copper Kettles so a comprehensive discussion is not possible in part (b). Your answer should discuss potential issues.

* Based on Ian James, 'Performance Management', *Financial Management* (November/December 2009).

Question 2

Rivervalley Waders Ltd makes three different types of products – plastic waders, rubber waders and oilskin waders. The selling price and variable costs for the three products are as follows:

	PLASTIC WADERS €	RUBBER WADERS €	OILSKIN WADERS €
Selling price	70	120	135
Direct materials	12	16	36
Direct labour	12	30	36

The company has the following orders for the month of January:

	PLASTIC WADERS €	RUBBER WADERS €	OILSKIN WADERS €
Units	2 500	1 000	750

Direct labour cost is €12 per hour and labour is in short supply. The company estimates that it will only have 6 200 labour hours available in January. Additional labour hours will not be available until February and the company is concerned that it will not meet its orders out of the available labour hours. Fixed costs are estimated to be €20 000 in January.

Required

a   Calculate the shortfall in labour hours
b   Determine the best production plan, assuming that Rivervalley Waders Ltd wishes to maximise profit
c   Calculate the profit that could be achieved from the plan in part (b) above
d   Discuss any qualitative factors that Rivervalley Waders Ltd would need to consider in determining its production plan
e   Rivervalley Waders Ltd believes that if it increases its labour rate per hour, it will be able to overcome its shortfall in labour hours. Calculate the maximum labour rate per hour which should be paid to overcome the shortfall. Explain your calculations

Notes to students

1   It is necessary to calculate the labour hours per unit first.
2   In part (d) discuss any other factors apart from quantitative factors which you would need to consider in your production plan. For example, consider the customers' reaction if they can only obtain part of their order from Rivervalley Waders Ltd.
3   In part (e) consider the fact that Rivervalley Waders Ltd will want to pay a labour rate per hour which will ensure the company at least breaks even.

Question 3*

Sean Murphy, a carpenter, designs and makes furniture. At present he produces beds, wardrobes and dressing tables. He is planning his production levels for the next three months based on firm orders, which are as follows:

	BED	WARDROBE	DRESSING TABLE
Units ordered	2 800	3 200	3 100

His selling prices and costs per unit are as follows:

	BED €	WARDROBE €	DRESSING TABLE €
Selling price	350	320	330
Raw materials: wood	50 (5 kg)	40 (4 kg)	42 (4.2 kg)
Other raw materials	32	25	38
Labour costs	36	32	36
Variable overheads	4	4	4

All materials and labour are variable costs. Sean's fixed costs are €75 000 for the three months. Sean is concerned about the wood. He can obtain only 35 000 kg of wood at the current price of €10 per kg for the next three months.

Required

a Calculate the shortfall in wood
b Determine the best production plan, assuming that Sean wishes to maximise profit
c Calculate the profit that could be achieved from the plan in part (b) above
d Sean is concerned about fulfilling all his orders and sources some wood from a supplier at a cost of €15 per kg. This would overcome the shortage in wood. Based on your solution to part (c) above, would you advise Sean to obtain the wood at the higher price? Support your answer with relevant calculations

Notes to students

1 The kg of wood per unit are given in the question so there is no need to calculate them again at the start of the questions.
2 Raw materials: wood, other raw materials, labour costs and variable overheads are all variable costs.

* Based on question 6.26 in Catherine Gowthorpe, *Management Accounting*, 1st edition, South-Western Cengage Learning, 2008.

For answers and additional test questions, see www.gillmacmillan.ie. Search for Management Accounting and click on the link in the right-hand column.

11 Capital Investment Decisions

Learning outcomes of Chapter 11

At the end of this chapter, you will be able to:

- use quantitative analysis to decide between capital projects
- explain the concept of the time value of money and compounding and discounting
- apply investment appraisal techniques based on future cash flows, i.e., payback period, net present value, profitability index and internal rate of return
- apply investment appraisal techniques based on future profits, i.e., accounting rate of return
- identify the benefits and drawbacks of investment appraisal techniques

Introduction

In **Chapter 9: Cost Volume Profit Analysis** and **Chapter 10: Relevant Costing and Decision-Making**, you applied marginal costing techniques to making short-term decisions.

The types of decisions made in the short term include pricing decisions, shut-down decisions, accepting or rejecting contracts, limiting factor decisions and decisions on whether to sell products at the split-off point or to process further and then sell.

In this chapter we will consider decisions which will have a longer-term impact on the organisation. Each organisation will have to decide what is long term and short term for it.

These decisions can involve substantial investment in capital projects such as new machinery, equipment and research opportunities. A company may have more projects available for investment in than it has capital to invest. A choice between alternative investment opportunities may have to be made.

You will learn investment appraisal techniques such as net present value, payback period, profitability index and internal rate of return, which are based on future cash flows arising from investments, and accounting rate of return, which is based on future profits arising from investments. Each of these methods will be explained and their benefits and drawbacks discussed.

The concept of the time value of money will be explained and also how a business chooses an appropriate discount rate.

Decisions on capital projects

Organisations should make capital investment decisions in line with their mission statement and strategic objectives. For example, if a supermarket's objective is to expand its number of shops, capital should be made available to achieve this objective.

Organisations may have many more potential investment projects than they can invest in. When this is the case, the company must use capital budgeting as a decision-making tool.

CIMA Official Terminology defines capital budgeting as 'the process concerned with decision-making in respect of the choice of specific investment projects and the total amount of capital expenditure to commit'.

Profit-making organisations might make decisions regarding the purchase of a new asset, investment in research and development or the take-over of a business. Decisions in the public sector will have to be made on new schools, roads or transport systems. In this chapter the decisions are ones that affect profit-making organisations as their future costs and benefits can be quantified more easily than in non-profit organisations or the public sector.

As these types of decisions will impact on the organisation into the future, they cannot be appraised using only contribution. They should also include fixed costs. Capital investment decisions should be based on future profit or future cash flows. Capital investment requires the commitment of funds now for the potential return on the investment in the future. The techniques used in this chapter to appraise investment decisions have a narrow financial focus. They should be taken along with other non-financial considerations in assessing whether the investment project will achieve the long-term strategy of the organisation.

Cash flows and accounting profits

When making a capital investment there will be an initial cash outflow but the investment project should yield cash inflows over its life. For example, if the organisation purchases a new piece of equipment, the cost of the equipment will be the cash outflow and any cash savings made as a result of the new equipment will represent cash inflows.

There may be cash outflows over the course of the life of the equipment, e.g., disposal costs at the end of the investment period, repairs and maintenance and operating costs. Similarly, there may be cash inflows over the course of the life of the equipment, e.g., reduction in costs and disposal revenue at the end of the investment period.

Four of the capital investment appraisal techniques which we will use in this chapter use cash flows – net present value, profitability index, internal rate of return and payback period.

Depreciation is not included in investment appraisals which use cash flows as it is not a cash item. It is a financial accounting adjustment necessary to compute accounting profit. The fifth capital investment appraisal technique, accounting rate of return, is based on accounting profit.

The time value of money

Three of the investment appraisal techniques used, i.e., net present value, profitability index and internal rate of return, take into account the time value of money. €1 today is not worth €1 in one year's time if the money is invested in return for interest. We can look at an investment in two ways. It can be viewed in terms of its future value (use compounding) or its present value (use discounting). If, for example, we invest it in a bank account at an interest rate of 5%, the €1 will be worth €1.05 in one year's time (€1 x (€1 + 5%)). This is known as compounding.

We can deduce that if we want to earn €1.05 in one year's time, we must invest €1 today if the interest rate is 5%. This is known as discounting. Compounding and discounting are illustrated below.

With all the examples used in this chapter we will assume that all future costs and benefits are known with certainty. We will also assume that the objective of the organisation is to make as high a profit as possible on the investment project chosen. In the examples used, year 0 is the present or now, year 1 is one year from now, year 2 is two years from now and so on.

Compounding

Example 11.1

If savers invest €1 000 now in a bank account at an annual interest rate of 10% for four years, they will receive:

END OF YEAR	INTEREST	TOTAL INVESTMENT €
0		1 000.00
1	1 000 x 10%	100.00
		1 100.00 (end of year 1)
2	1 100 x 10%	110.00
		1 210.00 (end of year 2)
3	1 210 x 10%	121.00
		1 331.00 (end of year 3)
4	1 331 x 10%	133.10
		1 464.10 (end of year 4)

We can use a formula to calculate the compounding effect:

> Value of the investment at the end of year 1:
> $$€1\,100 = €1\,000 \times (1+10\%)$$
>
> The formula used is:
> $$\text{Value at end of year 1} = \text{Initial investment} \times (1+r)$$
> Where r = interest rate, expressed as a decimal

> Value of the investment at the end of year 2:
> $$€1\,210 = €1\,000 \times (1+10\%) \times (1+10\%)$$
>
> The formula used is:
> $$\text{Value at end of year 2} = \text{Initial investment} \times (1+r) \times (1+r)$$
>
> Or
> $$\text{Value at end of year 2} = \text{Initial investment} \times (1+r)^n$$
> Where r = interest rate
> Where n = the number of years, in this case two

> Value of the investment at the end of year 3:
> $$€1\,331 = €1\,000 \times (1+10\%) \times (1+10\%) \times (1+10\%)$$
> The formula used is:
> $$\text{Value at end of year 3} = \text{Initial investment} \times (1+r) \times (1+r) \times (1+r)$$
> Or
> $$\text{Value at end of year 3} = \text{Initial investment} \times (1+r)^n$$
> Where r = interest rate
> Where n = the number of years, in this case three

> Value of the investment at the end of year 4:
> $$€1\,464.10 = €1\,000 \times (1+10\%) \times (1+10\%) \times (1+10\%) \times (1+10\%)$$
> The formula used is:
> $$\text{Value at end of year 4} = \text{Initial investment} \times (1+r) \times (1+r) \times (1+r) \times (1+r)$$
> Or
> $$\text{Future value of an investment in n years} = \text{Initial investment} \times (1+r)^n$$
> Where r = interest rate
> Where n = the number of years, in this case four

Example 11.2

Calculate the value of an investment at the end of five years if €100 is initially invested at an annual interest rate of 5%. Use the formula illustrated in Example 11.1.

Solution to Example 11.2

The formula is:

Future value of an investment in n years = Initial investment x $(1+r)^n$

Where r = interest rate
Where n = the number of years, in this case five

$$€127.63 = €100 \times (1+5\%)^5$$

Discounting

Expressing future values in present-day terms is known as discounting. We can turn around the compounding formula to work out the discounting formula. The compounding formula is:

Future value of an investment in n years = Initial investment x $(1+r)^n$

Where r = interest rate
Where n = the number of years

Therefore:

Initial investment = Future value of an investment in n years x $\dfrac{1}{(1+r)^n}$

Where r = discount rate
Where n = the number of years

Note: in discounting *r* is referred to as the 'discount rate'.

Example 11.3

Use discounting to confirm that the present value of €1 464.10 received four years from now is €1 000 at a discount rate of 10%.

Solution to Example 11.3 (using discounting formula)

The discounting formula is:

Initial investment = Future value of an investment in n years x $\dfrac{1}{(1+r)^n}$

Where r = discount rate
Where n = the number of years

Therefore:

$$\text{Initial investment} = €1\ 464.10 \times \frac{1}{(1+10\%)^4}$$

$$\text{Initial investment} = €1\ 464.10 \times \frac{1}{1.4641}$$

$$\text{Initial investment} = €1\ 464.10 \times 0.6830134$$

$$\text{Initial investment} = €1\ 000 \text{ (rounded to the nearest whole number)}$$

Solution to Example 11.3 (using present value tables)

To simplify these calculations students can use the present value table in Appendix A, which is at the end of this chapter.

Using the information in Example 11.3 go to year 4 under the 10% column and multiply 0.6830 x €1 464.10 to find out the initial investment, i.e., €1 000 (to the nearest whole number).

In conclusion, €1 000 is the present value of €1 464.10 at the end of year 4 at a discount rate of 10%.

Choosing a discount rate

To use net present value and internal rate of return, a company must choose a rate of return for discounting future cash flows back to their present value.

It may choose the opportunity cost of the investment, i.e., the percentage return it would obtain in a bank, from investing in shares or from some other investment opportunity. For example, if it has €100 000 to invest, it could earn a return of 5% per annum in a bank account. If it decides to use the €100 000 to invest in a capital project, the return must be greater than the alternative investment option, i.e., the bank account.

The discount rate the company will use depends on its attitude to risk. If the company is risk-averse it may decide to invest its funds in a deposit account in a bank. Under normal economic circumstances, this is usually a risk-averse choice. In recent times, banks have proven to be risky and have required state guarantees for investors. Normally, deposit accounts in banks are a safe investment.

If the organisation is more of a risk taker it may opt to invest its funds in shares. The returns may be greater than from a bank but it is more of a risky option.

Usually, organisations use their cost of capital as their discount rate and they may also refer to it as the minimum required rate of return.

Investment appraisal technique: net present value

Once the discount rate is established for an organisation, it can use this in calculating the net present value of the investment.

Calculating net present value

Net present value (NPV) is the sum of the projected cash flows of a project discounted at an appropriate discount rate. If the NPV is a positive figure, the projected discounted cash inflows exceed the projected discounted cash outflows and the project should be accepted. If the NPV is negative, the projected discounted cash outflows exceed the projected discounted cash inflows and the project should be rejected. If the NPV is zero, the organisation is indifferent to whether the project is accepted.

When choosing between two projects, the project which has the higher NPV should be chosen.

Example 11.4

A company is considering investing in one of two mutually exclusive projects. Both projects would require an investment in equipment of €75 000 at the beginning of the project and the future cash flows are expected to be as follows:

	MACHINE A €	MACHINE B €
Year 1	30 000	27 000
Year 2	25 000	22 000
Year 3	22 500	19 500
Year 4	27 000	24 500
Year 5	–	37 000

Machine A will be sold for €35 000 at the end of year 4 and the Machine B will be sold for €15 000 at the end of year 5. The company's cost of capital is 20%. The company uses the straight-line method of depreciation for all fixed assets when calculating net profit.

Required

Calculate the net present value of the two machines using present value tables.

Notes to students

1 Remember that the investment outlay is now, i.e., year 0, and the cash inflows are from year 1 (at the end of one year from now) onwards.
2 When discounting the initial investment, the discount rate will be 1. This is because the present value of Machine A is €75 000 today.
3 Look up the present value table in Appendix A under 20% for years 1 to 5.
4 Machine A will be sold for €35 000 at the end of year 4. This is a cash inflow along with the €27 000 cash inflow in year 4. It is advisable to have two year 4s in the NPV table for Machine A and two year 5s for Machine B.

Solution to Example 11.4

Net present value table for Machine A:

YEAR	CASH FLOW	DISCOUNT FACTOR 20%	PRESENT VALUE
0	(75 000)	1 000	(75 000.00)
1	30 000	0.833	24 990.00
2	25 000	0.694	17 350.00
3	22 500	0.579	13 027.50
4	27 000	0.482	13 014.00
4	35 000	0.482	16 870.00
		Net present value	10 251.50

Net present value table for Machine B:

YEAR	CASH FLOW	DISCOUNT FACTOR 20%	PRESENT VALUE
0	(75 000)	1 000	(75 000.00)
1	27 000	0.833	22 491.00
2	22 000	0.694	15 268.00
3	19 500	0.579	11 290.50
4	24 500	0.482	11 809.00
5	37 000	0.402	14 874.00
5	15 000	0.402	6 030.00
		Net present value	6 762.50

Both machines have positive NPVs but Machine A's NPV is higher than Machine B's. This indicates that Machine A is the preferred option. The decision to invest in Machine A should not be based solely on NPV.

We should also consider the internal rate of return, payback period and accounting rate of return of both machines before we make our final decision.

Benefits of NPV

NPV takes into account the time value of money and also considers all future cash flows. NPV provides an absolute result rather than a percentage (like internal rate of return).

Drawbacks of NPV

NPV can be difficult to calculate as it requires an understanding of discounting, which can be difficult for non-accountants to understand. It also requires the company to have decided upon an appropriate discount rate.

Investment appraisal technique: profitability index

The profitability index is a method of investment appraisal that allows alternative investments to be ranked. The formula used is:

$$\frac{\text{Present value of cash inflows}}{\text{Initial investment}}$$

It represents the NPV of each €1 invested in a project. The higher the profitability index, the more desirable the project. The rule is if:

Profitability index > 1: accept the investment

Profitability index < 1: reject the investment

Example 11.4.a

Using the information in Example 11.4, calculate the profitability index of the two machines.

Solution to Example 11.4.a

Using the solution to Example 11.4 above, the present value of Machine A is:

YEAR	CASH FLOW	DISCOUNT FACTOR 20%	PRESENT VALUE
1	30 000	0.833	24 990.00
2	25 000	0.694	17 350.00
3	22 500	0.579	13 027.50
4	27 000	0.482	13 014.00
4	35 000	0.482	16 870.00
		PV of cash inflows	85 251.50

The profitability index of Machine A is:

$$\frac{€85\ 251.50}{€75\ 000.00} = 1.14 \text{ (rounded to two decimal places)}$$

Using the solution to Example 11.4 above, the present value of Machine B is:

YEAR	CASH FLOW	DISCOUNT FACTOR 20%	PRESENT VALUE
1	27 000	0.833	22 491.00
2	22 000	0.694	15 268.00
3	19 500	0.579	11 290.50
4	24 500	0.482	11 809.00
5	37 000	0.402	14 874.00
5	15 000	0.402	6 030.00
		PV of cash inflows	81 762.50

The profitability index of Machine B is:

$$\frac{€81\ 762.50}{€75\ 000.00} = 1.09 \text{ (rounded to two decimal places)}$$

Both machines have a return which is higher than the required rate of return of 20%, and both have a profitability index which is greater than 1. Machine A has a higher profitability index, 1.14, than Machine B, 1.09. Machine A would be chosen over Machine B.

Benefits of the profitability index

This method is a variation of the NPV method and subsequently takes into account the time value of money. It provides a simple answer – if the profitability index is greater than 1, the project is acceptable, and if less than 1 it should be rejected.

Investment appraisal technique: internal rate of return

The internal rate of return (IRR) is the annual expected return of the investment over its life. It is the discount factor at which the NPV of the investment is zero. It can be ascertained in a number of ways and the linear interpolation method is described below.

Example 11.4.b

Using the example of Machine A in Example 11.4, the NPV at a discount rate of 20% was €10 251.50. If we calculate the NPV at 22%, 24%, 25%, 26% and 28%, we find:

DISCOUNT RATE	NPV €
20%	10 251.50
22%	6 759.50
24%	3 446.00
25%	1 940.00
26%	434.00
28%	(2 461.50)

As the discount rate increases, the NPV decreases. Zero lies somewhere between 26% and 28%, i.e., the IRR lies somewhere between these two percentages.

We can ascertain the IRR using linear interpolation. At a discount rate of 26%, the NPV is €434 (positive), and at a discount rate of 28%, the NPV is –€2 461.50 (negative). As the discount rate increases by 2% (from 26% to 28%), the total distance between the two NPVs is €2 895.50 (from +€434 to –€2 461.50). The distance between 26% and the IRR is:

$$26\% + \frac{434.00}{2\ 895.50} \times 2\% \quad = 26.30\% \text{ (to two decimal places)}$$

Alternatively, the distance between the IRR and 28% is:

$$28\% - \frac{2\ 461.50}{2\ 895.50} \times 2\% \quad = 26.30\% \text{ (to two decimal places)}$$

Using the example of Machine B in Example 11.4, the NPV at a discount rate of 20% was €6 762.50. If we calculate the NPV at 22% and 24%, we find:

DISCOUNT RATE	NPV €
20%	6 762.50
22%	2 958.00
24%	(624.50)

As the discount rate increases, the NPV decreases. Zero lies somewhere between 22% and 24%, i.e., the IRR lies somewhere between these two percentages.

We can ascertain the IRR using linear interpolation. At a discount rate of 22%, the NPV is €2 958 (positive), and at a discount rate of 24%, the NPV is –€624.50 (negative). As the discount rate increases by 2% (from 22% to 24%),

the total distance between the two NPVs is €3 582.50 (from +€2 958 to
−€624.50). The distance between 22% and the IRR is:

$$22\% + \frac{2\ 958.00}{3\ 582.50} \times 2\% \quad = 23.65\% \text{ (to two decimal places)}$$

Alternatively, the distance between the IRR and 24% is:

$$24\% - \frac{624.50}{3\ 582.50} \times 2\% \quad = 23.65\% \text{ (to two decimal places)}$$

The IRR can also be calculated using a computer spreadsheet programme such
as Excel, otherwise it can be a tedious exercise.

If the IRR is greater than the opportunity cost of capital, the investment is
profitable and should be accepted. It will yield a positive NPV. If the IRR is
less than the opportunity cost of capital, the investment is unprofitable and
should be rejected. It will yield a negative NPV.

Benefits of IRR

IRR uses the time value of money in its calculations. The decision using IRR is
easy. If a project has an IRR greater than the required rate of return, it should
be accepted. If not, reject the project.

Drawbacks of IRR

It can be difficult to calculate the IRR, be precise about it or explain its
calculation to non-accountants. The IRR does not provide results as an
absolute value but as a percentage.

Investment appraisal technique: payback period

Payback period is the time it takes a project to recover its initial cost out of
future cash receipts. The premise is that the quicker an investment can be
recovered out of future cash receipts, the better the investment. The company
might have a target payback and would reject any project which has a longer
payback period. Payback uses cash flows in its calculations but does not use
discounting.

Example 11.4.c

Using the information in Example 11.4, calculate the payback period of the
two machines.

Solution to Example 11.4.c

Payback period for Machine A:

YEAR	CASH FLOW €	CUMULATIVE CASH FLOW €
0	(75 000)	(75 000)
1	30 000	(45 000)
2	25 000	(20 000)
3	22 500	2 500

The payback period, i.e., when the cumulative cash flows are zero, lies somewhere between years 2 and 3. The payback period is:

$$2 \text{ years} + \frac{(20\ 000}{22\ 500} \text{ x 12 months)} = \quad 2 \text{ years 11 months} \\ \text{(to the nearest whole month)}$$

Payback period for Machine B:

YEAR	CASH FLOW €	CUMULATIVE CASH FLOW €
0	(75 000)	(75 000)
1	27 000	(48 000)
2	22 000	(26 000)
3	19 500	(6 500)
4	24 500	18 000

The payback period, i.e., when the cumulative cash flows are zero, lies somewhere between years 3 and 4. The payback period is:

$$3 \text{ years} + \frac{(6\ 500}{24\ 500} \text{ x 12 months)} = \quad 3 \text{ years 3 months} \\ \text{(to the nearest whole month)}$$

Summary

Machine A has a shorter payback period of 2 years 11 months while it would take Machine B 3 years 3 months to recover its initial investment.

Benefits of payback period

Payback period is simple, quick and easy to understand for non-accountants. If the payback period on a project is shorter than the target payback period, the project should be accepted. If longer, reject the project.

Drawbacks of payback period

It ignores cash flows after the initial cost has been recouped. Consider Example 11.4.c, Machine A has the shorter payback period and would be recommended using this method. However, Machine B goes on to generate cash inflows in year 5. Should this not be taken into consideration in the investment appraisal?

It also ignores the time value of money and does not discount future cash flows into their present value. It also ignores the size of the investment project and its overall cost and benefit.

Investment appraisal technique: accounting rate of return

The accounting rate of return (ARR) does not use cash flows to appraise investments, it uses accounting profit. ARR calculates the return generated from net income of the proposed capital investment. The ARR is a percentage return. If ARR = 10%, it means the project is expected to earn 10 cent out of each euro invested. If the ARR is equal to or greater than the required rate of return, i.e., ROCE (return on capital employed), the project is acceptable.

There are many ways of calculating the ARR. The formula which we will use is the one defined by *CIMA Official Terminology:*

$$\frac{\text{Average annual profit from an investment}}{\text{Average investment}} \times 100$$

Example 11.4.d

Using the information in Example 11.4, calculate the ARR for Machine A and Machine B.

Notes to students

1 Cash flows are given in Example 11.4 for Machine A and Machine B. The ARR requires profit figures for its calculation. Ensure that depreciation is deducted from cash flows to ascertain profits.
2 The average profit is calculated by dividing the total profit by the number of years of the investment.
3 To calculate the average investment, take the book value of the investment at the beginning of year 1 (this is usually the cost of the investment) and then add the value of the investment at the end of its useful life, i.e., its scrap value. The answer should be divided by two. Don't be tempted to deduct the scrap value from the cost of the investment.

Solution to Example 11.4.d

Machine A

Depreciation is calculated using the straight-line method:

$$\frac{\text{Initial cost of the asset} - \text{residual value}}{\text{Expected life of the asset}}$$

$$\frac{€75\ 000 - 35\ 000}{4\ \text{years}} = €10\ 000 \text{ per annum}$$

Calculate the average annual profits:

YEAR	CASH FLOW €		DEPRECIATION €		NET PROFITS €
1	30 000	–	10 000	=	20 000
2	25 000	–	10 000	=	15 000
3	22 500	–	10 000	=	12 500
4	27 000	–	10 000	=	17 000
			Total net profit		64 500

The average profit per year generated by Machine A is:

$$\frac{€64\ 500}{4\ \text{years}} = €16\ 125$$

Calculate the average investment:

$$\frac{€75\ 000 + 35\ 000}{2} = €55\ 000$$

The ARR for Machine A is:

$$\frac{€16\ 125}{€55\ 000} \quad \text{x} \quad 100 = 29.3\ \%$$

Machine B

Depreciation is calculated using the straight-line method:

$$\frac{\text{Initial cost of the asset} - \text{residual value}}{\text{Expected life of the asset}}$$

$$\frac{€75\ 000 - 15\ 000}{5\ \text{years}} = €12\ 000 \text{ per annum}$$

Calculate the average annual profits:

YEAR	CASH FLOW €		DEPRECIATION €		NET PROFITS €
1	27 000	–	12 000	=	15 000
2	22 000	–	12 000	=	10 000
3	19 500	–	12 000	=	7 500
4	24 500	–	12 000	=	12 500
5	37 000	–	12 000	=	25 000
			Total net profit		70 000

The average profit per year generated by Machine B is:

$$\frac{€70\ 000}{5\ \text{years}} = €14\ 000$$

Calculate the average investment:

$$\frac{€75\ 000 + 15\ 000}{2} = €45\ 000$$

The ARR for Machine B is:

$$\frac{€14\ 000}{€45\ 000} \times 100 = 31.1\ \%$$

The ARR shows that Machine B is the better of the two options. However, Machine A actually produces a higher average profit (€16 125) than Machine B (€14 000). This is a weakness of this investment appraisal technique. It would be useful to know what the return on capital employed (ROCE) is for the whole company. If the company's ROCE is considerably higher than the ARR of Machine B, the company may need to reconsider the investment project.

Benefits of ARR

The ARR is very similar to the return on capital employed (ROCE) which is calculated for the whole company. It is easy to compare the investment projects ARR with the overall ROCE of the company. The ARR is easily understood and calculated.

Drawbacks of ARR

The ARR ignores the time value of money. It assumes that €1 spent or received now has the same value as €1 spent or received five years from now.

The ARR formula which we have used is the one defined by CIMA. There are many other variations on this formula, which can be confusing for students.

The ARR is based on profit and is the only investment appraisal technique which we will use that is based on profit. Profit is not the best method for appraising investment projects as it can be affected by the depreciation method which the company has adopted.

The ARR is expressed as a percentage and it does not take into account the relative size of investment projects being considered.

The investment appraisal techniques should not be looked at in isolation. A summary of the techniques applied to Example 11.4 is shown below:

	MACHINE A	MACHINE B	CHOOSE:
NPV	€10 251.50	€6 762.50	Machine A
Profitability index	1.14	1.09	Machine A
IRR	26.3%	23.65%	Machine A
Payback period	2 years 11 months	3 years 3 months	Machine A
ARR	29.3%	31.1%	Machine B

Four out of the five techniques recommend that Machine A should be chosen. In making its final decision the company should consider non-financial matters such as which machine comes with the best guarantee or has the better after sales service.

Chapter summary

In this chapter we explained how decisions are made on long-term capital investment projects. The time value of money was explained and its importance in capital investment appraisal discussed. We also discussed how a business decides on its cost of capital.

The following investment appraisal techniques were illustrated, along with their benefits and drawbacks:

Capital investment appraisal techniques which use discounting:	Capital investment appraisal techniques which do not use discounting:
Net present value	Payback period
Internal rate of return	Accounting rate of return
Profitability index	

Inflation and taxation are also important considerations in capital investment appraisal. For the purposes of simplicity they are ignored in this book. See Drury (2008) for a discussion on the effect of these items on capital investment appraisal.

Test questions

Question 1*

The following information relates to three possible investment projects. The company can only select one project.

PROJECT	X	Y	Z
Initial cost	€100 000	€115 000	€90 000
Projected cash inflows:			
Year 1	€40 000	€50 000	€50 000
Year 2	€35 000	€35 000	€30 000
Year 3	€30 000	€25 000	€45 000
Year 4	€30 000	€25 000	€50 000
Year 5	€25 000	€20 000	–

Cash inflows occur at the end of each year. Projects X and Y are expected to have a life of five years and Project Z, four years. Expected scrap values at the end of the projects' lives are as follows:

PROJECT	X	Y	Z
Scrap value	€5 000	€7 500	€4 000

The company's cost of capital is 10%. The company's policy is to depreciate projects on a straight-line basis.

Required

a Calculate the net present value for each project
b Calculate the payback period for each project
c Calculate the profitability index for each project
d Calculate the accounting rate of return for each project
e Summarise your findings and recommend which project should be accepted

Notes to students

1 Remember NPV, payback period and profitability index all use cash flows, while ARR uses accounting profit.
2 Use the present value tables rather than calculating the discount factor yourself.
3 You will need to calculate depreciation and deduct it from cash flows to calculate profit.
4 Try to fit all three projects into one NPV table.

5   Remember to have two year 4s and two year 5s in the NPV table, for scrap value at the end of the projects' lives.
6   Remember to add the scrap value on to the cost of the investment when calculating the ARR. Don't deduct it!

* Based on question 13.3 in Colin Drury, *Management and Cost Accounting*, 5th edition, Business Press Thomson Learning, 2000.

Question 2

A company estimates the following cash inflows and outflows for a new piece of equipment which it is considering buying:

YEAR	CASH FLOWS €
0	(400 000)
1	100 000
2	110 000
3	125 000
4	165 000

The company's cost of capital is 8%.

Required

Calculate the net present value, internal rate of return, profitability index and payback period of the equipment.

Question 3

Murphy Contractors Ltd has €75 000 to invest in a new machine. The managing director is trying to decide whether to invest in Machine A or Machine B. Details are as follows:

	MACHINE A	MACHINE B
Cost of the machine	€75 000	€75 000
Annual cash inflows years 1–4	€22 000	€20 000
Resale value at end of four years	€8 000	€12 000

The company's cost of capital is 8%.

Required

Prepare the net present value calculations for the two machines and recommend which machine Murphy should purchase.

Note to students

As the cash inflows are the same each year, you can use the Appendix B: Present value annuity factors table to calculate the present values of the cash inflows for years 1–4.

For answers and additional test questions, see www.gillmacmillan.ie. Search for Management Accounting and click on the link in the right-hand column.

Appendices to Chapter 11

Appendix A: Present value factors: present value of €1 after n years

YEARS HENCE	1%	2%	4%	6%	8%	10%	12%	14%	15%	16%	18%	20%	22%	24%	25%	26%	28%	30%	35%
1	0.990	0.980	0.962	0.943	0.926	0.909	0.893	0.877	0.870	0.862	0.847	0.833	0.820	0.806	0.800	0.794	0.781	0.769	0.741
2	0.980	0.961	0.925	0.890	0.857	0.826	0.797	0.769	0.756	0.743	0.718	0.694	0.672	0.650	0.640	0.630	0.610	0.592	0.549
3	0.971	0.942	0.889	0.840	0.794	0.751	0.712	0.675	0.658	0.641	0.609	0.579	0.551	0.524	0.512	0.500	0.477	0.455	0.406
4	0.961	0.924	0.855	0.792	0.735	0.683	0.636	0.592	0.572	0.552	0.516	0.482	0.451	0.423	0.410	0.397	0.373	0.350	0.301
5	0.951	0.906	0.822	0.747	0.681	0.621	0.567	0.519	0.497	0.476	0.437	0.402	0.370	0.341	0.328	0.315	0.291	0.269	0.223
6	0.942	0.888	0.790	0.705	0.630	0.564	0.507	0.456	0.432	0.410	0.370	0.335	0.303	0.275	0.262	0.250	0.227	0.207	0.165
7	0.933	0.871	0.760	0.665	0.583	0.513	0.452	0.400	0.376	0.354	0.314	0.279	0.249	0.222	0.210	0.198	0.178	0.159	0.122
8	0.923	0.853	0.731	0.627	0.540	0.467	0.404	0.351	0.327	0.305	0.266	0.233	0.204	0.179	0.168	0.157	0.139	0.123	0.091
9	0.914	0.837	0.703	0.592	0.500	0.424	0.361	0.308	0.284	0.263	0.225	0.194	0.167	0.144	0.134	0.125	0.108	0.094	0.067
10	0.905	0.820	0.676	0.558	0.463	0.386	0.322	0.270	0.247	0.227	0.191	0.162	0.137	0.116	0.107	0.099	0.085	0.073	0.050
11	0.896	0.804	0.650	0.527	0.429	0.350	0.287	0.237	0.215	0.195	0.162	0.135	0.112	0.094	0.086	0.079	0.066	0.056	0.037
12	0.887	0.788	0.625	0.497	0.397	0.319	0.257	0.208	0.187	0.168	0.137	0.112	0.092	0.076	0.069	0.062	0.052	0.043	0.027
13	0.879	0.773	0.601	0.469	0.368	0.290	0.229	0.182	0.163	0.145	0.116	0.093	0.075	0.061	0.055	0.050	0.040	0.033	0.020
14	0.870	0.758	0.577	0.442	0.340	0.263	0.205	0.160	0.141	0.125	0.099	0.078	0.062	0.049	0.044	0.039	0.032	0.025	0.015
15	0.861	0.743	0.555	0.417	0.315	0.239	0.183	0.140	0.123	0.108	0.084	0.065	0.051	0.040	0.035	0.031	0.025	0.020	0.011
16	0.853	0.728	0.534	0.394	0.292	0.218	0.163	0.123	0.107	0.093	0.071	0.054	0.042	0.032	0.028	0.025	0.019	0.015	0.008
17	0.844	0.714	0.513	0.371	0.270	0.198	0.146	0.108	0.093	0.080	0.060	0.045	0.034	0.026	0.023	0.020	0.015	0.012	0.006
18	0.836	0.700	0.494	0.350	0.250	0.180	0.130	0.095	0.081	0.069	0.051	0.038	0.028	0.021	0.018	0.016	0.012	0.009	0.005
19	0.828	0.686	0.475	0.331	0.232	0.164	0.116	0.083	0.070	0.060	0.043	0.031	0.023	0.017	0.014	0.012	0.009	0.007	0.003
20	0.820	0.673	0.456	0.312	0.215	0.149	0.104	0.073	0.061	0.051	0.037	0.026	0.019	0.014	0.012	0.010	0.007	0.005	0.002

Appendix B: Present value annuity factors: present value of €1 received annually for n years

YEARS HENCE	1%	2%	4%	6%	8%	10%	12%	14%	15%	16%	18%	20%	22%	24%	25%	26%	28%	30%	35%	36%	37%
1	0.990	0.980	0.962	0.943	0.926	0.909	0.893	0.877	0.870	0.862	0.847	0.833	0.820	0.806	0.800	0.794	0.781	0.769	0.741	0.735	0.730
2	1.970	1.942	1.886	1.833	1.783	1.736	1.690	1.647	1.626	1.605	1.566	1.528	1.492	1.457	1.440	1.424	1.392	1.361	1.289	1.276	1.263
3	2.941	2.884	2.775	2.673	2.577	2.487	2.402	2.322	2.283	2.246	2.174	2.106	2.042	1.981	1.952	1.923	1.868	1.816	1.696	1.673	1.652
4	3.902	3.808	3.630	3.465	3.312	3.170	3.037	2.914	2.855	2.798	2.690	2.589	2.494	2.404	2.362	2.320	2.241	2.166	1.997	1.966	1.935
5	4.853	4.713	4.452	4.212	3.993	3.791	3.605	3.433	3.352	3.274	3.127	2.991	2.864	2.745	2.689	2.635	2.532	2.436	2.220	2.181	2.143
6	5.795	5.601	5.242	4.917	4.623	4.355	4.111	3.889	3.784	3.685	3.498	3.326	3.167	3.020	2.951	2.885	2.759	2.643	2.385	2.339	2.294
7	6.728	6.472	6.002	5.582	5.206	4.868	4.564	4.288	4.160	4.039	3.812	3.605	3.416	3.242	3.161	3.083	2.937	2.802	2.508	2.455	2.404
8	7.652	7.325	6.733	6.210	5.747	5.335	4.968	4.639	4.487	4.344	4.078	3.837	3.619	3.421	3.329	3.241	3.076	2.925	2.598	2.540	2.485
9	8.566	8.162	7.435	6.802	6.247	5.759	5.328	4.946	4.772	4.607	4.303	4.031	3.786	3.566	3.463	3.366	3.184	3.019	2.665	2.603	2.544
10	9.471	8.983	8.111	7.360	6.710	6.145	5.650	5.216	5.019	4.833	4.494	4.192	3.923	3.682	3.571	3.465	3.269	3.092	2.715	2.649	2.587
11	10.368	9.787	8.760	7.887	7.139	6.495	5.937	5.453	5.234	5.029	4.656	4.327	4.035	3.776	3.656	3.544	3.335	3.147	2.752	2.683	2.618
12	11.255	10.575	9.385	8.384	7.536	6.814	6.194	5.660	5.421	5.197	4.793	4.439	4.127	3.851	3.725	3.606	3.387	3.190	2.779	2.708	2.641
13	12.134	11.343	9.986	8.853	7.904	7.103	6.424	5.842	5.583	5.342	4.910	4.533	4.203	3.912	3.780	3.656	3.427	3.223	2.799	2.727	2.658
14	13.004	12.106	10.563	9.295	8.244	7.367	6.628	6.002	5.724	5.468	5.008	4.611	4.265	3.962	3.824	3.695	3.459	3.249	2.814	2.740	2.670
15	13.865	12.849	11.118	9.712	8.559	7.606	6.811	6.142	5.847	5.575	5.092	4.675	4.315	4.001	3.859	3.726	3.483	3.268	2.825	2.750	2.679
16	14.718	13.578	11.652	10.106	8.851	7.824	6.974	6.265	5.954	5.669	5.162	4.730	4.357	4.033	3.887	3.751	3.503	3.283	2.834	2.757	2.685
17	15.562	14.292	12.166	10.477	9.122	8.022	7.120	6.373	6.047	5.749	5.222	4.775	4.391	4.059	3.910	3.771	3.518	3.295	2.840	2.763	2.690
18	16.398	14.992	12.659	10.828	9.372	8.201	7.250	6.467	6.128	5.818	5.273	4.812	4.419	4.080	3.928	3.786	3.529	3.304	2.844	2.767	2.693
19	17.226	15.678	13.134	11.815	9.604	8.365	7.366	6.550	6.198	5.877	5.316	4.844	4.442	4.097	3.942	3.799	3.539	3.311	2.848	2.770	2.696
20	18.046	16.351	13.590	11.470	9.818	8.514	7.469	6.623	6.259	5.929	5.353	4.870	4.460	4.110	3.954	3.808	3.546	3.316	2.850	2.772	2.698

12 Performance Measurement and Issues in Management Accounting

Learning outcomes of Chapter 12

At the end of this chapter, you will be able to:

- explain the content of the performance report
- explain how performance should be linked to the objectives and mission statement of the organisation
- understand why large organisations use a divisional structure
- argue the benefits and problems of a divisional management structure
- discuss performance measurement in the three different types of divisions
- explain how performance is measured in a non-profit organisation
- appreciate the use of non-financial performance measures
- understand the balanced scorecard approach to performance measurement
- discuss the future role of management accounting

Introduction

This chapter examines internal performance reporting in businesses. It explains that internal reporting should be linked to the objectives and mission statement of the business.

A divisional structure is explained and performance measurement in the three types of division is discussed. The chapter goes on to explain how performance can be measured in non-profit organisations.

The importance of using non-financial measures of performance is discussed and the role the balanced scorecard can play in performance measurement is outlined.

Performance reporting

Internal performance reporting is necessary in a business for making decisions, planning activities, communicating information and motivating and rewarding staff. Information in the performance report should be produced in timely fashion. It can be reported daily, weekly, monthly or whenever it is required.

The performance report can be communicated electronically by email to the relevant managers and staff in the business or produced by managers using performance reporting software. It may also form part of the monthly management accounts. The information in the performance report should be timely and produced easily and cost-effectively. Its benefits to the business should outweigh its costs. As it contains sensitive information its publication should be restricted. It should not be published outside the business.

Linking the performance report to the objectives of the organisation

If the organisation's objective is making profit then the performance reporting system should report profit measures such as gross profit percentage, net profit percentage and return on capital employed (ROCE), along with non-financial measures. Not all organisations have a profit motive. In non-profit organisations performance measurement and reporting needs to establish whether the targets and objectives of the organisation have been met. Non-profit organisations include the public sector, charities, churches, hospitals, local government and others.

In **Chapter 6: Budgetary Planning and Control**, we discussed how budgeting, planning and control are linked to the mission statement and strategy of a business. If a performance reporting system is to be successful it should be linked to clear and measurable objectives, also referred to as key performance indicators, KPIs. For example, if one of a hospital's objectives is to reduce patients' waiting times when they attend out-patient clinics, a measure must be put in place to see whether this objective is being achieved. The outcome, i.e., the time lapse between the patients' appointments and when they are seen by a doctor, should be measured. The results can be published in the hospital's weekly performance report and a decision may be taken to allocate funds to improve this outcome.

Performance reports should measure the organisation's success in achieving its objects or KPIs. Measures may be quantitative or qualitative. *CIMA Official Terminology* defines qualitative factors as 'factors that are relevant to a decision but are not expressed numerically', and quantitative factors as 'factors that are relevant to a decision and are expressed numerically'.

A profit-making organisation may decide to link its performance measurement and reporting system to rewards. If managers and staff achieve the objectives, they may achieve a reward, e.g., a bonus. For this system to be fair, managers and staff should be aware of the objectives of the business and should be held accountable only for what is within their control.

Responsibility in large organisations

In large organisations, financial control and performance measurement can be complex. The organisation may be spread geographically or extended after take-overs. The organisation may decide to adopt a divisional organisation structure, freeing up senior managers' time to deal with strategic matters. Divisions then manage their own finance and operations and report periodically to head office. The objective of divisionalisation is to achieve the objectives of the company and to make day-to-day management of the company more achievable. Managers given more responsibility are likely to be motivated and will have authority to react quickly to opportunities and make quicker decisions.

The problem with divisionalisation is that sub-optimal decisions may be made by an individual division, i.e., decisions which benefit one division over another. There is a danger that managers will concentrate on short-term gains and neglect long-term goals. Other problems of divisionalisaton are setting transfer prices between divisions which are fair and duplication of effort among divisions, e.g., payroll and HR.

Divisional managers should be responsible only for finances and operations which are under their control. This is referred to as responsibility accounting.

If divisional managers are responsible for costs in their division but are not responsible for revenue, each division may be a cost centre. They will report on costs in their performance measurement report. Actual costs will be compared with budgeted costs and variance analysis will be carried out.

If divisional managers are responsible for both the costs incurred by their division and the revenues generated by their division, each division may be a profit centre. They will report on costs, revenues and profits in their performance measurement report. Actual profit will be compared with budgeted profit and variances investigated. The performance measurement report should clearly show what costs and revenues are within the control of managers and what costs and revenues are not.

If divisional managers are responsible for costs and revenues but also investments, each division may be an investment centre. They will report on costs, revenues and investments in their performance report. The divisional manager will be held responsible for earning a return on the division's investments.

Cost centres, profit centres and investment centres are all examples of responsibility centres. Each division or centre should be aware of the strategy, objectives and targets of the organisation. Divisions should work together to maximise the returns for the organisation as a whole, this is known as goal congruence.

Measuring performance in non-profit organisations

Non-profit organisations do not have a profit motive so performance would not be measured in terms of ROCE or gross profit percentage. Non-profit organisations would be conscious of controlling costs and obtaining value for money. Their main objective is to achieve their plans and objectives as laid out in their mission statement and strategy plans.

Jones and Pendlebury in *Public Sector Accounting* (2010) distinguish the following elements of performance:

- Inputs – being resources consumed, measured primarily using costs but also non-financial measures.
- Outputs – being services provided, measured primarily using non-financial measures.
- Outcomes – also being services provided, but primarily using unmeasured qualitative judgements.

There is a danger that performance measurement may become fragmented and isolated into financial performance measures and non-financial performance measures. The organisation should attempt to measure how successful it has been in achieving value for money. When measuring value for money in an organisation we should assess whether economy, efficiency and effectiveness have been achieved, otherwise known as the three E's.

Economy is defined by *CIMA Official Terminology* as 'acquisition of resources of appropriate quantity and quality at minimum cost'. Economy is concerned with the cost of inputs and obtaining them at the lowest acceptable cost. For example, in a hospital, inputs may be the cost of tendering for cleaning services. It does not necessarily mean that the lowest tender should be accepted. The services provided and quality of service should also be an influence in the choice of contract. Economy is measured in financial terms.

Efficiency is defined by *CIMA Official Terminology* as 'achievement of either maximum useful output from the resources devoted to an activity or the required output from the minimum resource input'. Efficiency aims to maximise the output for a given input. For example, how many telephone calls were answered by an employee. Efficiency can be measured in financial and non-financial terms.

Effectiveness is defined by *CIMA Official Terminology* as 'utilisation of resources such that the output of the activity achieves the desired result'. An organisation may be efficient but not effective. In a profit-making organisation, effectiveness can be measured in terms of gross profit percentage, etc., outputs can be measured in terms of sales revenue. In a non-profit organisation, outputs cannot be easily measured in monetary terms. For example, in a hospital, the number of operations performed does not necessarily have a monetary value. It is necessary to state the objective in a measurable term, e.g., the hospital aims to perform 10 operations a day. This is a way of judging whether the target set has been achieved.

Non-financial performance measures

Traditionally profit-making organisations concentrated on financial performance measures, e.g., gross profit percentage, which they published in their annual financial statements. Financial measures tended to be historic and reflected past performance. Recently the shift towards customer service and quality has resulted in organisations measuring non-financial measures of performance. These measures, along with financial measures, should provide management with information on how effectively they are achieving their objectives.

Non-financial measures will vary from business to business. Two of the most widely used measures are quality of service and customer service.

The balanced scorecard

The balanced scorecard was developed by Robert Kaplan and David Norton in a series of articles in the *Harvard Business Review*, starting in the January/February edition in 1992. The balanced scorecard uses both financial and non-financial measures to examine the performance of an organisation. Measures are listed under four perspectives – financial, customer, internal business, and innovation and learning perspectives.

Targets are set out under each perspective and actual performance is measured against each target. Targets represent the KPIs of the business and should be linked to the organisation's mission statement and strategy. The aim of the balanced scorecard is to measure whether the strategy and objectives of the organisation are being achieved. The four perspectives are linked and achievement of targets in one perspective may lead to achievement of targets in other perspectives. For example, if employee satisfaction is improved this may result in a better quality of service provided to customers and the profitability of the organisation may also improve.

The following is an example of the layout of the balanced scorecard:

FINANCIAL PERSPECTIVE	CUSTOMER PERSPECTIVE
Target	Target
Performance measures	Performance measures
INTERNAL BUSINESS PERSPECTIVE	INNOVATION & LEARNING PERSPECTIVE
Target	Target
Performance measures	Performance measures

The four perspectives of the balanced scorecard

Customer perspective: 'How do customers see us?'

Kaplan and Norton in 'The Balanced Scorecard – Measures that drive performance' (1992) state that customers' concerns tend to fall into four categories: time, quality, performance and service, and cost. Managers need to decide what the customer objectives or targets are for their organisation and develop performance measures in the balanced scorecard. Examples of targets and performance measures relating to customers are:

TARGET	PERFORMANCE MEASURES
Sell new products	Percentage of sales from new products
Reduce delivery time	On-time delivery as a percentage of all deliveries

Internal business perspective: 'What must we excel at?'

Kaplan and Norton state that internal measures should stem from the business processes that have the greatest impact on customer satisfaction – factors that affect cycle time, quality, employee skills and productivity. For example, if a customer target is to reduce delivery times, we need to establish what internal processes contribute to its success or failure. Delivery times may be affected by bottlenecks in manufacturing or lack of raw materials. The internal business perspective should set targets and measures to ensure these factors are improved. Examples of targets and performance measures relating to the internal business are:

TARGET	PERFORMANCE MEASURES
New product introduction scheduled vs planned	Actual new products introduced
Improve quality in production	Defect-free units as a percentage of completed units

Innovation and learning perspective: 'Can we continue to improve and create value?'

Kaplan and Norton state that a company's ability to innovate, improve and learn is tied directly to the company's value. A company needs to continually innovate and improve operating efficiencies to survive and to create more value for customers. This could involve investment in staff, recruiting qualified staff or investing in training and development of existing staff. The innovation and learning perspective is also referred to as the 'learning and growth' perspective. Examples of targets and performance measures relating to the innovation and learning perspective are:

TARGET	PERFORMANCE MEASURES
Improve staff morale	Satisfaction levels among staff using surveys
Use latest technology	Spending on latest technology

Financial perspective: 'How do we look to shareholders?'

Kaplan and Norton state that financial performance measures indicate whether the company's strategy, implementation and execution are contributing to bottom line improvement. Shareholders in the business will look to the financial statements to see whether the company's strategy is successful. The financial statements should reflect the success or failure of strategies implemented by the company. There may be a time lapse between the implementation of strategies and targets and the reflection of their financial effects in the financial statements. Examples of financial targets and performance measures are:

TARGET	PERFORMANCE MEASURES
Long-term survival	Liquidity
Increase profitability	Return on investment

When developing a balanced scorecard it can be easy to decide on targets for the organisation as these reflect the mission statement and strategy of the organisation. It may be more difficult to choose the right performance measures. They should be selected with caution and should concentrate on factors that enhance performance in the target areas.

Benefits of the balanced scorecard

1   Only important measures are included in the balanced scorecard. As a target is achieved, it is dropped from the balanced scorecard and another target to be achieved is added.
2   It translates strategy targets into performance measures. Strategy targets may be financial or non-financial and the balanced scorecard can accommodate both.
3   It brings together the four perspectives into one report. It does not place undue emphasis on any one perspective. It should reflect the fact that the implementation of a strategy may affect the four different areas of the balanced scorecard.
4   The balanced scorecard can be published as frequently as required – daily, weekly, monthly, etc.
5   Managers are forced to consider all aspects of the business when reading the report. For example, they can observe the effect on financial results of implementing a new policy of customer service.
6   It balances past, present and future performance in one report. The

financial perspective measures the impact of past decisions on financial performance. The customer and internal business perspectives measure the effect of decisions on current performance. The innovation and learning perspective measures targets which need to be achieved now to ensure future success.

Problems with the balanced scorecard

1   Targets can be easily set but there may be difficulty in developing performance measures to achieve those targets. For example, a target may be to improve customer service. This is very broad. The company needs to consider which areas of customer service need to be improved, e.g., delivery times, after sales service, customer enquiries.
2   The relevance of the balanced scorecard may be damaged by having too many targets and measures in one report. The aim of the balanced scorecard is to measure performance in the business. Its benefit should not outweigh the cost of gathering information.
3   The balanced scorecard can be costly to develop and implement. It requires investment in expertise, information technology and managers' time.

Management accounting into the future

Traditionally management accountants were based in manufacturing industries and many of the techniques explained in this book were developed when manufacturing was very labour intensive. Recently manufacturing has diminished in developed economies and shifted to the developing world. The growth of the global economy and the use of the Internet in global communications mean that management accountants do not have to be based at the location where manufacturing is taking place. They can work as part of a multi-national corporation and oversee operations at many different locations spread throughout the world.

Traditionally the management accountant focused on past, mainly financial, information to make future decisions. They were involved in so-called number crunching and preparing information at a very low level or operational level in the organisation. Advances in information technology mean this information is now processed and available using software packages.

There is increasing demand for management accounting techniques in non-profit organisations and particularly the public sector. This has arisen from the demand for more transparency in these sectors and concerns about the spending of public funds. Performance measurement systems such as the balanced scorecard can provide useful information for reporting and decision-making in the public sector.

What now is the role of the management accountant?

In **Chapter 1: Introduction**, the changing role of management accounting was discussed. The changes mentioned provide a challenge to the management accounting profession. Some of these issues have been addressed by the involvement of the management accountant in strategic decision-making. Information provided at a strategic level assists managers in developing strategies for the business and provides information to support those strategies. For example, if a company's strategy is to expand its product range, the management accountant will analyse existing and new markets and competitors' strategies in developing new products.

In this chapter we have concentrated on some recent developments in the area of strategic management accounting. They involve the analysis of strategic information used by businesses for decision-making internally and externally. There is no one definition of strategic management accounting. The balanced scorecard and activity-based management/costing are examples of strategic management accounting techniques which are described in this book. Other strategic management accounting techniques would be life cycle costing, target costing and value-chain management. These techniques are outside the scope of this book.

These strategic management accounting techniques represent a shift from low level or operational accounting information traditionally provided by the management accountant to a higher level or strategic level of information. Management accountants are increasingly becoming strategic information providers. This has been reflected in the syllabi of professional accounting bodies with some accounting bodies including 'Strategic' in the titles of their management accounting subjects.

In response to the changing role of management accountants CIMA has tailored its syllabus to train accountants in business and financial strategy. It states that it teaches skills for strategic advice. It has also recently included a topic called 'The Global Business Environment'.

Chapter summary

This chapter is split into two areas – performance reporting and a discussion about the future role of management accounting.

Performance reporting within an organisation is discussed in terms of financial measures and non-financial measures of performance.

Consideration is given to performance reporting in non-profit organisations and the importance of achieving value for money.

The balanced scorecard is described as a method of reporting performance which links key areas of the organisation – financial, customer, internal business and innovation and learning.

The chapter concludes with a discussion on strategic management accounting and the future role of management accounting.

Test questions

Question 1

a List non-financial measures which identify the effectiveness of:
  (i)   A health clinic's adherence to appointment times
  (ii) Ability of patients to contact the health clinic by telephone
  (iii) Implementation of a new immunisation programme for children
b Discuss the importance of non-financial measures of performance evaluation and problems that may arise in using such measures

Question 2

The mission statement of a hospital reads: 'The hospital is committed to providing the highest-quality healthcare through service excellence and to being the community's healthcare provider of choice.'

Management at the hospital have identified the following strategies they would like to fulfil during the next year:

- provide high-quality services to patients
- increase utilisation of services within the hospital
- motivate, retain and train staff
- roll out a training course in theatre practice for nurses
- value for money

Required

Design a balanced scorecard suitable for presentation to senior managers. Your scorecard should clearly indicate one target under each of the four perspectives. Each target should have two measures of performance.

Question 3

You are the management accountant in a national television company which is funded through licence fees and advertising. Programmes are made in-house, commissioned or bought in. The range of programmes must fulfil a remit set down by government – news, current affairs, young people, drama, sport and religious. The advertising budget has fallen dramatically over the past year and the company is losing market share to other commercial companies.

The company is currently running a producer training course and 10 staff are on the course. It will take six months and it is in its third month. Trainee producers are assessed halfway through the course. The drama department is unique in that it needs to invest now in script development to produce and transmit drama programmes in two years' time.

The company's objective is to 'fulfil its viewer remit, develop a schedule of high-quality programmes within its budgetary constraints and retain a highly skilled workforce'.

The company produces monthly management accounts and year-end financial statements. As management accountant you are concerned that the company is over-emphasising the measurement of performance in terms of financial data and is ignoring non-financial measures of performance.

Required

a Explain your concerns regarding the over-emphasis of financial results in performance measurement
b Draw up a list of four appropriate non-financial performance targets which will enable you to determine whether the company is meeting its objectives. For each target, suggest a way of measuring it.

For answers and additional test questions, see www.gillmacmillan.ie. Search for Management Accounting and click on the link in the right-hand column.

REFERENCES

CIMA, *CIMA Offical Terminology*, CIMA Publishing, 2005.

Clarke, Peter and Mullins, Tracy, 'Activity Based Costing in the Non-Manufacturing Sector in Ireland: A Preliminary Investigation', *Irish Journal of Management*, (2001), 1–18.

Clarke, Peter, Thorley Hill, Nancy and Stevens, Kevin, 'Activity-Based Costing in Ireland: Barriers to, and Opportunities for, Change', *Critical Perspectives on Accounting*, vol. 10, (1999), 443–68.

Cooper, R. and Kaplan, R., 'Measure Costs Right: Make the Right Decisions', *Harvard Business Review*, (September/October 1988), 96–103.

Doyle, Geraldine, Duffy, Lisa and McCahey, Melissa, 'An Empirical Study of Adoption/Non-adoption of Activity Based Costing in Hospitals in Ireland', Conference of Irish Accounting and Finance Association, University College Dublin, 2009, 1–42.

Drury, Colin, *Cost & Management Accounting: An Introduction*, 6th edition, Thomson Learning, 2006.

Drury, Colin, *Management and Cost Accounting*, 7th edition, South-Western Cengage Learning, 2008.

Greenberg, P. S. and Greenberg, R. H., 'Who Needs Budgets? You Do', *Strategic Management*, (August 2006), 41–5.

Hope, J. and Fraser, R., 'Beyond Budgeting: Building a New Management Model for the Information Age', *Management Accounting*, (January 1999), 16–21.

Hope, J. and Fraser, R., 'Who Needs Budgets?', *Harvard Business Review*, (February 2003), 108–15.

Innes, J., Mitchell, F. and Sinclair, D., 'Activity-based Costing in the U.K.'s Largest Companies: A Comparison of 1994 and 1999 Survey Results', *Management Accounting Research*, vol. 11, (2000), 394–462.

International Financial Reporting Group of Ernst & Young, *International GAAP 2009*, vol. 1, chapter 20, section 2.2, Wiley, 2009, 1,296.

Jackson, A. and Lapsley, L., 'The Diffusion of Accounting Practices in the New "Managerial" Public Sector', *The International Journal of Public Sector Management*, vol. 16, no. 5, (2003), 359–72.

Johnson, H. Thomas and Kaplan, Robert S., 'Relevance Lost: The Rise and Fall of Management Accounting', *Harvard Business School Press*, (October 1987), chapters 1–5, 7–8, 11.

Jones, Rowan and Pendlebury, Maurice, *Public Sector Accounting*, 6th edition, Prentice Hall, 2010.

Jones, T. C. and Dugdale, D., 'The ABC Bandwagon and the Juggernaut of Modernity', *Accounting, Organizations and Society*, vol. 27, (2002), 121–63.

Kaplan, R. and Cooper, R., *Cost & Effect Using Integrated Cost Systems to Drive Profitability and Performance*, Harvard Business School Press, 1998.

Kaplan, Robert and Norton, David P., 'The Balanced Scorecard – Measures that drive performance', *Harvard Business Review*, (January/February 1992), 71–9

Macintosh, Norman B., *Management Accounting and Control Systems*, Wiley, 1994, 1–8.

Seal, Willie, Garrison, Ray H. and Noreen, Eric W., *Management Accounting*, 3rd edition, McGraw Hill Education, 2000.

Steven, Grahame, 'Lessons from History', *CIMA Insider*, (May 2002), 19–20.

Steven, Grahame, 'Management Accounting – Decision Management', *Financial Management* (July/August 2005), 39–40.

Storey, Roger, *Introduction to Cost and Management Accounting*, Palgrave, 2002.

Upchurch, Alan, *Cost Accounting Principles and Practice*, Financial Times/Prentice Hall, 2002.

INDEX